Children, Gender, Video Games

Children, Gender, Video Games

Towards a Relational Approach to Multimedia

Valerie Walkerdine

First published 2007 by
PALGRAVE MACMILLAN
Houndmills, Basingstoke, Hampshire RG21 6XS and
175 Fifth Avenue, New York, N.Y. 10010
Companies and representatives throughout the world

PALGRAVE MACMILLAN is the global academic imprint of the Palgrave Macmillan division of St. Martin's Press, LLC and of Palgrave Macmillan Ltd. Macmillan® is a registered trademark in the United States, United Kingdom and other countries. Palgrave is a registered trademark in the European Union and other countries.

ISBN–13: 978–0–230–51717–2   hardback
ISBN–10: 0–230–51717–X   hardback

This book is printed on paper suitable for recycling and made from fully managed and sustained forest sources.

A catalogue record for this book is available from the British Library.

A catalog record for this book is available from the Library of Congress.

10   9   8   7   6   5   4   3   2   1
16   15   14   13   12   11   10   09   08   07

Printed and bound in Great Britain by
Antony Rowe Ltd, Chippenham and Eastbourne

Contents

Acknowledgements

This book itself is an assemblage. While my name appears as author, this backgrounds the fact that I feel more like the director of a film, in that a number of people contributed to the work which is written up here. The research was funded by the Australian Research Council Large Grant scheme. The data was collected by Angela Thomas, David Studdert and Ken McMullin, as well as myself. Carolyn Williams came onto the project at a very difficult time and I am enormously grateful to her for her role in helping to salvage it. She helped with the major part of the data analysis and later analysis was carried out in collaboration with Peter Bansel. Some final additional analysis was undertaken with Louise Madden. I owe a big debt of gratitude to all these people, who ultimately made the book possible. Louise Madden and Merryn Smith also helped with final editing. Jessica Ringrose and David Studdert gave me supportive and helpful feedback on the manuscript and I am grateful for their input. Lisa Blackman, Cathy Urwin and Gabrielle Ivinson provided support, friendship and laughter as I sat typing the first draft in a lovely house on Lanzarote. I am grateful to Lisa Blackman and David Studdert for the many helpful conversations. Last but not least, I wish to thank all the children, parents and after-school club workers in Sydney who enthusiastically shared their video game experience with us. To all, my heartfelt thanks.

1
Introduction

It is a spring afternoon in an after school video game club in the inner western suburbs of Sydney. Twenty-four young children excitedly play console video games in twos or threes. Researchers join them and in one case two boys, Sam and Timothy, are playing a hectic game of Star Wars Racer, while their game is being videoed by the team. We see Sam telling Timothy that he wants to play a Jedi, to which Timothy, the better player, tells him firmly, 'you can't be a Jedi in this'. Persisting, Sam tries to 'use the force' to gain enough playing power to beat Timothy. Meanwhile, Timothy has subtly ensured that nothing is left to only his skill at playing in his quest for winning, by turning off the console and starting again when he thinks he may not win. This takes no more than a few minutes, but a huge amount has happened within that time. How do we understand what has happened and what it means?

Video games are the world's biggest selling entertainment. They out-gross film receipts and yet only 5 per cent of video games devised make a profit (Wikepedia: http://en.wikipedia.org/wiki/Game_development). What makes them such big sellers? Why and how do children, the video game generation, play them? While there is no shortage of material on this topic (see Roberts et al., 1999), the debate about whether games are good or bad for children and young people continues to rage and games get blamed for any manner of social ills from addiction to murder. Clearly this makes them important. In this book, I take children playing some recent video games as a case study to think about a number of key issues of how we conceptualise our ways of being or indeed what we become in a complex life world. In this world, new technologies and international communication flows collapse some central notions of what it means to be a child in terms of traditional accounts of development. For example, Piagetian accounts understand development as occurring

1

through action upon an object world towards a state of disembodied rationality, but video games demand an entry into a complex virtual space, not solid objects, and often children are the experts at these games, not adults. This means that our taken for granted ideas about what develops into what need considerable rethinking. To do this, I bring work from cultural and social theory into dialogue with debates about learning, media effects and gender studies, among other things. In attempting to understand some of the issues at stake in this group of young children (in Sydney) learning to play and playing a set of, at that time, top-rated games, I am struggling to deal with some central issues about subjectivity. For example, do children learn skills that are psychological in nature in order to play, or through playing, games? Do they have to have a certain developmental level in order to play effectively? Do girls and boys play in the same way?

I want to look at these questions certainly, but I want to radically rethink what it means to think about subjectivity. In doing this, I want to go beyond a set of distinctions between psychological and social, between what's inside and what's outside, between macro economics and micro interaction, for example. My argument is that video games are an important cultural, social and economic phenomenon and the way I want to think about this is to consider how the practices of game playing themselves produce what it means to be a player and how playing is made up of complex interrelations, relations often obscured by our habitual way of reading action as a person playing a game. Rather than think this way, I want to explore the relationalities themselves, to understand how games get to be played and how the complex relations of playing, and the place of games in a global world constitute what it means to play and to be a player.

If we go back to the example with which I opened the chapter, you will note immediately that I present the account as one of two protagonists acting, which is a standard way that we all recognise and find easy to follow. This casts the boys as actors who are the authors and originators of those actions and the games and equipment as bit part players. But I could have presented the account in a different way. I could have foregrounded what the technology does, what appears on the screen, the bodily movement of two players. If we think about it in a different way, so much is going on. There is the setting of the school club, the console, the screen, the movements of hands on controllers, the talk, to name just some of the aspects. We are used to thinking about these by foregrounding the players as subjects who act, but actually the whole scene itself is a complicated mixture of many different things all working together, things that we usually background both in terms of what we notice and what we put into an account. If we think about it like one of those psychological illusions, where the duck can become the rabbit or vice versa, then we can perhaps see that what becomes the ground and what the figure are interchangeable. Or think of it another way. When I was an undergraduate art student, a staple first year task was to make us draw only the spaces around objects to highlight how full the space itself is and that it is not nothing or an absence. I am here not so much saying the space around objects is full or that ducks can become rabbits but that what we see and concentrate on is only a partial picture and that this way of looking is motivated by what we assume a human subject is, that is the assumptions we bring to bear on how we understand what we look at. So, I am saying that if we approach video game playing another way, the solidity of the players can also break down as we begin to look at different things within the frame. If we emphasise relations over subjects, the solidity of subject and object boundaries begins to fragment. I am interested in that fragmentation because it allows us to focus on the complexity of what happens in ways that show us connection rather than separation into discrete persons acting upon objects. We would then see hands, bodies, screens, consoles, voices, for example, moving together to produce game play. This manner of approaching this situation challenges a Cartesian view that it is the separate action of human actors behaving rationally in the world which gives the world meaning, and instead opens up the possibility of understanding the complex connectednesses of the world in ways that have been hidden by our Cartesian insistence on subjects and objects. In other words, how might we look and engage in a different way, which does not start with subject and object as simply a given frame to be placed onto everything, but let us understand connections between hands, eyes, voices, screens, consoles, bodies – in a different way, a way that does not automatically separate them into a figure and a ground or a subject acting upon an object.

I have been inspired to take this route by work emerging within different disciplines in the social sciences which connect with my own longstanding attempts to go beyond Cartesianism (e.g. Henriques et al., 1984). However, I found this is not an easy journey to take and the momentum of my attempt to work in a different way builds up as the book progresses.

To do this I am working with data collected from a project on children and video games, conducted in Sydney Australia between 1999 and 2003, funded by the Australian Research Council. This project involved 48 children aged between 8 and 11 who played console games top rated in their age group for Nintendo 64 and Sony Playstation. The children were video-taped during after school club sessions, and were also interviewed, along with their parents. It is necessary to say here that of course I recognise the specificity of the work. Video games are a fast changing field. The games played may be specific to the time of their release and play. Of course, different games also differ according to the platform on which they are played. Yet, I feel that there are points worth making about children and multimedia that have not been sufficiently made and so I will risk generalising from these particular games in these particular situations to talk about three aspects that I think are central: the relational issues I began with, issues of gender, and issues of embodiment and affectivity. I will discuss these as the book progresses.

Masculinity

I begin by engaging with the centrality of masculinity for the study of video games and this leads me, in the end, to focus on the importance of masculinity and femininity and to criticise the absence of concerns about gender in most of the approaches that have inspired my attempt to think about things differently.

One central claim is that many of the games are one site for the production of contemporary masculinity and that an exploration of the relationalities that make up game playing has to take this on board first and foremost. Although there is now much more work on video game play than even a few years ago, there are relatively few systematic studies of children playing games, and those that there are do not place masculinity centre stage. To do this I develop a relational approach, which utilises insights from post-foundational work in the social sciences, which attempts to rethink experience and which attempts to displace subjectivity from centre stage to discover that what we think of as subjectivities are an effect of complex relations themselves. I am thinking here of work in the social sciences which moves from complexity theory (Urry, 2003), Actor Network Theory (Latour, 2005), the return to phenomenology (Csordas, 1994), the use of Deleuze (1994) and the relational and post-modern turns within psychoanalysis (see Elliot and Spezzano, 1999). Although these are all very different approaches, I believe that they share an attempt to go beyond Cartesianism and explain the present globalised world with its complex interconnections. In addition, I want to draw on this approach to understand the production of learning and the learner within video game practices, both drawing on and going beyond current debates about learning within cultural and situated practices (Cole, 1999; Lave and Wenger, 1991).

This is clearly a large undertaking and the book looks first at masculinity, and then goes on to issues of femininity, regulation, (especially how parental regulation of game playing is subtly gendered), violence, and finally to complexity and to learning.

Ideology

I begin by engaging with a classic split within cultural and media studies, between the passive consumer and the active maker of meaning. I want to start here in order to demonstrate that it is necessary to go beyond this distinction, which has cropped up a lot in recent discussions about video games and children. In reviewing it, I want to show that there are other places to start if we are to radically rethink how to approach children and multimedia. In order to think about the context in which we might approach video game playing by young children as relational, I want to begin by thinking about a central debate and dispute within the field of media and cultural studies; that is, between the study of a cultural product and practice such as video game play as concerned with ideology, an ideology which makes possible a certain kind of subject, and as a cultural phenomenon in which players create their own culture as a spontan eous and subversive activity. This tends to be characterised in terms of a passive versus an active subject, and has also become important in debates about children's culture, in what are understood as psychological accounts, which are opposed to the idea of children as active makers of their own culture (James and Prout, 1990). I want to review this division in order to go beyond it, to suggest that it is quite unhelpful, not only in its divisions between activity and passivity but for the ways in which ideological subjects or creative subjects are separated from an economy which is seen as a distant force acting upon them. I argue rather (see Chapter 7) that the economic is deeply embedded in the very everyday practices through which children and adults become game players.

One of the most important developments in media studies was the 1970s take-up of the work of French social theorist Louis Althusser. Using the psychoanalysis of Jaques Lacan, Althusser argued forcefully that subjects had to get beyond the Imaginary and into the Symbolic Order where the power of the Law was located. This work presented the workings of ideology and what came to be known as a theory of the subject, absolutely centre stage in the understanding of the social, and was critical of a stress on what Althusser called state apparatuses, such as schools, as only vehicles for the production of subjects ready to become workers and enter economic relations. What is important for my purposes is the radical split that this instantiated between ideology and economy, arguing that subjects were created in ideology, having reference to the economy only in the last instance, which never came. This paved the way for the significant take-up of this approach within media studies, especially film studies, and it also prefaced a move from an engagement with production to the study of identity as produced through consumption.

The idea of mass-produced fantasies and possibility for identification was linked to earlier work on the mass media, notably by members of the Frankfurt School (e.g. Adorno, 1950) who had looked at the central importance of post-war mass consumption for producing identities.

However, many cultural theorists have opposed the pessimism and determinism of the Frankfurt School and Althusserian arguments. Cultural Studies, as developed by Stuart Hall, his students and colleagues at the Centre for Contemporary Cultural Studies at the University of Birmingham in the 1970s, emphasised not simply the understanding of ideological processes but the understanding of possibilities for radical political transformation and action within a context in which everyday cultural processes and practices are the site for the production of resistant readings and identities. In this, they stressed the possibility of active, resistant readings of ideology through the development of resistant subcultures. This tended to set up an uneasy opposition in media studies in which active, resistant audiences, for example, were set against an idea of passive film audiences being entirely produced through ideology, although this was a misreading of the 'activity' of the unconscious. As we shall see, versions of these debates resurface with respect to children and video games. The rise in marketing techniques based on an appeal to identity creation for small market segments within current capitalism, also led to much more stress within cultural studies on consumption than on production, and meant rather a lack of interest in the production of workers and economic relations themselves. I will address this issue in Chapter 7.

However, it could also be argued that the debates in the post-war period, and in the 1970s and 80s were predated by American developments much earlier in the century. It could be argued that psychology and mass consumption have been put together from much earlier within the twentieth century. In a convincing argument, made in a BBC documentary series *Century of the Self*, Adam Curtis (2002) puts together the case that American government of the masses could be said to build upon earlier crowd psychology (Le Bon, 1897), by developing an opposition between irrationality and rationality, in which irrationality was understood as the remnants of the animal and primitive, the Enlightenment project of producing rational citizens for a rational government. For Le Bon, it was necessary to move away from the irrational sway of the crowd to the production of the rational and solo individual. Freud (1922) drew upon Le Bon's writings in his work on group psychology as did the early social psychologists (see McDougal, 1941). Curtis argues that the Americans took up Freud's work in a different way in relation to government. Freud's nephew, Bernays, who had migrated to the USA, deployed marketing techniques to develop a mass market and mass consumption. His idea was to play on the unconscious desires of the people and associate those with the purchase and ownership of commodities. This produced the possibility of a government which linked capitalism with democracy and produced a quietened population, apparently sated by consumer goods and wealth. While this was seriously destabilised by the Wall Street crash and the depression of the 1930s, the power of the irrational was demonstrated by the unhappiness of returning servicemen from the Second World War. Freud's daughter Anna was drafted in to develop a programme of citizen support which aimed at fortifying the ego or rational side of the equation by emphasising the strengthening of the ego over the forces of the id. It thus becomes clear that the opposition between rational and irrational is deeply caught up in the politics of government, with an address both to the power of the irrational in the production and sustaining of mass consumption, while at the same time drawing on discourses and practices of rationality to produce a population whose irrational was not out of control or devoted to anti-social and anti-government activities. This opposition between passive consumption of ideology and active resistance can therefore be understood to be a completely specious one in the sense that both strategies have been, and are demanded, within liberal democracies based on consumer capitalism, and both require active, participating consumers or citizens. Yet, this opposition is reprised endlessly in debates in media and cultural studies, as we will see, and certainly so in debates about video games.

Going beyond the oppositions between activity and passivity

In the work which I am developing in this book, I think it is necessary to go beyond the impasses of the dichotomies created between activity and passivity, and ideology and economy. I want to suggest that we should not bracket off the economy but should understand its particular place in the cultural and social practices of the present. I do not wish to oppose ideology and economy, nor to propose a single theory of the subject, but rather try to think about how specificity is a product of complex relationalities. I want to show how these dichotomies have been quite unhelpful in the field of media and cultural studies and in particular in relation to the study of children and media, in this case video games.

Children as active makers of meaning

The new sociology of childhood opposes traditional psychological conceptions of children, claiming that developmental psychology presented children as passive, whereas the new sociology aims to understand them as active makers of their own culture and meanings (James and Prout, 1990). David Buckingham (2000) takes up this approach with great vigour in relation to children as media audiences.

The work of Henry Jenkins in relation to audience research typifies the approach of the active maker of meanings. Jenkins (1998) carefully studies the culture of Trekkies, that is, people who are fans of the television series *Star Trek*. He demonstrates that the fans do not passively identify with the ideology of *Star Trek*, but actively build a whole set of cultural practices and new meanings around the *Star Trek* characters and narratives. For example, some fans write new stories, which can be quite subversive, such as a gay relationship between Captain Kirk and Dr Spock. In other words, Jenkins argues that just as in any other social sphere, the fans as people are creative – they create things out of what they have available. It matters not that what they have available is *Star Trek*, what matters is that they can use it as raw material to create something new, just as the 19th century workers in E. P. Thompson's (1968) account, created the working class. While Jenkins wants to demonstrate that people do indeed create history in circumstances not of their own choosing, and by stressing the activity and creativity of audiences downplays the determinism of ideology theorists, I feel that there is a defensiveness in his position. It is as though demonstrating the veridicality of the active audience minimises the importance of the media and popular culture as makers of meanings. And like cultural studies theorists before him, he understands activity as almost synonymous with resistance.[1] In relation to video games, Jenkins has further developed this approach in Cassell and Jenkins (1998) and Jenkins (2004). It is the idea of activity which is central to the opposition to the approach that has become known as media effects, that is, the idea that the media has deleterious effects upon children, such as video games making children violent, for example. This work, while terribly important, sets up a very strong dichotomy between activity and passivity and a very strong defence against the idea that the media is harmful to children. Jenkins (2004) puts it this way:

We have to recognise a distinction between 'effects' and 'meanings'. Limbaugh and company see games as having social and psychological 'effects' (or in some formulations, as constituting 'risk factors' that increase the likelihood of violent and antisocial conduct). Their critics argue that gamers produce meanings through game play and related activities. Effects are seen as emerging more or less spontaneously, with little conscious effort and are not accessible to self examination. Meanings emerge through an active process of interpretation; they reflect our conscious engagement; they can be articulated into words; and they can be critically examined. New meanings take shape around what we already know and what we already think, and thus, each player will come away from a game with a different experience and interpretation. Often, reformers in the 'effects' tradition argue that children are particularly susceptible to confusions between fantasy and reality. A focus on meaning, on the other hand, would emphasise the knowledge and competences possessed by game players starting with their mastery over the aesthetic conventions that distinguish games from real world experience. (pp. 1–2)

While I agree in large measure with Jenkins' assessment of the effects approach as extremely crude, his argument runs a set of risks because it still assumes a rather Cartesian subject. In addition, it deftly reprises the opposition between different strategies of government based on rational and irrational, discussed earlier in the chapter. Indeed, we could say that Jenkins protests too much and is only in fact taking up a position on one side of a dichotomy, a position in which it is vital to argue that the population is rational precisely for fear of the power of its opposite. Indeed, we could also argue that this is a false opposition. Video games and other media manufacturers need the creativity and rationality of game players just as they need to draw players into the fantasy of the game and its characters. This suggests that the two strategies of government deftly outlined by Curtis can here be implicitly cited within this very hollow debate. So, this opposition could be said to be eliding another, the complex place of the rational and irrational in the making of the subject of liberal democracy within global consumer capitalism.

Indeed, it is plainly ridiculous to assert that issues of fantasy, except somehow rational fantasies, do not have a place in the active, rational, meaning-making game player. Jenkins' subject is an active maker of meanings, but the subject is rational, in control. This leaves his argument open to the psychological claims of effects researchers, about fantasy and reality. In Jenkins' formulation, meanings are made actively by conscious subjects in specific practices in which subjects master the aesthetic conventions of games and which distinguish games from what he calls 'real world experience', which we must assume to be different practices with different aesthetic conventions. I would argue that those other practices are important because the knowledge and competences players bring to the games are produced through active meaning-making in other practices (Walkerdine, 1988). In the approach I use, there is no 'real world experience' which is not also to be understood through the specific meanings generated in quite specific sites and practices, but, further than this, we are still left with the child as active maker of meaning, which assumes a Cartesian subject who generates meanings. If Jenkins is obliquely referring to the cultural studies tradition discussed above, then we need to rethink what it means to experience (Stephenson and Papadopoulos, 2006). However, we still have the active subject as the centre point, at centre stage, and in this book I try to move this on, so that subjectivity becomes understood as part of the complex interplay that I am struggling to develop in this book. In relation to this, I would argue that Jenkins lacks an account of subjectivity. Subjectivity in his approach is already assumed – it is a subject who consciously makes meanings. Indeed, this is where we need to go beyond the so-called splits between the active and passive subject. We have to take on board the strategies of governmentality in the making of citizens. These inscribe subjects within practices designed to produce both the rational and desiring subject. When we account for the making of the video game player we do not start with a clean slate. The meanings subjects make and the meanings in which subjects are inscribed need to be thought of as part of one and the same process. How might we begin to produce a more complex account which does not result in this dichotomy between ideological and personal meanings? I approach it through an engagement with work on affect, which emphasises the embodied relation between sensation and meaning, such that meanings are not only inscribed in discourses and modes of governance but are also part of constantly shifting affective relations.

Fantasy

In Chapter 2, I explore what it would mean to think about meaning-making in a different way. In addition to this, I specifically want to address fantasy. The idea of distinguishing fantasy from reality comes from a developmental psychological paradigm which derives from psychoanalytic approaches to the central role of unconscious phantasy in development. Acknowledging the unconscious and indeed fantasy does not mean we accept effects research. Fantasy is centrally present in the cultural and social fantasies which are mobilised for us within our everyday practices (e.g. Zizek, 1997). This is the terrain of Lacanian work and a central prop to post-Althusserian accounts of ideology. I therefore ask what it would mean to take this work seriously while not moving away from the idea that game players do indeed make meanings in the context of themselves being already inscribed in complex signifying practices through which all life is lived and which give us the meanings through which we come to be. Jenkins (2004) mentions another piece of work on children and video games by Jim Gee (2003) in which Gee describes game players as active problem solvers. But, as Jenkins describes, Gee sees the most powerful dimension of the game as being what he calls 'projective identity'. He argues that the taking on a role from the game allows us to see the world from an alternative perspective. For Jenkins this means that 'identity is projected (chosen or at least accepted by the player, actively constructed through game play) rather than imposed . . . whether the game's ideas are persuasive depends on the kid's backgrounds, experiences and previous commitments. Games, like other media, are most powerful when they reinforce our existing beliefs, least effective when they challenge our values' (p. 4). Clearly, Gee assumes that the player projects his or her identity outwards, understood as an active pursuit. It is this which allows both Gee and Jenkins to understand this as not an ideological imposition onto a passive child. But I feel that their account is so defensive. It is as though the spectre of 'effects' has to be kept at bay at all costs. Yet, I feel it is precisely this which in fact opens the door to effects. It is the refusal to recognise that engagement with fantasy and imagination in the making of identity is complex and that the dichotomies of active and passive do not adequately account for it. I am suggesting that in thinking about the relation between players and imaginary identities and other fantasies, we need to approach from a position which allows us to think about the circulation of fantasies within cultural and social practices and the active engagement of players, as well as their mobilisation in practices. There is no necessary opposition in practice between children as so-called 'passive' consumers and 'active' makers of meaning, in that these are both produced as aspects of techniques through which fantasies are mobilised by techniques of mass marketing, and active rational citizens are demanded for liberal democracy. We should hardly be surprised if we find these two techniques jostling together just as they have done since the early part of the twentieth century. That capitalism demands the engagement of our fantasies to market goods that keep liberal democracies afloat, while liberalism demands rational active citizens who are not swayed by the animal irrational, is simply one of the paradoxes of liberal government. Indeed, we can so easily point to the Enlightenment project which demands the rational citizen and separates the rational and civilised from the irrational, animal, instinctual and primitive. This is a discourse that Freud plays directly into and on which Bernays drew in developing mass marketing techniques in the early decades of the 20th century.

Subjectivity and the media

How can we go beyond the opposition of active and passive?

In *Daddy's Girl* (1997), I present a number of examples of the ways in which media texts and popular cultural practices have a particular place in the making of feminine subjectivities. Little girls and their mothers watching the musical *Annie*, a father and his sons and daughter watching *Rocky 2*, a girl having a talent competition in the back garden, for example. I set this against the massive eroticisation of little girls within popular culture, an eroticisation which is both ubiquitous and barely acknowledged. I try to put the two things – girls in the media with girls relating to the media – to show how there is a complex set of relations, not a set of simple determinations nor a set of active resistant subjects. I suggest that we have to look both at texts and at the practices in which those texts are consumed as well as the complex interplay of this with the economic. It is this relationship that I try to take further in this book.

Embodiment

In addition to all the above concerns, we need to think about the fact that playing video games, like all engagements with new media, and unlike film and television upon which classic media theories are based, demands an interaction with the media form, which is itself embodied in that we sit at computers and, consoles, we type, we handle controls. This actively engages the body in a way hitherto not an issue. One way of thinking about these new media has also followed a utopian versus dystopian path, with some writers announcing addiction, the end of childhood, etc. and others presenting a disembodied world in which everything is possible – one can become another persona online, change sex, develop a new personality. This worldview, often linked to William Gibson's cyberpunk novels, sees the new technologies as disembodied, indeed freed from the confines of the body. In a very insightful analysis, N. Catherine Hayles (1999) argues that this view draws upon a long history in which the interaction between human and machine is modelled as one of a disembodied mind, which itself draws on the Cartesian mind/body split. Attempts to produce machine intelligence, cognitive science, all draw upon this split. Conversely, Hayles argues that the human–machine interactions are deeply embodied precisely because they require a bodily interaction with the computer, game console or whichever machine. In that sense, we might compare it with riding a bicycle or driving a car. Indeed, we could say, in response to previous debates about audiences within media studies, that it is the new media which demand that we concern ourselves not only with the relations of psychical to social and cultural but also with the relation between body/mind and machine. In addition to this, we can look to insights from the field of science studies, particularly Actor Network Theory, which remind us that scientific discoveries are not made by single scientists with great insight but through complex practices and networks, even though those practices and networks become invisible in a Cartesian logic which understands the production of science as a work of the mind of the scientist. Such a model persists in a view of child development in which accomplishments are understood in a stagewise progression, which gradually both disembodies them to take them from a work of action to a work of mind, and understands that mind as increasingly capable of an abstract thought, through which the world is made anew as a work of thought. This view is central in all classical developmental psychology but particularly in derivatives of Piaget (1972). In that respect, I want to think of previous work of my own which attempted to critique such accounts of child development (e.g. Walkerdine, 1984; 1988) by understanding what is described as cognitive development as being about the achievement of rationality, itself produced within specific practices, with a certain historical specificity. With that in mind, I want to think about the emergence of the discourses and practices about children and video games and the ways in which those practices produce what it means to be a game player, as well as the activity of playing. In my book *The Mastery of Reason* (1988), I argue that school mathematics as taught to primary school children is a discourse with particular properties, which has to be actively mastered. The mastery of it conveys a fantasy of omnipotent control of a calculable universe – the fantasy of the world written in the language of mathematics, or, more generally, as a work of thought. To be inculcated into this discourse requires an embodied engagement with a new set of relations of signification, which must be made to link with other relations within other discourses and embodied within other practices. The shift from one relation of signification to another is carried, I argued, through semiotic chains, with links often made by the body of either the child or teacher. That body is itself never in a simple object world as described by Piaget, but in objects always understood and contained within discursive practices, with complex relationalities embodied within them.

When I started thinking about the project which led ultimately to this book, I was interested in developing that work in relation to video games. However, since then I have expanded that remit. In particular, I think that new work on embodiment can considerably enhance the small steps I was taking around 20 years ago. In particular, I have found the work of Mark Hansen (2004) on embodiment and new media helpful. He argues that new media should be understood as embodied, not disembodied. It is precisely through the senses that we interact with new media. He uses phenomenology to develop a theory of affect based on Bergson (1911).

He argues along with N. Catherine Hayles (1999) that this approach is a sort of rationalism that is central to Cartesian thinking and which sees thought as increasingly divorced from actual physical action. Of course, games are about complex embodied relations. How do we think about that? Using Hansen's approach allows us to see all thinking as embodied and not separate from interaction – therefore opposing the Enlightenment approach to the greater abstraction of thought reaching its apogee in virtual media. We can take this further by thinking about experience and embodiment as connected to flows and complex networks. The work of Deleuze (1994) has been used recently in thinking about experience as always an embodied act of becoming, in which the flows across bodies keep the body and the social world in which it exists, and which gives it meaning, in constant flow and movement.

I will discuss the work of Hansen in much more detail in Chapter 2. Suffice it to say here that I suggest that we can link Hansen's and Deleuze's approach to embodied affect with work within contemporary psychoanalysis and approaches to relationality more generally, but we must be careful not simply to go back to a relationship between action and object which misses out the discursive practices and therefore the meanings within which such action is framed.

The research project and the organisation of the book

The children in the research were self selected as children who enjoyed video games enough to join an after-school video games club. The games chosen were those rated for the age groups in question and were the most popular games on the market for that age-range at the time. We chose after-school clubs because they facilitated the observation of playing in a social context and were technically easier to work in than in individual children's homes. The after-school clubs kindly allowed the project to run video game clubs in their normal after-school clubs for a number of weeks. In all there were 60 hours of video recording, during which time children played in pairs, threes and fours, some single sex, some mixed sex. During the fieldwork, we made fieldnotes on the playing and videotaped children in turn playing the games. In addition, the children and their parents were interviewed in their homes using a narrative-based interview technique. Chapter 2 sets this work in the context of recent research on video games. Chapter 3 presents an analysis of masculinity, arguing that video games are one site for the production of contemporary masculinity. Chapter 4 takes this analysis further by considering how we might understand girls' game play if games are a site in which masculinity is produced and practised. Chapter 5 considers the debates about violence and video games and argues that games neither make children violent nor act as a cathartic space in which violence is contained, but rather games are one space in which the regulation and self management of when to act and when not to act is accomplished. Chapter 6 considers parental regulation of game playing and discusses how it is that parental regulation of girls' game play appears to be more strict than the regulation of boys' game play. Chapter 7 attempts to place game playing practices in the global flows of multinational capitalism and Chapters 8 and 9 take that account further by relating it to debates about how children learn to play games. Finally, Chapter 10 offers some concluding remarks.

2
Video Game Research

A central issue in my own past work has been an address to subjectivity. I have approached this over many years (see Henriques et al., 1984) by bringing together the idea of subjectivity as constituted through a process of subjectification, in which multiple positions are held together through affective unconscious dynamics. This approach has informed previous work on children and the media, notably my work on girls and popular culture (Walkerdine, 1997). What I want to do here is to recap how this work relates to earlier media analysis and to then go on to think about firstly, the debates about the interactivity of video games and secondly, to engage with how new work from the social sciences might help us to think beyond the position I have taken in the past.

As I argued in Chapter 1, in the 1970s, what is now known as Screen Theory was particularly important (cf. Blackman and Walkerdine, 2001) because it attempted to understand the ideological place of the media through the production of subjects, using Althusser's turn to psychoanalysis to provide a theory of the subject. In particular, this work turned to the unconscious identifications afforded by the process of spectatorship. This work was important in pointing to the ways in which masculinity and femininity, far from being stable givens, were the result of a great deal of psychic work, which itself was never resolved. So, for example, analyses of Hollywood Westerns (Neale, 1983) showed how the hero of a Western classically got beaten several times before he triumphed in the end. Neale argued that this screen struggle paralleled the psychic struggle to embody masculinity. The fact that the hero had to get beaten several times shows that masculinity required constant work to appear to become that which was forever elusive. The triumph of the hero at the end of the movie was therefore understood as pleasurable because it appeared to offer resolution to the struggle – I *am* a man, I *am* the hero. In this sense then, it was argued that movies mirrored and captured what Lacan saw as the endless psychic work of masculinity. This work, as I will show, has been important to my thinking about masculinity and video games. However, it is important to note that within media studies this work was criticised for assuming the overwhelming importance of identification with a media text, which assumed a direct relationship between subjectivity and the psychic work of media. Two positions were most frequently put forward. One (Geraghty, 1991) stressed the importance of social fantasy as productive and active, while the other (e.g. Jenkins, 2004) argued that spectators worked creatively with what they had available and turned it into something else (see Chapter 1). Some of this criticism fails to engage with what is really meant by unconscious processes and psychic work, looking too readily to conscious choices made by spectators, while ignoring unconscious affect. However, that aside, this latter work served to make clear that Althusser's idea of a theory of the subject and a simple process of interpellation needs to be complicated and should at least take on board the complex intertextuality and multiple sites in which subjects are located and the active part they play. However, this latter tended to assume, as Jenkins (see Chapter 1) does, that active means rational and that we therefore do not need to take any account of unconscious or affective processes. It is precisely because of the power of such processes that I, together with the co-authors of *Changing the Subject* (see Walkerdine, 1984), attempted to link Foucauldian multiplicity and subjectification with desire and affect. In this sense, this work allowed the possibility of understanding the ways in which apparatuses of governance position subjects and allowed us to understand how the impossible multiplicity of positions demanded of subjects are held together. Understanding how the media played into this required both an engagement with media texts and a view on how the positions afforded were lived. In this, our work went some way to reconciling the demands of both Screen Theory and television researchers (Blackman and Walkerdine, 2001). However, to further complicate things, recent work on new media has stressed that we cannot simply map studies of television and film onto so-called interactive media such as video games.

It is to the concept of interaction that I will now turn. One of the principal issues raised by video game researchers is that because games are interactive, it is impossible to simply use ideas of identification taken from work on film and television. But what does interactive mean in this context? It is a source of some debate amongst video game researchers, with, on the one hand, some researchers describing games as interactive and others suggesting that this is false. I will simply give a flavour of the debate in this context. For example, Marie-Laure Ryan (2001) characterises games as both interactive and immersive. This builds on work in hyptertext (Bolter and Grusin, 1999) and hypermediacy theories. Both are understood as a work of mimetic desire, the attempt to depict a reality that is multiple, surrounded by multiplying media and sources of information. Work on hyperfiction presents it as the fulfilment of poststructuralist theory (Van Looy, 2003) because it appeared to offer decentering, a writerly text and difference. In this sense, we could suggest that it presents multiplicity and could be argued to mirror the multiplicity of sites of subjectification. On the other hand, opponents have argued that it is like being lost in a maze and trying vainly to extract meaning. Thus, one can equally argue here that multiple narratives with no clear fixed plot line can be quite unpleasurable because they offer no clear narrative solution that appears to resolve the problem of identity (for example, the work of masculinity which I described earlier). Van Looy argues that the dispute revolved around the difference between looking at and looking in. However, this would appear to make the pleasure derived from video games unlikely, so we have to understand its pleasure in another way. Ryan understood immersion as the transportation to a virtual world. This is what led media theorists to argue for the liberatory potential of virtual reality, in which one could be whatever one liked in this constructed world. In that sense, it also builds upon the idea of the cinema as immersive because one is transported to another world in a darkened room, with the film the source of light. However, Ryan opposes immersion to interaction, that is, the interaction between a person and a machine. She offers basically two kinds of interaction – internal and external. 'In the *internal* mode, the user projects himself [*sic*] as a member of the fictional world, either by identifying with an avatar, or by apprehending the virtual world from a first person perspective. In the external mode, the reader situates himself [*sic*] outside the virtual world. He either plays the role of a god who controls the fictional world from above, or he conceptualizes his activity as navigating a database' (2001, 7). Ryan describes these two aspects as the 'cornerstones of a phenomenology of reading, or more broadly, of art experiencing'. So, immersion sits alongside play and reflexivity. It could be argued that this characterises the debates between those who have stressed the identification potential of movies versus those who stress what spectators do in their active engagement with the medium. What Ryan does effectively is to show the way in which we need to unite both elements together and not simply present both in an eternal and sterile opposition. So, for Ryan, the player is both inside and outside at the same time, in a virtual world and playing at controlling that world. Manovich (2001) argues in fact that new media objects do indeed oscillate between these two poles, by creating illusion only to remind us of their artificiality, incompleteness and constructedness. It could be argued that what is pleasurable initially is sufficient immersion to set up a fantasy of being the avatar in the virtual world, combined with the constant work of attempting to be what Ryan calls the controlling God. We have met this controlling God figure before within my own work. In my 1988 book *The Mastery of Reason*, I described the pleasures of mathematics, following Rotman (1988) as the omnipotent fantasy of control over a calculable universe. This is a fantasy of masculinity – it is one of the fantasies of the achievement of masculinity that Neale attempted to describe with respect to Hollywood Westerns. But Ryan and others' work demonstrates that there are two kinds of fantasy working together – that which takes us into the world and that which has us controlling it. Psychoanalytically, this takes us to the *mise-en-scène* of desire but takes us in and out of it all the time as the omnipotent God figure who is ultimately in control of everything. Some years ago, Urwin (1989) noted that children in her therapy practice used superhero toys to produce omnipotent fantasies of control. They did so in circumstances in which they felt small, dependent and helpless. The fantasies therefore served to defend against those feelings by presenting the pleasure of fantasising being huge and in total control. We could argue that this is one central fantasy of masculinity played out in many different ways.

However, understanding engagement with new media as interactive assumes that there is a subject acting upon an object and vice versa. But this view rather fixes the subject and object and describes everything that happens in between, rather than understanding what she calls subjects, objects and interaction as part of a complex whole. This is in opposition to an approach which understands subjectivity as made possible through the relation of practices of subjectification and the plays of affect, desire and fantasy through which the contradictions between these positions are held together. The assumption of a prior but active subject is a standard psychological position which assumes that the subject is formed and can exist outside of discourse (Henriques et al., 1984).

I want here to take the reader back to the work of two media theorists, N. Catherine Hayles (1999) and Mark Hansen (2004), mentioned in Chapter 1. The early work on virtual reality with its idea of immersion, understood this as a work of mind because in fantasy the mind would be able to go where the offline body could not venture, in order to construct new possibilities for identity not available in the offline world, such as men playing at femininity and vice versa. It is for this reason that immersion was understood as potentially liberatory. Hayles argues that this approach develops out of a long cybernetic tradition which understands it as associated with cognition and with mind in a disembodied way. The Platonic metaphysics, developed by Descartes and enshrined in the rise of science from the seventeenth century, presents a disembodied thought as the way of understanding the world, which it is both separate from and has mastery over. In this sense, video games are presented as a work of thought par excellence. In her excellent survey, N. Catherine Hayles (1999) demonstrates how ontologies of the virtual developed which understood it as a disembodied work of thought. This is further developed by Mark Hansen's (2004) work on the new media as deeply embodied. This problem is a central constituent of traditional developmental theory. For example, Piaget understood children as acting upon an object world to develop structures of thinking which mirrored the underlying mathematical structures of the natural world. He envisaged these structures being internalised in a such a way as to produce forms of thought, which became the basis for a disembodied abstract rationality, which effectively formed the basis of the liberal rational subject. I have critiqued this approach in a number of places (Walkerdine, 1984 and 1988 for example). As I mentioned in Chapter 1, Mark Hansen argues that new media should be understood as embodied not disembodied. It is precisely through the senses that we interact with new media. He uses phenomenology to develop a theory of affect based on Bergson:

> As I see it, digitization requires us to reconceive the correlation between the user's body and the image in an even more profound manner. It is not simply that the image provides a tool for the user to control the 'infoscape' of contemporary material culture . . . but rather that the 'image' has itself become a process and, as such, has become irreducibly bound up with the activity of the body . . . Specifically, we must accept that the image, rather than finding instantiation in a privileged technical form (including the computer interface), now demarcates the very process through which the body . . . gives form to or *in-forms* information. In sum, the image can no longer be restricted to the level of surface appearance, but must be extended to encompass the entire process by which information is made perceivable by embodied experience. (p. 9)

In particular, Hansen stresses the importance of affect for our engagement with the new media. It is precisely towards an anti-Cartesian approach that he gestures, by telling us of the profound way in which our engagement with new media are bound up with the body. He argues that there is a fundamental shift in our relation to the digital media away from a model dominated by perception, because we engage with it with our bodies rather than simply looking at it. From the point of view of a shift to embodiment and beyond interactionism, his approach is tremendously important. He argues that the body itself forges the digital image through affectively expressed sensation coming into contact with the digital. In other words, we feel things with our bodies because it is our bodies which do the manipulation and in this sense, as he argues, it is our bodies which construct the image. Central to the idea of affect is both sensation, or what bodies feel, and the sensational and ideational relations it fixes both within and between bodies. This is very important for being able to rethink the psychoanalytic/discursive relation with which I have been working up to the present. Hansen argues that we transform disembodied information into embodied information imbued with meaning (pp. 12–13) and that looking at a virtual image (as in games) is not like looking at an object in 2 or 3D because the viewer can't turn it around to view from different angles, not can it be 'an objective, technical image observable from a distance, but a dimensionless, subjective "image" . . . that can be experienced only internally, with the body of the sensing organism itself' (p. 176). In other words, I think that he is saying that it is not like Piaget's famous three mountain problem, for example, which he used to demonstrate the development of children's concepts of Euclidian space, because it is impossible to gain a perspective about it or view it as an object, but only to sense it and immerse oneself in it. More than this, Hansen argues that our interaction with digital media involves the non-geometric intuition of spaces *'that themselves need not be geometric or otherwise correlated to visually apprehensible reality'* (p. 177) (my italics). In such cases, he argues, it is the digital (or virtual reality) interface itself which functions to fold the transpatial dimension of consciousness back onto the physico-empirical mode, except that there the latter denotes the location of consciousness not in the external world but *within the space of the body*. This is why he calls it an intuition of the space of the body, to take the place of an extended geometric space. In other words, we have to feel our way around rather than logically work it out with a conscious rationality. He argues that the engagement with the digital is basically a sensori motor activity. If this is the case, we are definitely in territory which absolutely challenges a standard western developmental psychological sequence towards disembodied abstraction and rationality. Piaget drew on Bergson by linking sensori motor experience, action, affect, but he built it into a naturalised sequence in which action was stripped of context and meaning and in which there was a gradual moving away from the so called unreliability of the senses (Plato, 1977). Piaget's whole point about development was that the senses deceived young children, who had to develop logical reasoning which worked things out in a way that went beyond the senses. It was this which he saw as the basis for a reasoning subject (which, as I have argued elsewhere was the centrepoint of the liberal subject, see Walkerdine 1984). In this way, Hansen's approach is extremely radical because he takes embodied sense data as the basis of action. In part, he does this because of the way in which he argues that the digital 'object' is not something that can be viewed in Euclidian space, like a mountain – we can't get behind it and view it from another perspective, so instead we have to feel our way around the space, navigating it with our embodied responses. What is interesting is that Hansen utilises approaches which, in the end, return to work being carried out at the inception of the human and social sciences and thus take us back beyond the rational subject to rethink what 'interactivity' might look like.

Central to the way we feel our way around virtual space is the concept of affect. That Hansen stresses the primacy of sense data and embodiment means a reworking of the relation between mind and body, rational and irrational, action and thought. Hansen refers to the work of the social theorist Henri Bergson. In his book, *Matter and Memory* (1994), Bergson argued that bodily affects are actions upon the body. He argues that Bergson claims that pain is an action of the body on itself. Exemplary of internal sensation per se, pain involves a certain separation of a sense organ from the body as a whole. Yet despite some differentiation of the sensory from the motor, the body can escape pain by moving (i.e. motor activity) but it can't necessarily move away from the sensation. Affect, according to Bergson, is a separate sensori motor system internal to the body, the body's effort on itself. There can be no perception without affection. Affectivity constitutes an interval between an isolated sensory organ and the action of the body on that organ. As spatiality, or spacing, where the body is felt from within rather than seen from without, affectivity is a permanent and diversified experience of oneself, 'in a body which becomes in this way the body of someone and not only that of a living and acting being in general. What is more, affectivity infiltrates perception in a way that renders the latter irreducibly bodily and that reveals the full richness – the multimodality or, we might say, high bandwidth – of embodied perception' (p. 226). When we perceive something we also feel it – we have to translate the vision into feeling – action. 'The affective body does not so much see as *feel* the space of the film; it feels it, moreover, as an energised haptic spatiality within itself' (p. 232).

His approach to sensation is to understand the body. For Bergson, the body is both intermediary between self and the outside world through which the world is knowable and is also the way through which the world is processed. The body is both a screen for the outside and also what takes shape at the centre of perception. But this taking shape is constantly blurred by the motion of the body, because the body is understood as a moving limit between future and past. Bergson understands that not as a psychoanalytic unconscious, but that memory, is related to the totality of events which precede it and come after it. The unconscious is nothing other than a non perceived object or not imagined image. Mind enters contact with matter through the function of time and the body possesses the material capacity to turn intensity of time – i.e. sensation – into action. Thus, Hansen, following Bergson, defines affect as an action of the body on the body.

However, in understanding affect, I want to turn to another body of work, which comes from the same historical period, the work of one of the founders of psychology, Wilhelm Wundt. Wundt (1904) argued that emotions were created out of a composite of sensation or feelings in the body linked to representations of objects in perception or memory. Emotion was understood as composed of bodily feelings plus ideas or 'ideational processes', the ideas to which the feelings have attached themselves. In this way, Wundt and others were able to pursue a rational or cognitive approach to the science of emotions, which became the forerunner of cognitive approaches to emotion within twentieth-century academic psychology. This work in psychology built upon earlier concerns with sensation (Blackman n.d.) and I have already alluded to the post-Platonic concern that sensation itself was not a good guide for thinking. This view, originating with Plato, separates sense data from thinking, rationality from irrationality and instantiates the classic split within psychology between affect and cognition. It is further developed with Descartes' stress on the autonomous rational individual who is the author of 'his' own 'rebirth without the intervention of a woman'. In other words, what I am saying is that the split between sensation and thinking, instantiated as a split between thinking and emotion, or rationality and irrationality, is the place at which the mind is separated from the body. It is the mind or later cognitive processes which are understood as a better guide to action than sense data, embodied feelings or sensation. The civilised human being, then, from the post Enlightenment period, is one who is able to move away from sensation. For Hansen to refer back to a body of work which stresses the primacy of affect and sensation is to seriously rethink the affective/cognitive split.

This is important for a rethinking of the use of psychoanalysis within Screen Theory. The latter's use of psychoanalysis stressed unconscious identification with the 'ideational representatives' in Wundt's terms. But what it misses out is how those connections are made. For Hansen they are made through affect, that is, bodily sensation and, in relation to video games, that sensation is the basis for the navigation of virtual space. So, we could say that spectatorship of film is also embodied, but that this has tended to be downplayed by an engagement with psychoanalysis which stressed Freud's chains of association or Lacan's unconscious structured like a language. This is again a stress on the ideational representatives as a way of getting at the affect. Freud argued that 'psychoanalysis unhesitatingly ascribes the primacy in mental life to affective processes, and it reveals an unexpected amount of affective disturbance and blinding of the intellect in normal no less than sick people' (1913, 175). Freud's stress on what Wundt had called the 'ideational representatives' (the ideas to which feelings had attached themselves) and their relation to psychopathology led to a central emphasis on *phantasy* (unconscious fantasy) and a theory of unconscious defences against unbearable sensations through the production of *phantasies*, thoughts, and actions which kept the unbearable at bay, thereby producing neuroses. It is evident that Freud equally sustained the idea that affect was the irrational which got in the way of rational processes. For Hansen, as with others working on affect, the issue becomes one of how to think about the affective in a different way. There are interesting parallels between this work and work on the body from neuropsychology (e.g. Damasio, 1999) and Elizabeth Wilson's reading of somatics (Wilson, 2004). Returning to Freud, we can see that his move in relation to Wundt's two part account of affect as sensation and ideation was to posit an unconscious as a place where these were linked together. In particular, it is in relation to the concept of unconscious phantasy and a set of defences that Freud develops this link in most detail. Freud therefore presents us with a model of affect which is more complex than either Bergson or Wundt, in that the defences act as a mechanism through which sensation and ideation are linked. In particular, Freud engaged with the central importance of pleasurable and unbearable bodily sensation. His account begins with the difficulties encountered by infants for whom an absence of being held and 'contained' provides the site of sensations which are both unsymbolisable and unbearable. To understand this, Freud posits a realm of phantasy which comes into the gap between pleasurable holding and unpleasure. It is through the mechanism of unconscious phantasy that unpleasant sensations are borne by the infant. Freud posits that unconscious processes and phantasy become the central mechanisms through which affective life is lived and that no sensation can be understood except through its relation to ideation through the unconscious. This is very different from both Bergson, on which Hansen relies, and a cognitive psychological approach to emotion, which simply links sensation and ideation. I want to argue that in order to fully understand the issues raised by video game researchers we need to take the concept of affect much further than Hansen is willing to do, that is, into unconscious processes.

However, Hansen also argues that the affective response does not arise when we place ourselves within the image, as it does in film, nor does it arise through our movement toward or away from a space that presents itself as autonomous (as in antiquity), rather, the affective response takes place within our bodies: 'an internal interval that is radically discontinuous with, but that nonetheless (and indeed for this very reason) forms an affective correlate to the digital topological manipulation of space' (p. 232). That is, we create the space in and on our bodies.

How then can we relate this body of work to Hansen's proposal that it is through an embodied affective engagement that new media operates? Hansen argues in a sense that Ryan's idea of our dual interaction with a virtual world is never disembodied in the sense that we are always experiencing the virtual space through feeling our way around it. This breaks the distinction that Ryan sets up between two kinds of interaction. In this case, it would mean that a fantasised internal interaction in a *mise-en-scène* would be literally felt not simply imagined. This links to an interesting paper by James Newman (2002) in which he argues that video games are not interactive and that the pleasures of video game play do not flow through the joystick: 'what I am saying is that the pleasures of videogame *play* are not principally visual, but rather are kinaesthetic . . . what it feels to be in the *Tomb Raider* or *Vib Ribbon* gameworld is, however, of paramount importance' (2002, 2). I think Newman's point about feeling is precisely that which Hansen's work leads us to. But feeling is not simply a sensation, but is, as Wundt argued over a century ago, the connection of a feeling with an ideation. What it feels like in a gameworld is a complex issue, because the bodily sensations never exist alone but are accompanied by what we take those feelings to mean, both in terms of pleasure, pain, anxiety but also fantasy. This is the classic idea of the defence from psychoanalysis. When Urwin argued that children gained pleasure from omnipotent fantasies of being a superhero it was because they defended against the pain and anxiety of being small, dependent and perhaps frightened. What this means is that feeling one's way around a virtual space in Hansen's terms and the feeling discussed by Newman is not simply a kinetic, or indeed kinaesthetic, experience but an affective one. In this sense, affect means we look at three aspects – the sensation, the ideation of that as pain, for example, and the defence against the pain which is the fantasy of pleasure – that pleasure is the pleasure of control or being somewhere or someone else. I am suggesting that this triple way of thinking about the centrality of affect to new media is absolutely essential to our understanding of the pleasures afforded by video games and the ways that they make subjectivity possible. As I develop this approach in later chapters, I will argue that affect is not simply about sensation, ideation and fantasy but that these are contained within complex relational dynamics, which flow in and through the life world, as well as being unconscious intersubjective dynamics.[1] Bob Rehak (in Wolf and Perron, 2003) argues that the avatar merges spectatorship and participation in a way which transforms both activities. 'Avatars differ from us through their ability to live, die and live again. Their bodies dissolve in radioactive slime or explode in a mist of blood and bone fragments, only to reappear unscathed at the click of a mouse.' He says that the technology means that this is easily accomplished and that this constant rebirth represents a 'vicious circle of ego confirmation'. This ego confirmation is, in my terms, a fantasy – it is that which appears to establish that we exist as a Cogito (Lacan, 1977) but is central for the sensation of being a solid person acting in the world. Constructing a building, or casting a spell, is done through a mouse click. This is the omnipotent fantasy I described earlier, which Donna Haraway has also named the 'god-trick' of the scientist. I suggest it is fundamental to the fantasies of contemporary masculinity. As Rehak says, 'If our extension through various media is predicated on the body as root metaphor, then the body becomes an inescapable aspect of fantasized experience. Images of self demand recognition through identification. Yet, once established, this identification must be demolished so that players can remember where and who they "really are" and the cycle can begin again' (p. 124). In Rehak's analysis, however, there is a 'who they really are', as though the need to understand the constancy of the subject over time and space were itself the real and the other simply a fiction. This then suggests that the real is somehow outside of the practices through which subjectivity is produced. As I have argued above, this 'ego confirmation' is as much a fantasy as anything else – there is no real of the subject which stands outside. This theme is further developed by Marti Lanti (in Wolf and Perron, 2003), who understands games as the corporeal pleasures of becoming machine. She argues that games are about projecting oneself into a space defined by its otherness from the subject. So what degree of alterity can the projection take and therefore what desires does it answer to? She says that all avatars are defined by their mastery in the field so that even trying on femininity for men is a 'kick-ass' experience, not one of passivity (p. 168). Games accustom players to the newness of the new technologies by coupling the game world's cyborg bodies and subjectivities (reassuringly) with their own bodies, making the virtual and physical complementary rather than mutually exclusive realms. Joysticks, game controllers, pedals and various steering systems further foreground haptic interaction and simultaneously encapsulate players in a game world complete with bodily sensation (pp. 168–9).

Newman argues that being in a virtual environment, in Hansen's sense, feeling your way around, is as important as playing a character. This in fact reminds us of work in Screen Theory (Cowie, 1997) which argued that the *mise-en-scène* of desire was absolutely central to fantasy rather than a simple idea of identification with a hero or heroine. So, we could say that the feeling of the controls flow into the feelings of the body navigating around virtual space, link to the pain or pleasure these invoke and thus to the fantasies and skills embodied for overcoming. As we will see, there is an interesting relation between those children who invoke a powerful position within a game and those who are able to have the skill to control and win the game (see Chapters 8 and 9).

However, central to the way I am reading this research, is that part of my threefold characterisation of affect is that sensations understood as painful are defended against in the unconscious. I want to argue that the unconscious and embodied fantasies that these invoke are about masculinity. The double experience game researchers write about, as being simultaneously inside and outside the game, allows the possibility of Neale's idea of the hard work of masculinity to be lived not through identification with the hero but through the mastery of the technology – the ego confirmation, the god-trick. This makes video games powerful and pleasurable, but it also makes them gendered in a complex way. If it was Plato who argued that intuition and sensation had to be abandoned in favour of thought which was able to reason (the centrepoint of what Piaget naturalises as a developmental sequence, as I said earlier), Hansen's bringing back feeling ushers in another discussion. The Platonic distain for feeling was also a distain for the female body, which was associated with a greater proximity to feeling, associated with irrationality linked to the relation of female cycles to the moon – hence lunacy. If we prioritise intuition and sensation, are we not bringing in the feminine? How does this square with the idea that games offer masculine ego confirmation and a fantasy of completeness? We will see that 'feeling your way around' the virtual space has to be counterpointed by the ego confirmation precisely to confirm masculine rationality, control and dominance. Staying immersed in a scenario or having a fantasy not accompanied by technical skill does not produce a competent game player. As I argue in Chapter 4, this places girls in a complex position, in which their feeling for others – sensitivity (another derivation of the idea of sensation) – constantly opposes the investment in skill to win. As I will argue in the final chapter, we need a more developed account of connection and separation to understand this.

Locating embodiment

Having established an affective relation as the way of acting in relation to virtual space, we need to situate this activity within a wider framework. There is not an isolated body and an isolated virtual space. This activity happens in wider webs or networks of relations. In order to understand this further, I want to introduce the work of the sociologist Bruno Latour (2005), and the development of work usually referred to as Actor Network Theory; also the work of those sociologists who are returning to the work of Deleuze and Guattari, to understand complex social relations and flows within the contemporary present. The reason for doing this is that just as Hansen stresses the shift in virtual space and thus our relation to space, so the relation of wider social space has also shifted dramatically. That is, we exist in global spatial and temporal relations which constantly invoke relation and movement. We may speak from Europe to a call centre in India to pay a bill, and people, labour and commodities move rapidly around the world, whether for work or play or asylum. We may have our phone calls routed via satellite connections to remote countries. Although imperialism and mercantile capitalism established such relations and movements many centuries ago, a globalised market and shifting geopolitical relations change our relation to them, or rather, how and who we are in those relations. This body of work attempts to engage with the issue and I suggest we turn to it to understand game playing more fully. The embodied experience of playing does not take place outside of a larger relationality that links the player to other players, to networks of practice, to relationalities of meaning and to embodied connections. It is for this reason that the approach I am advocating is more complex and networked than that proposed by Hansen. Thus we can rethink intersubjectivity, relation and affect as the basis of subjectivity and sociality which is never actually separated from a context, a practice, is always embodied. The loss of embodiment is simply a chimera which elides and obscures the relations which make it possible, be they workers to capital, women to men, social relation to individual achievement, as Latour (2005) tells us.

The work of Latour and Actor Network Theory attempts to engage with the issue of the way in which social production flows through complex sites, often across global spaces. Video games involve complex relations of production, marketing and consumption across many sites worldwide. What I will describe in Chapter 7 is that game playing is linked all the time in complex ways to economic practices in global patterns of production and consumption. In this sense then, there is no way that the embodied relationalities of playing are separate from those other global flows and relations into which economic practices enter. In addition, we could argue that affective relations equally pass through all of those sites and are not simply about one embodied player and a machine. For Latour, machines can also act in relations, and work using Deleuze (1992) argues that affective relations are mobilised and flow across sites. So, we would expect complex affective relations to be central to the complex relations into which video game playing enters. More than this, the two-fold internal and external interactions mirror the pulling in of the consumer, and the pulling out again in order to be a rational citizen in control of his/her emotions, and thus the oppositions of activity and passivity in debates about children and game play.

For my part, coming to dialogue between the ways in which I have been thinking about subjectivity and media, and the more recent ways of thinking I have introduced, is what flows through this book. I begin in the next chapter with an engagement with masculinities and then go on to discuss the implications of my analysis for femininity. I think about regulation, about violence, and then go on to situate these within a wider frame of economic practices, of learning, and finally of an account of relationality. Thus my argument and dialogue develop in tandem with the book's chapters.

3
Video Games and Childhood Masculinity

Introduction

As we have seen in the previous chapter, I am arguing that the pleasures of video game play can be understood in relation to Hansen's kinaesthetics, together with an understanding of affect which incorporates psychoanalytic insights. By looking at research on video game play, I have suggested that the move of at once navigating virtual space and being immersed in it is also engaged with as a kind of god-trick which presents the player as both inside and outside at the same time; inside feeling their way around and being immersed, and outside doing the controlling, which we could understand as an omnipotent fantasy of control, a masculine fantasy. Indeed, we could speculate that because feeling your way around, as I argued in the last chapter, is characterised as feminine, and intuitive, the god-trick of being outside as well as inside is necessary to shore up a feeling of masculinity against its encroachment by the feminine. With this in mind we might explore how video game play provides one vehicle (among many) for the achievement of contemporary masculinity. Remember, that when I say its achievement I am also talking about a fantasy, a fantasy which requires constant work in order to provide some semblance of its success, a success which is always ultimately out of reach and which therefore has to be practised again and again. The pleasure in games which appear to offer one aspect of a route towards the achievement of masculinity is that they seem to offer a certainty that confirms masculine identity. Masculine identity in this analysis is composed of a set of unstable relations between the practices in which masculinity is performed and flows and the fantasies through which those performances are lived. Masculinity is multiple, produced in multiple sites and requiring different and contradictory performances. There is always an Other to masculinity – that which it has to be seen *not* to be. And there is always that which is longed for – a powerful fantasy of the achievement of masculinity, for ever out of reach.

What this means, as I argued, is that feeling one's way around a virtual space in Hansen's terms and the feeling discussed by Newman is not simply a kinetic, or indeed kinaesthetic, experience but an affective one. I pointed to three aspects of affect – the sensation, the ideation of that as pain, for example, and the defence against the pain which is the fantasy of pleasure – that pleasure is the pleasure of control or being somewhere or someone else. I am suggesting that this triple way of thinking about the centrality of affect to new media is absolutely essential to our understanding of the pleasures afforded by video games and the ways that they make subjectivity possible.

How are these three aspects, the sensation, ideation and unconscious phantasy, experienced in relation to masculinity? I am suggesting that the sensation of moving around virtual space is also its colonisation. Much research over many years has argued that boys' and men's take up of space often leaves no room for girls and women – from playgrounds to talk. Sue Austin (2005) argues that women have to be space, that is, they have to provide the kind of emotional containment which allows the autonomous subject to feel that they can have space to become an individual (to in fact provide ego confirmation). This means that it is hard for girls and women to have space of their own and they continually oscillate around being the one who facilitates others (i.e. is nurturant) and being 'a subject', as well as literally taking up space. I will explore this issue in Chapter 4. We could argue that boys' explorations of virtual space can also be considered as a right to be in the space, to take it up, to explore its frontiers. Affectively, in classic psychoanalytic terms, this taking up of space is, as in Urwin's discussion of fantasy play in the last chapter, also a moving away from the space of maternal containment, the space of dependence. So, the sensations and ideations of the exploration of virtual space could also be experienced as providing a space of which one is potentially in control. We could predict that pain would come from feelings of frustration or inability to master the space. It would bring into the body sensations with ideations, of painful dependency. As I explore later in the chapter, this is precisely what happens for some boys in the study, at least as reported by some mothers. Classic psychoanalytic dream analysis when applied to media research (e.g. Cowie, 1997) has argued one of the issues about unconscious fantasy as revealed in a remembered dream narrative, is that the dreamer can take many positions at once or at different points in the dream. Cowie argues that within the mise-en-scène, the dreamer can be the protagonist but can also be someone who watches action, or indeed someone who both is inside and outside of the dream at the same time – the classic point at which the dreamer recognises while dreaming that they are in a dream. We could argue that in the game play, the three positions outlined by other researchers are that the player feels their way around virtual space, identities, or otherwise embodies an avatar in those games requiring one, and simultaneously stands outside and controls – Rehak's ego defence. This is a complex position, or rather, a complexity of at least three positions at once. The goal of play would be to establish sufficient skill level to be able to control and win as often as possible. Just as in Neale's analysis of the Hollywood Western, this requires many defeats in order to be competent enough to compete with others and win. So, I suggest that we may see the video game as a development of the Hollywood Western, though a development which doesn't simply produce men who fantasise being the hero, but rather, who can embody a skill level which will give them rational control. We could say therefore that the games combine several types of fantasy: the fantasy of the hero, the fantasy of the Cogito, the knower and the god-trick, the fantasy of omnipotence. If this is anywhere near correct, it would make them extremely potent as they would involve the triumph of pleasure over pain and the sense of skill and control. As we will see, boys who simply fantasise having the power to win as if magically (by playing a talismanic avatar for example) but do not have the skills to win, find it hard to gain kudos amongst friendship groups. I want therefore to explore some examples of how this is lived.

I am arguing therefore, that the production of the successful player is not simply about the development of certain kinds of cognitive skills, because we cannot understand those skills outside the production of a particular form of the subject. That subject, the successful game player as rational masculine subject, is a fictional character created out of a number of demands and practices all of which add up to a great deal of hard work to form the masculine, games simply being one site of its production. This does not mean that girls and women cannot embody and perform masculinity. The learning of successful moves and strategies is simply part of that creation. As I will argue in Chapter 8, I suggest that this figure is only the fictional foregrounding of relationalities which make him seem real, there is no psychology of skill acquisition in any simple sense. The desire to learn the skills, the friendships which support it, the magazines consumed, identifications, defences, the cultural and social practices which produce the successful game player are as much about this as they are about complex relations in themselves.

After Deleuze and Guattari (1987), we could call this an 'assemblage'. This idea is different from Foucault's 'textual subject' precisely because it understands the processes of subject production as happening in an affective realm and through a constantly shifting set of relations. In that sense, it is not fixed or static but constantly moving and changing. This means that we need to move from the textual subject in Foucault, with multiple subject positions, to an assemblage, which is literally assembled from the bricolage of discourses, practices, cultural processes and objects which attach to certain feelings. Deleuze and Guattari (1987) give the example of 'home', which could be an arrangement of furniture, or what we make in an airline seat by bringing ipods or books to read, to a song sung to a child before it goes to sleep. In other words, an assemblage includes aspects which we would otherwise have relegated to the inside, like feelings or unconscious processes, and the outside, like objects and setting. Deleuze stresses the importance of something which flows and changes because he is attempting to develop an approach which stresses flow and movement over fixity. This means that we can think in these terms about the constant hard work of practising that is needed to fantasise the achievement of masculinity through the accomplishment of being a skilled player, even though that status of skilled player is never properly achieved and has to be reworked again and again.

In addition to the performative aspects, there are several defences necessary to create this assemblage. These could be understood as a defence against femininity, against dependence, sometimes understood through the fantasy of omnipotence and the skills of mastery and control. How are these produced? I want to explore each of these issues in order to understand how they operate for boys.

For young boys, the production of a heroic and autonomous masculinity requires affective work, one which is formative in producing them as men. We can expect dependency on mothers and attempts to get outside the grip of mothers, and equally we should expect both anxiety and frustration about not being able to win combined with a desire to become the winner. We have established that unlike the relation to film and television, identification with a hero is not enough. In order to have some semblance of appearing to achieve the fantasy of autonomous masculinity, the hard work must involve sensation and ideation. The practising of skills necessary to win in games is therefore crucial, but it must be accompanied by an investment in wanting to be the winner. Evidence of this is very clear within the data from both playing and interviews.[1] Let me begin with mothers.

I want to argue that the fantasy and performance of masculinity requires a disavowal of dependence, particularly with respect to the work of mothers. It was quite common within the interviews for boys to make statements about their game prowess that were completely contradicted by their mothers – the boys tend to present themselves as working things out on their own whereas the mothers tend to stress that the boys are still children, dependent on them. In particular, the mothers tend to contradict boys' versions of how they learn and play games. For example, Daniel's view that he looks at the manual as one strategy when he doesn't know how to do something, presents him as the rational Cartesian subject who thinks his way to the solution of problems. This is contradicted by his mother: 'Daniel's explanation of how he went through things in his manual. He wouldn't sit down and look at the manual in a pink fit. He would say "I cant do it" and leave it.' Mothers are also the ones who 'tell on' the boys, who make clear that they are not always strong and brave and able to win at the games all the time, but get angry, frustrated, fail, have tantrums and want their mummy! The mothers are the ones who give the lie to action masculinity, who lay bare its other side, especially its other emotional side. Just as in Descartes' idea that rationality was a kind of rebirth without the intervention of a woman, so mothers are the ones who puncture the fantasy of a masculinity produced without others, especially without them. Many mothers talked about their sons' anger and frustration. However, this does not stop mothers being constituted and constituting themselves as, as one mother put it, 'the lowest of the low' when it comes to games. They are powerful as adults in the lives of the children and yet most present a sense of incompetence. Another mother says when her children ask for help: 'if you can't do it, I can't do it.' And another: 'Oh Tobias, I don't know anything about that.' Tobias is sent to his dad. Only one mother claimed to know a lot about games and took a different position. Thus, in general, the ambivalent position of mothers on whom boys are dependent but on whom they can look down, helps produce a positioning in which masculinity is understood through its difference from the feminine. There are two dragons in the top favourite characters for the boys, but Eduardo is quite clear that Spiro is a 'boy dragon'. 'If I was like him', he says, 'I would flame. I might even flame my little mummy.' Note here the use of the diminutive to describe his mother. In this fantasy, he is a large dragon able to control and to punish his 'little mummy'. In the case of boys' dependency on mothers, this is accomplished both through disavowal and in the case of competence as a player, through the ways in which mothers themselves perform incompetence.

Masculinity as a defence against femininity

I want to argue that masculinity is constituted as Other to femininity, which has to be produced as its opposite. The boundaries of masculinity have to be policed to ensure that the performance of masculinity is not intruded upon by femininity, from which it must be differentiated. The performance of action masculinity in game playing can therefore be understood as containing its Other. The work of masculinity is to provide an assurance that masculine identity cannot possibly be confused with the feminine.

Harry is one of the few boys who admits to liking playing a female character. He has a good knowledge of game narratives and has a long speech in his interview about why Coco in Smash isn't sexist. Jacob says that he likes war movies, hates love movies. What is interesting about this is that of course what he dislikes are 'women's movies' – he has to position himself as masculine, which means a disavowal of the feminine. This is also evident in Jacob's remarks that 'boys get much more good and girls fight like girls on computer games and (in dainty voice) "do this and take this and take that" and the boys go like this, "get this" ' (aggressive voice). Peter says 'boys are more muscly than girls. Girls are all going "I think I'll shoot him, bang". But then the boys, the big boys, go dinnh, dinnh (gun noises).' 'I just don't like the idea of seeing a girl walking around with big muscly', and 'men are naturally stronger than women'. His mum says he gets this attitude from his dad. Dyllon 'can't stand Barbie' or girl characters unless they can be killed or can have weapons. In fact, most boys were almost beside themselves when it was suggested by a male interviewer that they might play the game of Barbie. John says that girls seem too serious, not strong enough and not humorous enough, while David thinks girl characters are boring. Daniel says 'when girls play they go "oh can you help me? I don't know this part". Instead the boys go like "oh come on, hurry up and move it".' The performance of action masculinity has a clear script. Its narrative lines are clearly articulated as different from those ascribed to femininity. Discourses of sex difference sit alongside endlessly repeated narratives of helpless heroines and action heroes. Of course, these narratives are often dented by female success, a success which must be kept at bay at all costs in order to affirm the difference and superiority of masculinity.

Although it is the mothers who give the lie to boys' autonomy and mastery, their anger and frustration with an inability to play as they would like does come through clearly in the interviews. Far more girls than boys express anxiety about not being able to play and parents do not talk a great deal about boys' anxiety. However, the desire to control and become the master implies an anxiety that cannot be allowed to gain the upper hand. It is the fear of failure that is most often expressed. For example, Nate's father talks about Nate's distress at his failure:

> 'Yeah, this one game that he really enjoys playing, what's it called, Final Fantasy 7. I'm not real familiar with the game but I believe it is a strategy type game and you save levels so that you can resume play and you don't have to restart the thing and he got a long way through it once and something went wrong with his save and he lost the level and he spun right out and there was tears and it was the biggest disaster under the sun because he'd so many hours getting to this and he couldn't save it or he hadn't saved it or whatever it was. That was a really big tragedy in his life.'

Nate himself talks about feelings of panic if his avatar cannot win. All of the expressed anxiety on the part of boys is about whether they can succeed and win or about whether they will lose or fail. For example, Ned says 'I am usually anxious. If there is a password or I am . . . a boss on a fighting game I feel really anxious. If I am about to get past a part I have never got past before I feel excited.'

In the following extract, the interviewer asks Ned's father:

> Is there any time you have observed Ned playing the games and after playing the game or during games his behaviour changes?

> **Father**: Yes, when things don't work out.
> **Interviewer**: What does he do then?
> **Father**: He usually talks to himself: 'Oh this is unreal. It can't be happening.' And this sort of thing. And I just say 'well just settle down, it is only a game.'

Many mothers talk of the frustration of their sons, as this mother says: 'Um, during, he if gets frustrated with that machine I reckon he would just about throw it through the window if he could, he gets very cranky with it.' Many boys talk of their frustration and anger at not being able to play as they would like. Indeed, Joe describes the frustration he feels when he can't do it at first and then how he learns to play so that he won't get frustrated. Simon says 'Like if I don't get to the end about when I am on my last . . . and I lose that one I get real cranky?' The interviewer asks what he does then, to which he replies, 'Just go thumping down the stairs . . . I can't get past this.'

But for some competent boys, playing is itself seen as a way of relieving tension and stress – by restoring their sense of success and winning, they feel less stressed. Some parents of boys particularly stress the importance of learning to compete and win through games, as one father says:

> Obviously, during those rare occasions when I win the games, he will obviously be upset . . . I understand that one because I could also sense his being competitive in nature. And of course you would also feel bad if you had been playing that game for many, many times than your opponent and then you lose in that particular occasion, you would feel bad and I think it is natural and um what I have done during those occasions is just encourage him, oh it is just a small difference in score and it was just my luck this time.

> **Interviewer:** So you rationalise it, put it in context?
> **Father:** Yeah I would make him feel good.

Certainly many boys present a strong liking for and desire for winning and some confidence in their powers of success. This means that many boys say that they practise on their own until they feel that they are competent enough to play with others. One mother makes it clear that if a boy is good at a game 'you are a hero – if they can go to a high level, everyone is your friend'. Conversely, some girls see boys as showing off, bragging and over-boastful and over-confident. This practice is absolutely compatible with a defence against the sensation and ideation associated with failure and dependence. To be boastful and over-confident is a practice which shores up a fragile and anxious sense of superiority. It is in this sense that we can understand the high fives, the shouts of 'we rule' and so forth, which offer a Hollywood movie style heroics to accompany a fantasy that all is as it should be – the boys are winning.

William says to another player who complains he is 'crap at this', that you have to practice: 'My words say have a try. Just what, practice, practice, practice.' In another game, this time of Pokemon Snap he demonstrates his prowess by teaching a girl how to play.

> See, I'll show you a little Pokemon sign. They're just pidgies. So you press A. Just press A. See? Pokemon food

> **Prudence:** Cool
> **William:** Wait. Go up there. Wait. Just wait. I'll show you a Pokemon sign, but you can't take a picture of it cause Professor . . .
> **Prudence:** [Mumbles]

William: No wait. Just go that way. That way. Down [Standing up and using console]
Prudence: Oops
William: Turn that way. Wait. Go down. Go down. Go down. You're going up.
Prudence: Which way's up?
William: [Pressing console] Oh. What's that?
Prudence: Thunderstone
William: Put an apple on it. God, I've never seen that. Boy. What is it? Never seen that. Is that Butterfink? Weee . . . Now can I go?
Prudence: I wanna get that Butterfink
William: Are you okay now?

[Pause]

Prudence: Another Butterfink
William: You don't take pictures like that. You press Z. And then press A. Press Z. Press Z. And press A. See? That's how . . .

What I am particularly interested in here is the way in which masculinity is presented as the achievement of game mastery through high skill levels, accompanied by actions and discourses which confirm the boy as 'on top'. Thus, we are confronted with the apparently self-made hero or autonomous rational subject of the Cogito. In both cases, and I suggest they come as a pair, the idea of being self made through hard work and practice, is both the affective work of the achievement of the fantasy of masculinity and a denial of its impossibility. By impossibility I mean two things – firstly, that the work has to be endlessly repeated, but that also it obscures relationality. That is, it is the practices which offer the appearance of success which have to be socially and psychically sustained, but both mothers and girls note that boys are not as good as they claim and mothers point out boys' dependency on others for help. I am therefore proposing that this version of masculinity is not only a fiction and fantasy in the psychoanalytic sense, but that it is a fiction which circulates endlessly in the life world because it is needed to form the basis of male dominance. However, this serves to endlessly obscure the fact that what is achieved is achieved relationally. There is no brilliant genius, no winner confirmed by practice, except that the fantasy that there is circulates to confirm a fantasy that is actually counter to what happens.

In addition, we can also note that some boys talk about how they imagine themselves already ahead in the kinaesthetic ways that Newman

(2002) mentioned. So Samuel says that he looks at the road and the car when playing a racing game, and watches the signs at the corner so that it shows you which way you are turning. Several boys say that they imagine the next space. So that while they are kinaesthetically in one space they are also imaginatively in the next one.

The same issues are also present for some fathers, as in the following interview with Tyrone, a single father of a learning disabled child. He tells the interviewer he is addicted to the game Metal Gear Solid.

> **Tyrone:** Well I was addicted to the Metal Gear Solid game, I just had to finish and it was every night I had to sort of you know, searching for all the magazines, the cheats and everything when I was stuck. I even called an expensive, you know those numbers the help things to try and find out how to get out of such a level. And yeah for a moment I was very much addicted to it.
>
> **Int:** How did you feel in that circumstance?
>
> **Tyrone:** Um, it was exciting because you are in another world. You are the character and it was, I used to look forward to it. I would come back from work and after doing my usual routine and this and that, put the kids off to bed and it was my time, here I am, I am sort of Snake sort of thing in this adventure, so I liked it.
>
> **Int:** But you didn't feel uneasy or stressed or frustrated when you couldn't get to the next level?
>
> **Tyrone:** Yeah, yeah, I think the first time I got the game, I think for the first week I sort of, it was in my mind all the time, thinking how am I going to get out of that level and thinking, this is in bed trying to fall asleep. And yes . . .
>
> **Int:** What is the downside of that then? Yes . . . okay but it makes my life a . . .
>
> **Tyrone:** It was, my life was pretty . . . not adventure, it had the mundane sort of thing, so it added a bit of adventure to it.
>
> **Int:** So you don't see that as a negative thing then, you think maybe it is a bit of a positive thing?
>
> **Tyrone:** Yeah I think so.

One of the things that is interesting about this extract is that in daily life Tyrone is a single parent of two young children, one of whom has learning difficulties. He is a working-class man in a part-time poorly paid job, who is also doing the work of bringing up children by himself. Metal Gear Solid is the place in which he can escape from the boring and very demanding aspects of his everyday life and become an action hero.

In taking on the persona of the character Snake, he becomes for a short time, the virtual embodiment of an action hero. I would contend that this has to be read against the positioning of him as rather on the side of the feminine (a nurturant parent who has to spent a lot of time looking after children). Metal Gear Solid is what defends against the possibility of being engulfed by this feminisation.

I want to take up the issue of fathers again by looking at the intercorporeal aspects of performing masculinity. The performance of masculinity is always embodied within practices which confirm its existence against the threat of the Other, the threat that it does not exist and the desire to embody it. Becoming a competent video game player for children is one route towards a technologically mediated action man narrative. Thus, the consumption of video games has to be entwined in a complex intercorporeality in which the game narratives constantly recall others through both association of sensations and of ideations and the link between them.

Creating the assemblage: action masculinity as intertextual and intercorporeal performance

Throughout the video recordings of game playing, boys (and occasionally girls) make constant reference to the action movie genre. In this way their performance of game playing is made to signify within a wider intertextuality and intercorporeality of media products and practices in which action masculinity is constituted. So, for example, there are several examples of handclaps/high fives where players congratulate each other on success. Or, for example, when Bobby and Dyllon are playing, they constantly position themselves within action-masculinity narratives, making statements like 'do it dude' and 'let's bust out of this place'. Similarly, boys also position themselves through a mixture of action-masculinity and sporting narratives, as in Peter's 'make room for me – I'm the king', and 'I'm a legend', and Bobby's 'I'm invincible'.

I want to draw particular attention to Nate who, on two separate occasions uses the phrase 'hasta la vista'. In the first instance he is playing Star Wars Racer with another boy. In this game the players have to steer racing pods that fly around a track. The steering demands considerable skill. At the moment at which he is about to overtake another pod, he says 'come to papa'. In fact, he fails, crashes and explodes, which is accompanied by 'Oh'. He then tries again to overtake another pod. As he approaches the craft he says slowly and decisively, 'hasta la vista', accompanied by a wicked little laugh and the cry 'heehaa, oh, far out' as he succeeds and comes into first place. In the second example, Nate and John are playing Zelda, using the 'Inside the Deku Tree' scenario. This is a game which is far from being a simple shoot-'em-up but nevertheless the boys certainly get excited, with Nate saying 'now you can kill things' when they manage to get a sword. In fact they need a sling shot, which is to be used to kill a spider. Nate uses the phrase 'hasta la vista' twice, as he is taking aim to kill the spider.

This is a phrase used by the Arnold Schwarzenegger character in Terminator 2. This is a very interesting and complex reference. Terminator 2 begins with a doomsday scenario in which there has been a nuclear war. A computer, Skynet, used to run defence, has learnt to develop itself and take over. When humans attempt to destroy it, it launches missiles against Russia because it understands that Russia will retaliate against the Americans. Basically the plot is that John Connor, now a child, is a future resistance leader who has to be saved against a terminator, a cyborg sent by the computer to destroy him. The task of the second terminator, played by Schwarzenegger, is to protect him. The movie is about that and about changing the course of history to prevent nuclear war. In some ways, this is a classic video game movie. Released in 1991, it features John and his friends playing video games at one point. But, more particularly, because the central battle is between two machines (cyborgs) who cannot be destroyed in that they are killed and then come back to life, it is just like a video game. In addition, the humans are simply there to direct the terminator not to do a great deal of the fighting. The phrase 'hasta la vista baby' appears twice within the film. The first occasion is when John tries to humanise the Schwarzenegger terminator by teaching him some slang. He says: 'if you want to shine them on (presumably kill them), you say hasta la vista baby'. In the final scene of the destruction of the evil terminator, Schwarzenegger shows that he has learnt by saying the phrase when attempting to terminate him. Although it appears that the terminator has been terminated at this point, he does come back one more time. The complex play between machines that have to be humanised to say the phrase 'hasta la vista baby' and the humanised machine actually being omnipotent, makes it all the more interesting. If we analyse the relationship between the use of the phrase by Nate and in the film, what is striking is the way in which Nate uses the phrase as a prelude to victory, a final blow, an omnipotent fantasy. Nate *is* the terminator, or at least fantasises being so. However, there is also a narrative about boys and parents in Terminator 2 and I want to make reference to this in the analysis that follows. John Connor has never known his father and his mother has become a strong remote fighter. She says at one point that the terminator, the cyborg, is the best choice as father for John because he will always be there and always protect him. At the end of the film, both terminators have to be terminated. John is desperate not to lose this 'father figure', but killing him off is, in fact the only solution to save the planet. It is masculine rationality, the invention of the omnipotent machine, which has produced this problem in the first place. It is only a humanised masculinity, the masculinity of the son, which can save it. In her important analysis of the Terminator movies, Susan Jeffors (1993) argues that the film keys into American concerns about the loss of fathers and manages to save masculinity by changing it:

> though the Terminator must sacrifice itself in order to prevent a destructive future, the film's plot makes clear that *it's not his fault*. Because the mechanised body from the movie's past has been shown, largely through the oppositional framework of the script, to be a 'good Terminator', its elimination is constructed to be not vengeful but tragic. The Terminator had to sacrifice itself not because it was 'bad' or harmful or even useless, but because others around it misused its components. Comparably, audiences can conclude that the aggressive and destructive male body that became the target of both ridicule and hatred may not have been *inherently* 'bad', but only, in some sociologically pitiful way, misunderstood. And who, finally, does Terminator 2 suggest *does* understand this obsolete but loveable creature? None other than John Connor, the 'new man' himself. So while T2 may present John Connor as the saviour of the human race, John Connor is finally saving something else, something far more immediate than a mechanised future and something far more dangerous than a personally-targeted mechanised killing machine. He is saving masculinity for itself, not embodying the 'new' future of masculinity, but rescuing its past for revival. (p. 261)

While it would be difficult to claim that Nate is making a direct intertextual reference or indeed has any knowledge of the film, my point is rather that the now common usage of the phrase 'hasta la vista' carries with it a set of meanings about masculinity and, more particularly, the masculine control through the utterance of a playful phrase of saying goodbye before going in for the kill. Thus, the intertextual references themselves provide evidence of the ways in which game play is lived as part of a wider circulation of embodied meanings, which continually make reference to action masculinity. It also draws on scenarios of boys and men as buddies, acting together against a common foe. I explore one such example below.

Joe and Sam

The tape begins with Sam controlling Banjo Kazooey, a single player game that involves running around collecting items, etc. Joe is giving Sam detailed and insistent instructions, controlling most of the action. Joe suggests they swap over to Mario Kart, saying it's a better game, but also that it is two-player. Joe is an expert player of both games and very knowledgeable. When they start playing, Joe is very vocal. He really wants to win, and gives commentary on his state in the game, as well as about killing and enacting revenge on the other characters. Although he competes with Sam, he doesn't point out that Sam does much less well in all the races, or direct his killing at Sam. As the game goes on, Sam also becomes more and more vocal in a similar way and begins to challenge Joe with his weapons. Although Joe doesn't seem happy about this, he doesn't use his obvious resources of sarcasm, intertextual discourses or greater game knowledge to undermine Sam, but occasionally gently mentions that Sam might be spoiling his own chances to do better. Joe seems to subscribe to a practice that is visible in some of the girls' games to a greater extent – that when playing a very competitive or violent game, your companions are considered 'on your side', and are exempt from the worst of the attacking, which is reserved for the non-player characters, even though this isn't written into the configuration of the game, which allows them to be harmed by your weapons. This excerpt is taken from late in the game, after several small incidents of Sam taking on Joe's discourses around killing and competing with the other characters.

> **Screen:** The game is taking place on a race track, with various obstacles such as cliffs, sandpits and lakes awaiting those that stray from the path. Both boys are racing as characters that appear in other games, racing against six computer opponents who are also well-known characters. The karts are equipped with weapons of various kinds, and can collect better weapons as they go, to attack the other karts. This game has been going on about two minutes, and is nearly over. The screen is split into two parts, one for each boy, with the action of their kart shown in the middle, and information about their weapons and time in the race shown on the screen.
> **Screen: Sam:** Sam's kart drives through a large crystal with a question mark hanging in it, in the road. A box in the top corner of Sam's screen cycles through several pictures of different weapons, eventually settling on a blue, spikey turtle shell.
> **Talk: Sam:** I got a spike guy!

Screen: Joe: Joe's kart drives through a similar crystal, and a banana appears in his box, an inferior weapon.

Talk: Sam: I'm gonna use it when anyone comes to me.

Screen: Sam: A sign saying 'Lap 2' appears in front of Sam's Kart.

Talk: Sam: [*scream*]

Screen: Sam: Sam's kart spins out of control for a moment, and then regains its position on the road.

Talk: Sam: I'm gonna use it.

Talk: Sam: [*loud, threatening tone*] If anyone comes to me. I use it

Talk: Joe: No, but, it'll happen on me.

Talk: Joe: Look

Screen: Joe: Joe's Kart overtakes two karts, then shoves another player off the road and overtakes it.

Screen: Joe: Joe is in second place, and his kart is on fire and out of control, veering from one side of the track to the other.

Screen: Joe: Joe's kart slides on a banana skin dropped by another player and spins for a bit, he's overtaken by several other karts.

Talk: Sam: Yep. I'll just use it.

Talk: Sam: It's going fast. I'll have to be quick.

Screen: Sam: Sam's kart is right off the track, driving over a grassy area.

Talk: Sam: One [*screaming noise*] One [*farting sound with lips*] Two [*klick, klick*] Yeaogh/Now!

Screen: A smoky projectile flies past Joe's kart.

Talk: Joe: Oh that missed!

Action: Joe: Joe's whole body expresses happiness at the weapon having missed him, with a massive grin.

Talk: Joe: It hit someone else

Talk: Sam: [*very deep voice, accompanied with a distorted face, sticking out his lips*] Yes! Some of my bullets scored

Action: Joe: Joe very quickly takes his hand away from his control to scratch his head.

Talk: Joe: Good on you! You managed it hit someone else. Good.

Action: Joe: Joe frowns deeply as he watches the screen intently.

Screen: Joe: Joe's kart approaches the finish line, it's in third place, and is closely behind the kart right in front of it.

Screen: Sam: Sam's kart is far behind, and off the track driving through some bushes.

Talk: Sam: [*still in funny, deep voice* (detracting from the gravity of the words?)] Cause you're my best friend

Action/Control: Just as Sam speaks, Joe uses his control to pause the game, without making any acknowledgement in words or body of what Sam has said.

Screen: Joe: Joe's kart crosses the finish line in third place just as he pauses the game. His section of the screen becomes frosted in grey, with the title of the race track and a buried menu allowing him to continue the game or quit out of it. Sam's screen is frozen, but he doesn't have a similar menu.

Talk: Joe: I just need to scratch

Action: Joe: Joe rubs his eye with his hand in a large movement.

Talk: Sam: [*still in funny voice*] You're my best friend

Talk: Joe: Let's go

Talk: Sam: [*still in funny voice*] So I don't want you to die

Talk: Joe: [*smiling broadly, carefully and stylishly said*] I don't die

Here are two 'guys', two 'buddies' working together as a team to defeat the enemy. What interests me here is the way in which this is enacted in relation to the intertextuality of Hollywood. It seems to come from an amalgamation of buddy movies in which male friendship is established in adversity, each helping the other and triumph is expressed through gestures like high fives, back slapping and cries of 'we rule'. What is learnt here is that playing is action masculinity, is friendship, is the fictional space of the buddy movie. As these complex relationalities come in and out of the frame, we see that what it means to be a male player can also encompass highly stylised relations of masculinity.

However, success also depends upon the consumption of the other accoutrements of game-playing masculinity: game magazines, talks about games with friends, trying to impress by doing well at games, reading certain books, watching certain TV programmes and films, dressing in a particular fashion, behaving in a certain way to girls, women and femininity. Taken together, these are the practices which produce the successful game player. My aim is to demonstrate both how it is accomplished and what else is present as embodied desires, fears, fantasies. There is no skill without the investment in it because there would be no reason to practice. I am trying to say that the fantasy of the winner (e.g. Crash Bandicoot Champion) is an essential component, because imagining belonging to the group of winners is essential to this membership of action-masculinity. It isn't simply what practices the children engage in but what they fantasise engaging in and being. I am suggesting that it is the wanting to be that subject that drives these boys (and girls) on, and so their practices are a constant effort to become it, something that, in the Lacanian (Lacan, 1977) sense, is always illusory. I would argue that this fantasising is an essential part of what makes games pleasurable and therefore what draws men and boys in particular into the games. It is therefore a central marketing tool. As I will go on to argue in Chapter 7, without these fantasies and pleasures, it could be argued that video games would not be successful as a product. There is a complex relation between the economics of multinational capitalism, game design, fantasies and performances of masculinity and the acquisition of the skills necessary to become a successful player. It is that complex relation that I seek to unpick as the book progresses. I will explore the details of how playing is accomplished in Chapter 8.

I will return to examples of boys' play later in the book. My aim here is to signal the way that I am framing the issue of masculinity. I am not claiming that all games are masculine, but I am attempting to develop an argument about games in relation to masculinity, that is, that many games are one site for the production of contemporary masculinity. Games go well beyond movies because they allow what Ryan called internal and external interaction. If we can restate that, following Hansen's kinaesthetic as the feeling our way through virtual space, then this makes us engage with the fact that the modernist idea of development, as a progress of abstraction through action on concrete objects, no longer holds in any simple sense. But that does not mean that games do not allow the embodiment of fantasies of omnipotent masculinity. I have tried to show how they might indeed be both extremely powerful and pleasurable because they allow both engagement in the fantasy of being an action hero and its omnipotent control, which allows the fantasy of the achievement of masculinity through the disavowal of dependency on adults, especially mothers. I am suggesting that this works in relation to a number of self management practices for boys, which we could understand as working to produce the possibility of masculine performance on the one hand and a fantasy on the other. While I am proposing that this is very powerful indeed, virtually no game research seems to put this forward as its central issue, which I think downplays the aspect of masculinity in relation to game play. I suggest further that it is a crucial issue for girls and women, as I will explore in the next chapter.

4
'Remember Not to Die': Girls Playing Video Games

Introduction

Eight year old Erica instructs other girls how to play a particular game. 'Remember not to die', she says, 'all you have to do, is not die – how easy is that?' Notice how she uses the passive construction – she instructs her fellow players not to remember to kill but to remember to avoid being killed, 'not to die', the most basic aspect of game play. In this chapter, I explore what I see as the implications of the complex positioning of femininity in video game play for young girls.

While there is growing address to gender and video game play (e.g. Kennedy, 2002; Fromme, 2003), most of it involves analyses of the games themselves and hardly any engages with what happens when playing, and even then there is little concerning the play of young children. While there is plenty of interest to be said about the construction of the games themselves, it is in playing the games that the three-fold approach to affect discussed in the last two chapters may be understood. I argued in the last chapter that games, through their particular engagement with kinaesthetics and the double inside/outside fantasy, provided a basis for the complex work of the achievement of contemporary masculinity. Understanding masculinity as both affect and performance is also to assume that its production is managed and regulated. What I want to argue in this chapter is how that understanding sits in relation to the girls in this research. There is no reason why a girl may not find pleasure in a performance and position usually understood as masculine. Indeed, it is my contention that the regulation of contemporary femininity demands it, as we shall see. This does not mean, however, that it does not pose problems for girls and it is the complexities of the issue that I would like to explore here. Contemporary masculinity, then, becomes those sets of affective relations, performances and discursive practices through which masculinity is known and accomplished. This does not map masculinity onto male bodies but sets up a gender difference which is constantly marked and therefore is differently lived in relation to girlhood and boyhood as differentiated. However, along with a long tradition of feminist psychoanalytic work, I argue that the achievement of masculinity and femininity is always out of reach (e.g. Rose, 1983). As I argued in the last chapter, this idea can be related to recent work on the assemblage. This means that performativity can be understood in relation to unconscious fantasies, that work to shore up anxieties about not being masculine or feminine enough, or indeed being too masculine or too feminine, evoked somatically through embodied affect, linked to a long history of associations, both within history and biography and in the life world. I have asserted here that many games are the site for the production of contemporary masculinity because they both demand and appear to ensure performances such as heroism, killing, winning, competition and action, combined with technological skill and rationality. My central claim is that in relation to girls, this constitutes a problem because contemporary femininity demands practices and performances which bring together heroics, rationality, etc. with the need to maintain a femininity which displays care, co-operation, concern and sensitivity to others. This means that girls have complex sets of positions to negotiate while playing – how do you win while caring for others who may lose, for example? So, I aim to explore how the demands of contemporary femininity are lived out in the ways that girls actually play games in the club. In what follows I discuss the management and regulation of contemporary femininity in relation to issues in my observations of game play and some aspects of the interviews.

In order to progress in most of the games the children play in the club, the children have to kill or destroy something, even if it is only to get to the next stage, although in some games such as Star Wars Racer, it is more important to drive well to avoid being destroyed and therefore out of the game. It is the way that Erica puts her instruction in the passive voice that seemed to me to contrast with the boys' constant injunctions to practise enough to be good enough to win, as I explored in the last chapter. Here Erica is talking not about winning but about avoiding being killed. In order to practise enough to win, it is necessary to go way beyond a competence in which the only concern is to avoid being killed. Of course the passive voice is reminiscent of that ascribed to femininity, with the active voice ascribed to masculinity, to action on and in the world. For reasons that I explore in Chapter 6, many of the girls did have a poor competence which meant that they often failed to get beyond a basic stage of the game, though it was by no means true for all of them. However, pursuing my idea that some games are one site for the production of contemporary masculinity, I wondered if Erica's use of the passive voice told us something about femininity and games. Classically, the feminine is rescued by the masculine – and rescue in order to be protected and cared for has been a central issue in the analysis of romantic narratives for women (Radway, 1984) as well as in my own work on comics for girls (Walkerdine, 1984). How then might she take on the active voice, become the hero? Much has changed in the 20 years since I wrote my paper 'Some day my prince will come' (Walkerdine, 1984), about the selfless heroines of girls' comics. Girls are offered girl power and a much greater sense of their own possibility of becoming. In addition, we are presented with female heroes in Hollywood films (though see note 3), though romantic narratives are as common as they ever were (Gill, 2006). In addition of course, there are many female avatars in video games which appear to offer spaces for the performance of heroics, action and competition. However, this assumes a kind of voluntarism – that is, that what we need to do is to offer performative spaces for girls and all will be well. This means criticising a notion that a central issue for girls is the kind of games available (Cassell and Jenkins, 1998) because this approach does not engage with the affective relations of which I wrote above. That is, if performativity in games about competition and winning is a fantasy, which guards against anxieties, this is where we have to look to produce a more complex explanation than simply assuming that girls can and should take up previously masculine positions. When they do not, we pathologise them, which I think is an inappropriate way to understand the issue. This is one reason why I feel that simply looking at female avatars, or different kinds of games, or indeed that girls perform heroics, is, by itself, not enough, because it returns us to assumptions about reading off what girls and women do simply from the relations within the text itself. In the girls' game playing in this research, it is the consistent engagement with both competition and co-operation that is striking, together with what look like attempts to hide the desire to win. Of course, when we to look at boys' playing we equally find anxieties, but it is my argument that the cultural practices marshalled for masculinity offer a different kind of resolution as the apparently successful accomplishment of masculinity. This does not mean, however, that the complexities of operating in a predominantly masculine space while attempting to keep alive a femininity which can in fantasy ensure the possibility of 'womanliness' (Riviere, 1986), is not a constant issue for all girls. If many games are one site for the production of contemporary masculinity it follows that the tasks for masculinity and femininity are different. To think about this,

I would like to combine a Foucauldian emphasis on self management techniques as Foucault elaborated in his later work (e.g. Foucault, 1986), together with an address to affect as discussed in the previous chapter. I propose that the performance of contemporary femininity may demand something in fact more convoluted and complicated than the fantasised achievement of masculinity – that is, the management of co-operation and competition, caring and winning. If the performance of masculinity is what is produced in relation to game play, then isn't the self management task for the girl that much more complex? Don't girls also at the same time have to perform femininity, attempting to keep going the oppositions and contradictions that are all too present? That is, they have to pursue the demands of contemporary femininity which blend together traditional masculinity and femininity. It is my argument that trying to do both these things while playing games is a very complex and difficult task. I am suggesting that it is possible to explain the complex performance displayed by girls if we take the argument I have been making as the basis for an explanation. It is with this in mind that I want to think about how the young girls played games, interpreting their play through a framework which assumes that they are managing contradictory positions of masculinity and femininity. Wanting to be the action hero of video games requires work, constant hard work, the work of practice, practice, practice. And of course, as many girls say, they are not very interested in that kind of work because its end point, action-heroic masculinity, is not the work they have to achieve – the work of femininity is different, but does involve managing the competing positions. One of the problems with the Foucauldian approach is that these positions seem static and we then think of an active subject doing the managing. Can we avoid this problem by going further than I went before in *Changing the Subject* (Henriques et al., 1984) to an idea that this 'management' is affective work, constituted through the affective relations of positions accorded in the practices, which are of course, at the same time, discursive?

Managing femininity

I want to begin by thinking about an observation made early on in the Sydney project by one of the researchers. She felt very disappointed when she was watching the girls play – she felt that they played in a different way from the boys, that is more sociably, with game playing as an accompaniment to other activities, such as chatting, and that they didn't play to win or with the competitive edge of the boys. She was upset by this because she had been a girl at school who was good at mathematics, which had singled her out, and she felt disappointed that the girls were not displaying the technological enthusiasm she would have liked them to display. Subsequently, we analysed the way that the girls played very carefully and felt that there was no basis for suggesting in any simple terms that the girls played differently from the boys, in the sense that they wanted to win any the less or did not show interest in trying to play well. However, the researcher was not deluded – she was picking something up – a difference in orientation to games. This difference has been the subject of a growing body of literature (see Cassell and Jenkins, 1998 for a review) about girls and video and computer games. Much of this literature looks at a number of factors to explain girls' lower participation in games.

In my own work on girls and mathematics in the 1980s, (Walkerdine et al., 1989, 1998), it wasn't a simple matter of girls behaving more like boys – breaking rules etc. – to be understood as mathematical thinkers. Far from it – examples from that research demonstrated that it was certainly not a simple matter of girls behaving or performing differently. Performance which was praised by teachers in boys met with pejorative comments when displayed by girls. I am suggesting therefore that it is not simply a case of making video games 'girl friendly', nor in any simple sense that girls don't like or are no good at video games. Rather, I want to raise the difficulties of the management of femininity in the present.

I want to explore the complex ways in which some girls who were videotaped while playing games, usually in pairs, but sometimes in larger groups, managed the contradictory positionings outlined above. It should be said at the outset that there were girls who were very keen on winning – it was very far from the case that girls didn't want to win – but it was the case that no girl was as competent or indeed as interested a player as the top boys.[1] In their interviews all boys talk about the kudos of being a good player in terms of relations with other boys and so of the necessity to practise until they are good enough to win. Boys have to try to win but girls wanting to win risk losing their designation as feminine by coming too far onto the side of masculinity. No wonder then that many girls find this task too difficult, despite the injunctions for them to be empowered, and that most of them are not as good at games as the boys or, perhaps more accurately, as the boys would like to be.

Cute and cuddly characters: the self presentation of girls as disavowing violence and liking only cuteness

Of course we all 'know' that women like fluffy animals, cute and cuddly, as well as babies and small children. On first glance, this liking for soft and cuddly things speaks of non-violence, of softness and kindness. I wonder though whether it serves another purpose, that is, to divert attention away from power and aggression – we see cuddly kittens not dangerous tigers. Or perhaps being cute and cuddly is a way of tolerating oppression and powerlessness and making it into a virtue. Whatever the reason, many girls in the study chose cute and cuddly avatars as their favourites in the games which they played in the club. These were the top-rated games for their age-group. The five favourite avatars chosen by the girls are Kirby, Donkey Kong, Pikachu – 'he's the cute and cuddly one', Princess Peach and Angelica. One of the interesting things about the avatars is that they may be played in one particular game in the club but in fact many of them circulate between games, so we can only speculate about what makes these the girls' favourites. But it is interesting that both Princess Peach and Angelica are female (Princess Peach with characteristics of hyperfemininity with pink dress, blonde hair and a crown), while Pikachu and Kirby are round, cute and cuddly and of no clear gender, though both with excellent special powers. Donkey Kong is a gorilla and rather coded as masculine. Apart from Donkey Kong, what is noticeable about these avatars is their either absence of, or ambiguous, masculinity. It may be that these are the most proto-feminine avatars available to the girls. Princess Peach in particular has characteristics which fit with the girls' stated interest in special magical powers. But the others combine cuteness with power and therefore may come closest to the possibility of competitiveness and classic femininity.

As we can see, it is not the case that girls always choose female avatars but their top avatars, if not female, tend to be of the cute and cuddly kind. Both girls and boys talk about female avatars as having less power – many boys cite Princess Peach as the most obvious example of this. However, the difficulty with interpreting this is that it depends on which version of which game is being discussed, since she appears in many games over a considerable period of time and so changes and evolves as a character. There is some debate amongst the children about whether she is a poor avatar, but generally it is assumed that if the girls pick her they are not going to win because she has poor powers. This is a mythology which seems to be quite prevalent amongst game afficionados. However, this doesn't stop some girls picking her because they like certain qualities about her, usually the fact that she is pretty and a princess.[2]

Some girls also talk about 'cuddly' or 'cute' avatars as male. For example, Rosa dreams of Pikachu, cute, as a pet: 'whenever he needs sleep or something I'd be really gentle with him'. Notice how she moves from 'being' Pikachu as she needs to play, to looking after 'him'. The girls operate as though they will be more able to cope with the male avatars if these are brought down to size, rendered less macho. This positions them very

clearly as mothering and caring, gaining power by looking after an emas-
culated cuddly male avatar. This suggests that this position is one in which
the cuddly male avatar is rendered powerless and the girl powerful. It is
a good way to manage the contradiction of femininity and masculinity in
that it gives the girl a position of power, but it is, of course, very restrictive.
In this scenario, there is no aggression at all – neither for males or females.
So, rendering the male avatar cuddly certainly cuts down the possibility
of the girl as object of violence but at a very high price.[3] Games do not
afford a subject position in which the heroine can look after the hero –
she is forced to compete to win. This may relate to why most of the girls
say they prefer fantasy play based on television characters to video games,
in that it offers them a greater range of fantasised positions. It is equally
interesting that a favoured position is a witch from TV shows such as
Charmed, in which the feminine power is produced by casting spells. It
would be informative to compare this to other female heroines from TV
shows, such as Zena or Buffy. I suggest that perhaps casting spells or fantasised overthrowing of, or defeating, men is different from having the
skills to play to win, or is at least complicated in actual play by the
demand to maintain a caring and co-operative femininity. Of course,
equally, we could see the demands of masculinity as obscuring its opposite
and projecting it onto women (Hollway, 1984).

The avatars that some girls favour seem to be versions of a classic
femme fatale. The version of 'cute with a poison sting' (Polly's choice of
Bilbasaur and Licka Tongue, seems to sum it all up). The *femme fatale* of
course exudes an active and passionate sexuality, but within classic
melodrama or thrillers she is often evil, and while she is allowed to be
active (gun toting, powerful, for example) she is never allowed to sur-
vive. Ruth likes 'a cute little person with a dress on, a crown, blondie
hair, nice shoes and a princess'. She is too scared to play a boy avatar and
she doesn't like them – 'big, huge moustache', 'big fat bully'. However, she
likes Techno 3 fighting girls, wrestling girls who are 'pretty and scary'.
So, an acceptable position seems to be the double positioning as cute and
powerful. Again, this is a useful way for a girl to resolve contradictions
of femininity and masculinity. It is my guess that it would be much
harder for many girls to like an avatar who had the metaphorical 'poison
tongue' but who was not cute, as this may be to cross too far onto the
side of masculinity. We could therefore argue, as I set out above, that the
girls' favourite TV characters, the sisters from *Charmed*, Power Puff girls,
Zena, Sabrina could all be described as possessing those dual characteristics.
I am suggesting therefore that the choice of cute and cuddly avatars and
femmes fatale are two ways of finding a position which attempts to resolve

the contradiction between femininity and masculinity which the girls must hold in some way.

In the next section, I want to think about the different ways that girls cope with attempting to perform masculinity while also performing femininity – that is, how they deal with these contradictions within game play itself.

Katie and Rosa

This analysis is based upon a detailed case study of two girls, Katie and Rosa, who both, in their different ways, exemplify an attempt to perform masculinity while maintaining a performance of femininity. It is my argument that there is not one single way of resolving the difficulties of this duality, and that to understand how it is that different girls perform in different ways we would have to look at the specificity of the case of each girl – something which is outside the scope of this chapter.

The girls are situated as female subjects in contexts where femininity carries certain privileged inscriptions and embodiments as well as some that are required to be disavowed. For example, it is clear from the interviews with both parents and children that boys, but never girls, are associated with violence and fighting and possible negative effects of video games (see Chapter 5).

As we have seen, the girls tend to position themselves as liking cute avatars and not liking the fighting in the games, but attention to the videos suggests an excitement and engagement in the activity of killing and competing that is disavowed through/in the girls' constructions of themselves in the interviews. I want to explore a number of examples of Katie and Rosa's play in order to explore the points I am making.

> **66. Katie:** If you kill yourself in half the time then you can go to another world . . .
> **67. Rosa:** Yer, I know, but then it will be game over, then it's your go
> **68. Katie:** No
> **69. Rosa:** It is
> **70. Katie:** I'll let you have another go
> **71. Rosa:** No, it's all right. I want you to.
> **72. Katie:** It's just if you don't like this level. But you have to tell me if you don't like this level and you're going to kill yourself, cause you can say that any time.
> **73. Rosa:** Wow
> **74. Katie:** Do you like [inaud.] or something?

75. **Rosa:** No I don't
76. **Katie:** Yes you do. This is your last lap, one before my turn, and then it's my go
77. **Rosa:** No it's not.
78. **Katie:** Yes it is
79. **Rosa:** Was only joking. Wow
80. **Katie:** Remember it's not like for the rest of the time its my go
81. **Rosa:** I know, but you're probably good at this
82. **Katie:** No I'm not. [*giggle*] Believe me, I don't go into this level

In this example Katie and Rosa are engaged in the issue of when Katie will get a turn. Open conflict or arguing is avoided as they each conduct a series of covert negotiations instigated by Katie and resisted by Rosa. There is nothing that passes as overt power-play as it is conducted in a friendly, non-confrontational manner – despite the complex work spent on positioning themselves as non-contesting subjects whilst actually contesting when Katie will get a turn. Katie seems to simultaneously suggest she is not interested in having a turn (deferring to Rosa) whilst working hard to ensure that she gets a turn. Katie reminds Rosa that even when she does get a turn 'it's not like for the rest of the time'. Rosa, on the other hand, simultaneously suggests she wants Katie to have another go, 'it's alright, I want you to', whilst resisting the possibility of it happening: she is dismissive of Katie's suggestion for play with 'Yer, I know, but then it will be game over, then it's your go.' In the face of Katie's continued attempts to negotiate her turn Rosa later positions herself as 'only joking'. When Katie finally gets her turn she giggles and disavows her competence, thus locating herself in her habitual 'feminine' position of incompetence. What I am suggesting here is that a feminine positioning necessitates this more passive/covert negotiation of power, especially in terms of a relation of coercion and resistance. This requires Katie to simultaneously express and disavow her desire to have a turn and for Rosa to simultaneously resist whilst appearing not to ('only joking'). When read as a performance of gender and the imperative for girls to be 'nice', 'friendly' and 'co-operative' it is no wonder that these different patterns in managing conflict emerge. Clearly the work that Katie and Rosa are doing around turn taking is situated in the imperatives of being 'girl' and this necessarily produces the negotiation of contradictory inscriptions – they are required to disavow the desire for control, authority and self-interest whilst simultaneously acting to achieve these things.

This ambivalence is also played out in terms of knowledge and mastery. Katie routinely takes up a position as 'dumb' although she has greater knowledge and familiarity with the game, while Rosa takes up the position of authoritative knower even when she is wrong or does not know. Katie seems to defer to Rosa's position – not in that she does not continue to assert the validity of her knowledge, but in that she does not challenge/ question/contest Rosa's position of authority. They are playing a platform game called Crash Bandicoot. In this game they have to control the avatar Crash Bandicoot to overcome obstacles to get to different levels. This involves, at its most basic, not dying, but also the obstacles are of a wide variety and some are animals or people who have to be destroyed. This is done by the help of various aids and skills.

> **108. Rosa:** . . . I think I'm gonna like this one better. I wanna do this one, the Great Wall of China.
> **109. Katie:** This is not the Great Wall of China
> **110. Rosa:** Well I didn't say it is. Oh no, this is . . .
> **111. Katie:** That's the one where you . . .
> **112. Rosa:** I know this isn't the Great Wall of China, I know. What happens when you fall in that? Is that water?

And later:

> **602. Rosa:** Now look who's the expert at this. You or me?
> **603. Katie:** Umm, you
> **604. Rosa:** Thank you. You gave my advice
> **605. Katie:** You always were the expert

Here Katie concurs with Rosa's positioning of herself as the 'expert'. This is not a position open to Katie as she positions herself as 'dumb/stupid'. Despite Katie's greater knowledge and familiarity, she is a tentative player who rarely takes risks. (Her successes in other game sessions are often a function of conservative play whilst the others take risks and then lose). She focuses her play on avoiding being killed and often pleads 'don't kill me'. She is the subject upon whom killing is performed. Rosa, on the other hand, is the subject who kills. She is a greater risk taker and is often impatient with Katie's caution and slowness. Rosa positions herself positively in relation to mastery and authority despite her lack of knowledge and experience and Katie positions herself as hopeless/useless/ incompetent, and by implication lacking mastery and authority, despite her comparatively greater knowledge and experience. When Katie watches Rosa play she is helpful, supportive and encouraging, constantly affirming what a good player Rosa is. When Rosa watches Katie play she is impatient, derisive and critical. This could be understood in terms of specific historically and biographically developed relationalities in which different ways of managing the contradictory performances of masculinity and femininity become sedimented. Rosa strays more into what might be defined as more typically 'masculine' performances (such as 'I'm a hard person'), whereas Katie displays more stable performances as 'helpful' but neither authoritative or masterful. Katie positions Rosa as 'crazy' and Rosa positions Katie as 'lacking' – slow, cautious, inept, scared, 'Oh this guy's easy, come on [*very impatient and derisive*] . . . You're too scared.'

> **125. Rosa:** Well, that's some . . . I dare you to go in that
> **126. Katie:** No. I don't want to kill myself. Did anybody notice here that this girl called Rosa, I know her? She's really crazy.

And later:

> **134. Katie:** You're crazy
> **135. Rosa:** What? Fall into that hole. Fall into that hole. Kill it. Just run, run, run. Do you ever want to get to this castle? Like, yes. Oh no.
> **136. Katie:** You must hate me sometimes.
> **137. Rosa:** No. Just, naar, only joking. I was joking when I said that. You see I'm a hard person. Does the frog kill you?
> **138. Katie:** No he kisses you [*giggle*]
> **139. Rosa:** And then you turn into, um, a charming prince.

And later:

> **176. Rosa:** You're not going to. Don't worry, there's not that much things anyway. Jump. What's wrong with you? If you could . . .
> **177. Katie:** Cause last time I jumped over, I nearly died. I need hundreds. Oh, I only got six there
> **178. Rosa:** Yer, cause you had a life, you got a life then. Oh you take your time.
> **179. Katie:** [*laughs*] What?
> **180. Rosa:** Gee, you take your time. Just run through the gate
> **181. Katie:** [*giggles*] I'm trying
> **182. Rosa:** Ah Ah, you're trying?
> **183. Katie:** Yer, I'm trying
> **184. Rosa:** [*mimics*] I'm trying
> **185. Katie:** I'm trying. I know I'm trying, I'm scared now. I'm scared.

Katie frequently describes herself as 'scared', 'I'm scared', 'I'm so scared', 'I'm scared now', 'this is scary', 'its too scary for me'. As a player she is scared of being killed and preoccupied with dying/avoiding being killed. In the following extract scared and dumb are positioned as continuous states.

> 197. **Katie:** I'm so scared. Is it going to hurt me?
> 198. **Rosa:** No darling [*patronizing/mocking adult voice*]
> 199. **Katie:** Oh, I'm . . . [*sings*] Dah, dumb, dumb. Dumb . . . scared.

Yet, as a watcher she explicitly encourages Rosa to kill: 'Try and kill that frog', 'Kill the frog. Scootch him. Smooch him. Smooch him', 'Kill him. Kill him.' But she also protests 'I can't watch, I can't watch.' Thus, when Rosa follows her entreaty to kill Katie hides behind her hands, arms, or turns away, maintaining her position as 'scared'. Despite the requirement of the game that play proceeds by killing, Katie resists this by either playing cautiously to protect herself or asking someone else to do the killing for her, encouraging the other to kill when she is observer. The contradiction/ ambivalence between this simultaneous disavowal and engagement is masked by the feminised performance of 'scared' and 'hiding'.

Rosa, on the other hand, shows no hesitation to position herself as 'killer'. Just as Katie is preoccupied with being 'scared', Rosa is preoccupied with 'killing': 'I can kill it', 'Yer I killed it'. She never talks about herself as in danger, as scared or as likely to be killed. It is important to remember that within the game killing is associated with mastery and winning and so Rosa often talks about which levels are hardest and about her success at getting to another level. Rosa is advantaged by Katie's 'scaredness' and reluctance to kill. In performing the killing for Katie, Rosa gets control of the game and the turn reverts to her even when it is not her turn. After one such episode Rosa is careful to remind Katie that even though Rosa is playing she is playing Katie's turn and that when the game is over it will still legitimately be Rosa's turn. In this way the issue of turn-taking continues to be an ongoing, if not always overt, struggle.

> 807. **Rosa:** I'm probably gonna have your go, my go, then. I'm probably going to have both of them you're so scared
> 808. **Katie:** Yer I know. I'm scared of everything. I'm scared
> 809. **Rosa:** Why, would you be scared? This is easy
> 810. **Katie:** Rrrrrrrrrrrr. Kill, kill, kill. Run, run, run. Kill. Can you try and go over there? Because I, I don't know
> 811. **Rosa:** No.

812. Katie: Ugabuga. Scary. Don't make me go through this again. Oh yer, I forgot, I'm not doing it [*giggles*] Oh, you're going to scare me like that, aren't you Lillypot? Oh, yer, and the fish are gonna to scare me too. Why's everyone trying to scare me?

813. Rosa: I don't know. Probably they hate you

814. Katie: Yes. I think that too. It's so amazing isn't it? Such an intelligent girl. Wooga, wooga. Get that thing. Get that thing. Kill the fish. Kill the things. Kill the boxes! [*giggle*] Kill the boxes. The boxes are so rude to us

815. Rosa: Oh, where am I going?

816. Katie: Ahh, get them, get them all, get them all, get them all.

I want to emphasise here the extent to which these exchanges appear to be very friendly. When watching the videos the girls appear to be messing around, having fun, using funny voices, joking with each other and getting along very well. The contestation of control/power is thus almost invisible and is more easily read on the page in terms of the complex and ongoing negotiation of positions. These positions centre on the issue of power and control and are played out through turn-taking. What the girls are negotiating is 'who will take control'. Here control is both literal and an inscription of power. They are engaged in an embodied performance of/with a technology that is manipulated through the 'control' or 'console'. They are playing a game for one player only and must thus take turns. The player has the 'control' – and is thus located in the position of control/power (and of course the attendant controlling fantasy discussed in the last chapter). The ongoing negotiation of who will have a turn is thus also about who will have control. Katie is mobile between the role of watcher and player, except when it comes to the 'scary killing bits' when she cedes control/play to Rosa. Rosa, on the other hand, is a very impatient watcher – she prefers to play and willingly plays Katie's turn for her. This fascinating construction ' playing her turn for her' masks the fact that Rosa is actually playing and in control. Both girls are aware of this, but the relation of power they have established through Rosa's dominance and Katie's acquiescence successfully keeps the power play covert. In the following continuing struggle to get Rosa to play level three Katie flatters her by telling her what a good player she is, at one stage resting her chin on her hand and fluttering her eyelids. Again, this flattery might be read as 'manipulation' through 'feminine wiles', so that various sites of heterosexuality can be assumed. It also serves to make safe the position that Katie takes in relation to Rosa, assuring Rosa that she has more authority. This desire for safety is consistent with the position that Katie takes up in relation to herself as a game playing subject – cautious, preoccupied with her safety, worried about dying and avoiding the scary bits. This can be read as a thoroughly 'feminine' inscription, and whilst she competes for power from this position she is ultimately acquiescent and silenced.

Playing a four-player game

Katie and Rosa are playing a four person game of Super Smash with Jess and Gilly. This is a game in which avatars attack each other with a variety of weapons. They each have a separate control and are playing separate avatars. They stay in the game as long as their avatar lives/survives. At the end of the game they engage in a perfunctory discussion of who has won and who came second, third and fourth. This position of winning is constructed for them, as the information is displayed onscreen at the end of the game. In saying that their discussion is perfunctory I'm not suggesting that they don't want or like to win – though they take quite different positions to winning. Rather, winning does not visibly confer any status on the winner. Status seems already established along other lines and is not affected in any major way by incidences of winning. Katie for example, positions herself as a 'dumb' 'loser'. Even though she sometimes wins, often through default or cautious play, she still positions herself as the loser. Clearly, the position she takes in the group is not contingent on her winning, but on her losing or positioning herself as the loser. Jess does not always win, but she has most authority in the group. All negotiations are conducted through her and she sits most centrally and acts most centrally to the play. Winning or losing does not alter the position of control/authority that Jess assumes. The positions the girls take up are reasonably stable across the duration of the video. The girls sit right to left: Rosa, Katie, Jess and Gilly. Jess and Katie are central in terms of physical position and dominance. They dominate the conversation and the activity. Rosa, on the outer right is relatively silent and intensely focused on the play. The bulk of her comments are play related self-talk directed at the onscreen characters. Gilly on the outside left says almost nothing and is most animated when she identifies her place at the end of the game. Jess and Katie are friends and their relationship, and Jess's status as the leader, are firmly established. Thus, though Jess and Katie dominate the talk, Jess's position as the one with most authority is unchallenged. All the girls are engaged in/by the play.

What struck me on first viewing was the position Jess takes up as a game player. She dominates the group, the space, the game and the noise level. She does the majority of the work in managing the group in terms of the selection of games and avatars, etc. ('Alright, you ready?', 'Everyone ready? Are they sure?'). She is loud, bossy, takes a lot of physical space, does air-punch type moves of victory, says 'whoo hoo' and other similar calls that seem to connote power and control. Jess typically says such things as 'Ar. Ar. Ar. Wait for a second . . . Fire, fire, fire. Come back, come back, come back. Yes. Oh bugger.' Katie on the other hand typically says 'Don't hurt me. I'm innocent', often in an affected whisper or an exaggeratedly 'girly' 'loser' voice. Gilly, though mostly silent, is more likely to make observations about her play and herself as player: 'That's me', 'I'm flying', etc. Rosa, like Jess, is intensely focused on the game and on the action of the game: 'Kick. Kick, kick, kick. Kick him up. Oh. Come on. Yer jump. Jump.' Unlike Jess, Rosa engages in little social talk directed at the other players or any audience other than herself. Even Rosa and Jess's laughter may be read as different from Katie's – the former is more robust and the latter would be understood as giggling.

I am attempting to argue that the successful game playing subject is 'masculine' (both in terms of the technology and the action of fighting/killing/winning) and that those girls who are most engaged with the games, who are most successful, or have the most power in the group, take up what might generally be identified as what we would read as traditionally more masculine positions. Gilly is silent. Katie is, in her own words, 'dumb', 'a loser', 'an idiot', 'scared' and is prone to giggling and squeamishness, 'Don't try and hurt me' and turning away when killing takes place. Jess is in control, loud, authoritative, skilled, knowledgeable and enjoys winning and killing; 'Weeee. Boom [*makes noises and then laughs*] I'm just bashing up everything.' Rosa, though less engaged in the social activity/talk of the group, is very focused on the killing activity of the game and her comments are therefore more focused on the specific activity of killing: 'I'll kill you, no matter if it's the last thing I do', 'Well I'm just killing everybody. Whoa. Cool, I'm just killing everybody', 'I love killing people' (accompanied by a sniggering laugh), 'I want to kill someone. No offence to everyone.' What I'm attempting to suggest here is that the successful game player is required to take up a visibly masculine subject position in terms of stereotypical inscriptions/performances of gender (Rosa 324: I can do whatever I want. I'm a grown man now mama' followed by 'I'm talking to me mama' in an affected/exaggerated masculine voice).

Each of these girls differently manages the contradictions of femininity and masculinity and thus appears to achieve what we could recognise through a psychologised discourse as different 'personalities'. But could we understand them instead as embodied, affective and performative engagements with these contradictions over a long period? We could understand this as unconscious and social and cultural relationalities or the continuous creation of assemblages. However, we must also recognise that the configurations change according to game and players, so we should be wary of treating these positions as too fixed, but more as an indication of how contradictions are resolved from moment to moment in the spatial and temporal flow of the game and across the many practices and relations which form embodied practices for coping. Rosa does not compete with Jess's social position (of power) within the group, but makes her own avatar compete with Jess's avatar within the game. This allows for some power play that is legitimised by the activity of the game, but is not obvious or confrontational within the social group. Again, the group looks cohesive, democratic and friendly.

Katie's performance during the group game is markedly different from that when she is playing in a pair with Rosa. This could be accounted for in at least two ways. One, she takes up different positions as a player and observer, more feminised when playing, and in the group she is always a player. Two, she is friends with Jess and may take up a more exaggerated feminine position around Jess's performance of authority. Katie giggles more, sucks her thumb and generally works harder to assert her fear and failure: 'I'm innocent', 'My enemy's myself', 'I'm dead, see what you do when you hurt people? They cry [*giggles*]', 'Don't hurt me please', 'I'm an idiot.' Completely absent from this episode is the type of power play that could be seen between Katie and Rosa in other exchanges. Jess positions herself as winner and Katie is positioned by Rosa as loser. However, careful scrutiny and insistence on Rosa's part reveals that Katie is actually second and Gilly third, leaving Jess in fourth place and Rosa in first. Jess is resistant to being fourth (last/loser) and Rosa clearly establishes her position as first. Interestingly, whilst Rosa positions herself as winner and cannot believe it when she has lost ('How can that be?', 'I damn well came fourth'), Katie positions herself as loser and cannot believe it when she is not ('Me? No I didn't . . . I never win'). Thus, the idea of fixity has to be challenged by the sense that these positions are fluid and changing – there is no fixed 'personality' but it is rather that relations are differently mobilised in different dynamic intersections across space and time (see Chapter 8).

This becomes clearer if we examine another four-player game in which a group of girls shift the dynamic of the play to accommodate the expressed fear of being killed of one of the group. Gina, Bronwyn, Melanie and Melissa are playing Super Smash, which is an extremely hectic game that takes place in a cramped single-screen area made up of several platforms, and involves attacking each other with an elaborate variety of weapons. The game screen is very chaotic, and the girls often don't seem to know where their characters are and what they are do. Earlier in the long game session, Melanie has frequently made requests not to be hurt or killed, or expressed fear. The others appear to take no notice of this in their talk and actions off-screen. Those from the earliest part of the game, are shown here, along with any apparent replies they receive. Despite the chaos of the game, when watching the other girls' onscreen actions, it seems that everyone has agreed not to attack the character she is playing. (It was impossible to find a clear point on the tape where this is originally negotiated, and it wasn't until we followed in detail the onscreen action that it became clear that the other girls weren't attacking Melanie's avatar.)

Screen: **Melissa**: Melissa's Kirby bounds up the platforms to the top of the screen.

264. Talk: Gina: Oh oh [*Appears to be Gina spotting the pink, glowing stick*]

Screen: **Gina**: Gina's fox bounds high up on the screen, nearly lands on the top platform, but falls off and lands at the bottom in a shower of red sparks. It continues to fight with Bronwyn's Pikachu on the bottom level, with both bouncing all over the area.

Screen: **Melissa**: Melissa's Kirby collects the glowing pink stick.

263. Talk: Melissa: A A A

Screen: **Melissa**: Melissa's Kirby bounces down from the top platform, and lands on the middle, left-hand platform close to Melanie's Link.

265. Talk: Melanie: Don't hurt me please Jess

266. Talk: Melissa: [*to Melanie*] Sorry

Screen: **Melissa**: Melissa's Kirby bounces up from the left-hand middle platform (which still has Link on it) and hangs in the air for a moment, surrounded by a glowing circle. The circle disappears and Kirby drops again onto the top platform.

267. Talk: Gina: Beep beep beep beep

Screen: **Bronwyn and Gina**: Bronwyn's Pikachu and Gina's fox continue to fight on the bottom level.

268. Talk: Melanie: [*To Melissa*] You're not sorry. You're just saying that

Screen: **Bronwyn**: Bronwyn's Pikachu bounds high up from the ground level platform to land on the top platform.

Screen: **Melissa and Bronwyn**: Melissa's Kirby bounces onto the top platform, above Melanie's Link and engages in a fight with Bronwyn's Pikachu which involves both bouncing all over the platform and showering each other with sparks.

Screen: **Melanie**: Melanie's Link bounces around on its platform, away from where it might have been in danger from Melissa's Kirby.

Screen: Gina: Gina's fox is still on the lower level.
Screen: Melissa and Bronwyn: Melissa's Kirby and Bronwyn's Pikachu both bound away from the platform.
269. Talk: Gina: I've got to go up
Screen: Gina: Gina's fox bounces up onto the platform that Melanie's Link is standing on, and then runs away from Link along the platform.
270. Talk: Melissa: I've gotta go down. Ur. Ur
Screen: Bronwyn: Bronwyn's Pikachu bounds down to the bottom platform.
Screen: Melissa: Melissa's Kirby bounces downwards from the top platform, travelling widely around the whole screen area, brandishing a long glowing stick – perhaps a laser? and lands on the rocky area at the bottom of the screen. Bronwyn's Pikachu is already there, and they battle together.
271. Talk: Melanie: Don't hurt me!
Screen Melanie/Gina: Melanie's Link and Gina's fox move around on the platform together. Link has a weapon in its hand, that looks like a sword or a light saber. It is pointing towards Gina's fox and seems to push it off the edge of the platform, where it falls through space and onto rocks at the bottom of the screen.
272. Talk: Gina: [*shooting sounds*] Oh you just killed me
Screen: Melissa: Melissa's Kirby bounds from the ground onto the right-hand, middle platform.
273. Talk: Melanie: [*giggling*] I didn't mean to
274. Talk: Melissa: I'm staying up here
Screen: Bronwyn: Bronwyn's Pikachu floats up to the top of the screen on a cloud, then drops down onto the top platform next to Melissa's Kirby [*perhaps the start of its new life after being killed by the lava?*]
275. Talk: Melanie: Can I come with you?
Screen: Gina: Gina's fox continues to bob at the top of the screen in its green circle.
276. Talk: Melissa: Oh fifth. Go down
Screen: Bronwyn: Bronwyn's Pikachu bounces down the right-hand side of the screen.
277. Talk: Gina: Go down, go that way. Oh, it's so dumb
Screen: Gina: Gina's fox in its green circle moves down, below the level of the rocky lowest platform.
Screen: Melissa: Melissa's Kirby quickly bounces down several platforms, travelling from the top of the screen to the bottom. Along the way it makes one bounce on the platform that Melanie's Link is standing on.

278. Talk: Melanie: Don't hurt me . . . Melissa
Screen: Gina: Gina's Pikachu carries on bouncing downwards and falls out into space, falling into the lava at the bottom.
279. Talk: Melissa: I'm not
Screen: Lava bubbles up from below the lowest level, and submerges all but the highest platform.
Screen: Gina: Gina's fox stands on the top platform and shoots beams of light off into space.
288. Talk: Melanie: I didn't hurt you did I?
289. Talk: Gina: No
290. Talk: Melanie: Cause I don't wanna hurt people
Screen: Melissa: Melissa's Kirby continues to fall towards the ground.
291. Talk: Melissa: Pikachu's winning
Screen: Bronwyn: Bronwyn's Pikachu bounces to the top of the screen, then down to the left, bouncing past Melanie's Link, and off into space.
292.Talk: Gina: Pikachu?
293. Talk: Melanie: I just slashed . . .
Screen: Melanie: Melanie's Link makes several slashing movements in the air, still on the left-hand middle platform by itself.
Screen: Bronwyn: Bronwyn's Pikachu drifts down and lands in the lava below the lowest platform, and is shot to the top of the screen surrounded by smoke.
294. Talk: Gina: I'm not killing anybody. I haven't killed anybody
Screen: Bronwyn: Bronwyn's Pikachu floats in a circle of light at the top of the screen for a moment, and then plummets again, in the foreground.
Screen: Gina: Gina's fox stands on the top platform and shoots balls of light out of the game screen.
295. Talk: Melanie: Don't kill me Jess
Screen: Melissa: Melissa's Kirby bounces off Melanie's Link's platform, and then bounces high into the air above the highest platform.
296. Talk: Gina: Do you think I should kill Jess? Pikachu's annoying. Pikachu, take this
Screen: Bronwyn: As Gina speaks, a cloud appears at the top of the screen, and Bronwyn's Pikachu falls out of the sky, and so does a large brown crate, to land close to Gina's fox, who is standing on the top platform.
Control: Melanie: In contrast to the other girls, who are using their controls very quickly, Melissa is only making occasional adjustments on hers, and is keeping her hands over the few Daniele buttons throughout.

Screen: Gina: Gina's fox repeatedly shoots, apparently at Bronwyn's Pikachu, but it's difficult to tell [*and perhaps she can't?*] because the figures appear to be on top of each other.

Screen: Melissa: Melissa's Kirby bounces up and down several times from the left-hand middle platform (where Link is still standing), bouncing through Gina's fox's line of fire, as the fox shoots off the left-hand side of the top platform.

Screen: Bronwyn: Bronwyn's Pikachu bounds to the opposite end of the platform from Gina's fox, and then bounces off the end onto a moving platform, which carries it towards the ground.

297. Talk: Melissa: Jump

Screen: Gina: Gina's fox shoots the crate in a shower of sparks, and it explodes and an object falls out of it.

Screen: Melissa: Melissa's Kirby bounds off Link's platform, to land next to Gina's fox on the top platform, then lies down flat on the ground.

Screen: Bronwyn: Bronwyn's Pikachu stands on the moving platform as it moves up and down and repeatedly uses a sword-like weapon that causes flashing lights directly in front of it.

Screen: Melissa: Melissa's Kirby bounds into the air from the top platform, floats in its glowing circle for a moment, and then falls from above the top platform, and drifts down towards the lowest platform.

Screen: Bronwyn: Bronwyn's Pikachu moves from the moving platform onto the lowest platform.

298. Talk: Gina: Fire. Hey, hey, hey. Oh damn it. Who did that?

Screen: Gina: The exploding box shoots Gina's fox into the air, and it flies from one end of the screen to the other, looks like it will fall off the edge of the game area, but as she finishes speaking lands on the very edge of the rocky ground at the bottom of the screen.

299. Talk: Melissa: Not me

300. Talk: Gina: Cause whoever did will pay. Oh damn it. Whoever did that?

Screen: Melissa: Melissa's Kirby is on the highest platform, striking at the object that came out of the box, which is still there.

Screen: Gina: Gina's fox bounces up one side of the screen, shooting Bronwyn's Pikachu and Melissa's Kirby as she rises and falls past them.

Screen: Bronwyn: Bronwyn's Pikachu bounces out over the right-hand edge of the right-hand middle platform, shooting at Gina's fox as it flies past.

Screen: Gina: Gina's fox twirls up to the right-hand middle platform, directly above where it was standing.

301. Talk: Melanie: It wasn't me
Screen: Large words fill the screen saying 'Time up'
302. Talk: Gina: I lost . . .
303. Talk: Melanie: I lost
Screen: Large words fill the screen saying 'Sudden Death!'
304.Talk: Gina: . . .I think
305. Talk: Melissa: Sudden death, oh
Screen: Large words fill the screen saying 'Go!'
Control: All four girls start to manipulate their controls.
Screen: Melanie and Melissa: A small area of the rocky ground is in view, with only Melanie's Link and Melissa's Kirby standing on it. Link repeatedly shoots bolts of light from a sword towards Kirby.
306. Talk: Melanie: Oh I didn't know
307. Talk: Melissa: We're still going
Screen: Melissa: Melissa's Kirby is lying on the ground, looking flat, orange and glowing.
Screen: Melanie: Melanie's Link continues to brandish its sword and shoot sparks, even though Kirby is not responding, and looks dead.
Talk: Melissa: Aaaw. You turned me into a rock.
Talk: Melanie: Did I?
Screen: Melissa: Melissa's Kirby returns to its usual shape and size, and bounces up to the middle platforms.
Talk: Melanie: Its because both of us are equal. Aaaw. You're going to kill me Melissa, you're going to thrash.

I have included such a long extract because I felt it was important to show how many times Melanie emphasises that she should not be hurt by the others and thus presents what comes over as an extreme anxiety which must be protected or contained by the others. All the other girls have agreed not to harm Melanie's avatar. This completely determines their relating. There is no attempt to teach Melanie, whose hands appear not to operate the controls well. There is simply a commitment not to exclude her by killing her avatar. This leaves Melanie well and truly positioned as the helpless, frightened female. It could be said that psychodynamically she manages to hold this position for the group, allowing them distance from it and that, in many ways, it is a very powerful position because, unlike the other girls, her avatar does not get killed. Even then, Melanie manages to act and this kills Melissa's avatar, yet Melanie acts as if this were entirely unknown to her with her comments 'oh I didn't know' and 'did I?' In psychoanalytic terms this could be understood as a disavowal of what Austin (2005) calls aggressive fantasies, as I will introduce below. This is something managed by Melanie but it is also managed by all of the girls together. In that sense it is created within an affective relational dynamic.

I argue that the successful player/manager of the technology of the video game is a masculine subject and that this subject position is performed more often by some girls than others. I also argue that it requires complex, covert negotiations of power that position girls ambivalently in the sense that they seem to struggle for power whilst appearing not to. Girls are also positioned ambivalently in terms of the taking up of a masculine position in one context, game playing, and a feminine position in another, the interview, which I discussed briefly, where fighting and winning are disavowed and the cuteness (and other appropriately feminine inscriptions) of avatars emphasised. I have been trying to explore the different constitution of shifting relations through which inscriptions of femininity and masculinity are performed. It might be thought from this analysis that Jess actually manages to maintain a position which is more comfortable with winning. However, from the interview material with Jess and her father, we understand that Jess is rather afraid of her abilities and ambitions. She says that she is scared of turning into 'someone mean' and violent through playing violent games (e.g. Duke Nukem) so she won't play them (she's heard the discourse of violent games turning children into playground killers on the news). Jess's father says she won't play Duke Nukem even though they have it at home – maybe she doesn't like it because of her fear of becoming someone she does not wish to become (not an issue raised by the boys). This is also an interesting commentary on the 'real effects' of discourse. If you believe the discourse (e.g. games will turn you into a nasty person) you will regulate yourself accordingly, i.e. not play violent video games. However, we must wonder how Jess manages to cope with the feelings of difficulty her dominating play brings up for her. It is clearly not straightforward or unproblematic for her.

And what of pleasure?

In relation to the complexity of self management tasks for girls, I want to explore the equally contradictory site of pleasure. We have seen that Rosa and Jess gain considerable pleasure from winning (which in the games she is playing in this case, means killing) in a way not unlike that of the boys. There is pleasure then for these girls in mastery. They can take up a masculine position, though not without having to almost simultaneously take up a feminine one as well. We saw that Katie liked to display an exaggerated squeamishness of taking a vicarious pleasure in others doing the killing while saying she is afraid. As we know from horror movies, we can take great pleasure in squeamishness, watching the horror through our hands (Kristeva, 1982; Clover, 1992).[4] What is the fascination? What is the vicarious pleasure? Is there any mileage in attempting to understand how Katie manages to take pleasure (was it in winning or in killing or both?) while operating as though she had nothing to do with it? All those fluffy cuddly creatures – of course so well satirised in the boiling of the family bunny by the abandoned woman in *Fatal Attraction*. Just as the Glenn Close character seeks her revenge with a murderous fury, murdering too the sweet and acquiescing part of herself, so Katie reveals that the violent must be kept in check to produce femininity, while for boys the opposite is the case – as the exaggerated denials of any interest in the game of Barbie make clear. The work of performing masculinity and femininity is affective work. It is also about the complexities of positions of power: the power of the mother over the child/man, the power of the *femme fatale*, the power of the pleasure in mastery, of omnipotent control, of winning, killing. Performing femininity and masculinity requires affective work to attempt to embody a position which is a necessary fiction in that it is the central constituent of the management and regulation of femininity and masculinity. So, what seems like power is, in Foucault's sense (Foucault, 1977) deeply compromised, because it is the way in which we are managed and regulated as autonomous citizens in apparent control of ourselves and our lives. I have argued that video games are sites in which masculinity is produced through a number of techniques and practices of self management. I have argued that the task of femininity is different and that this makes the playing of games a complex self management task for girls. We have seen how a number of girls take up different and shifting positions in relation to this. If the discursive work is also affective work, then girls have to deal with managing a femininity that demands both those positions traditionally associated with masculinity while simultaneously holding those traditionally associated with femininity. I suggest that this approach might be useful not only in relation to thinking about video games but also about debates about women and new technologies more generally.

Affective work

If we go on to think about the affective work involved in both masculinity and femininity in the light of the arguments raised above, I want to ask how we might think about the way the contradictions of femininity and masculinity are lived. In particular, I want to introduce the work of Sue Austin (2005), who makes an explicit link between some of my own earlier work and what she calls aggressive energies or fantasies. For Austin, aggressive fantasies can be understood as fantasies through which the discursive aspects of power are played out. That is, in line with my three fold approach to affect as sensation, ideation and fantasy, we can also add an 'energetics', the idea of something through which the relational dynamic flows and through which the affective power of the fantasy works. In particular, she makes reference to a paper of mine (Walkerdine, 1981), which analyses the way in which two four year old boys in a nursery classroom bring a female teacher 'down to size' by treating her to a sexist chant involving body parts. She retorts by treating them as boys for whom such things are to be expected and which she must contain. Austin asks what it would take for the teacher to be able to experience anger at this positioning of her and to stand up to it. How might she be able to experience what she calls the thrill of a good fight? I wonder if the game playing girls I have discussed above are able to experience this thrill unreservedly? What would it take and what would it mean for them to do so? Let us examine Austin's case a bit further.

She argues against a view of object relations which looks at aggression as a product of development, or problems as a result of a faulty inner life or psychic world. She attempts to engage both with Butler's (1997) idea of an inner topography or landscape in melancholia and the idea of a metaphysics of absence, by inverting Derrida.

She claims that self hate is the most common form of female aggressive energies. She talks about the 'Not I' within. In this respect she is trying to link the ways in which violence towards femininity is taken in and cannot be pushed outward again by women. She talks of the joy and energy of a good physical fight but how this energy is mostly experienced by women in the negative, as self hatred. In her analysis of the incident in the nursery classroom I discussed above, she argues that the small boys aggressively make the teacher into a sex object but that her only response is feminine nurturance. Thus she does not and cannot marshal her aggression in return. The teacher, Miss Baxter, is made in the image of nurturance. It is this quality which is projected onto her as a nurturant teacher who tells the boys off for being silly but does not retaliate about their sexism. So she condones their behaviour but she also cannot marshal her own aggressive fantasies in retaliation.

Austin gives the example of teachers in my work on girls and mathematics (Walkerdine et al., 1989, 1998) who simultaneously look for nice, kind and helpful girls and then say how much they hate those girls and indeed those characteristics inside themselves. They are of course brought up to validate the qualities ascribed to boys. That is, reason, naughtiness, leaps of imagination, and to regard those things inside themselves and girls as crazy. While the Other is always validated they can never easily cross the divide and experience the joy of aggressive energy.

To discursive work therefore Austin adds the necessity to understand, following Butler (1977), the inner topology. What it would mean to marshall that which has been denied? She argues that marshalling aggressive energies is central to the possibility of women's agency and their *jouissance*, which she opposes to *plaisir*, which can only be understood as the pleasure of being the object, of fitting the position accorded to woman. In relation to that inner topology,[5] women's aggressive energies also get mobilised to create a containing space – so the space they themselves take up can only ever be 'diverted into creating and sustaining these categories of perception and experience which have become normalised as truths' (p. 145). These categories are that maternal containment which is the prime marker of all psychological space in that it is maternal containment which is usually set up as the possibility of emotional space for human beings within most approaches to child development. The dangerous nature of femininity is thus reworked or tamed as the very basis of childhood, personhood. 'Space is not ours to take part in, since our substance has been used in the production of the concept of containment.' So women's aggressive energies have been dammed up and diverted.

Austin asks 'if the structure of femininity comprises solidified, disavowed aggressive energies, whose solidification and remanufacture is eroticised as being a "good thing" for the benefit of some imagined "Other", how might such energies be gathered together into something liveable, something which women can use in their inner and outer lives?' (p. 173). Her use of the concept of energy brings together both psychoanalytic accounts of psychic life as understood through the transmission of psychic energy and also directs us to a renewed interest in vital energies in recent sociological work (see Fraser, Kember and Lury, 2005). Although this is not the context for a detailed explanation of Austin's use of the concept of aggressive energies, it is worth noting that this makes very different assumptions from that of a pregiven propensity to aggression.[6]

As we have seen, girls can play video games with relish. However, the constant subversion of this relish into a maintenance of a femininity which is its opposite, is, in Austin's sense, diverting. It is at the very least not unproblematic for the girls in this research to display what Austin calls their aggressive energies, because they must maintain the very internal space which renders them nurturant and caringly feminine, which seems certainly to be the case here. More than that, such fantasies and energies can be displaced by some girls onto others to do their killing for them.

However, as I have argued in the past in relation to girls and mathematics (Walkerdine, 1989, 1998), it is not simply a question of allowing girls to behave in ways discursively sanctioned for boys, because that behaviour is differently read and evaluated when displayed by girls. In one case in a secondary school mathematics classroom, one girl was called a 'madam' by her male teacher for displaying the kind of performance praised as brilliant in her male peers. The discursive constitution and domestication of femininity has to be understood in relation to its other and opposite, the constitution of masculinity as unproblematically essentialising aggressive energies, precisely directed at that containing space which they both need and then disavow in the Cartesian rebirth, with respect to boys and with the help of their mothers. If the fantasy of masculine aggressivity is the Other of feminine nurturance, it is that which takes up the space provided by the sucking out of the affective space of the feminine. We might therefore ask why it is that the feminine is continually pathologised while the omnipotent fantasies of the boys, that they can indeed become the conquering action hero, are presented not only as unproblematic but is needed for the perpetuation of a technologically led mode of governance and multinational capital. Girls' aggressive energies are heavily regulated and pathologised (Ringrose, 2006). Why is boys' competitiveness lauded? Why is the possibility of their emergent sensitivities to others suppressed and their anxiety about being able to win disavowed and projected onto women? Why is the fantasy of winning and beating not itself considered more of a problem than the problems for girls? Or more particularly, what kinds of fantasies and anxieties are displaced by the acting out of omnipotence? In particular, we might look to precisely the performance of help and nurturance by the mothers, which must be disavowed in order to produce the self made man. Femininity may, as Austin suggests, create the psychic space which is taken to make masculinity possible, but it must equally be disavowed and denied as it produces dependency and infantilisation. Of course the idea that woman is the container, the mother, the muse, the vagina, and man the subject, the phallus, is very far from new. The issue here is the place of games and new technologies more generally in creating places and possibilities for the subversion of the oppositions and a move to something new.

In the next chapter, I will explore the issue of violence, which, as we shall see, is usually associated with masculinity.

5
Rethinking Violence

Violence is ubiquitous in western culture as a central part of action masculinity, but becomes the object of binary thinking, that is, good masculinity is central but bad masculinity is Othered – perpetrated by Others, who don't understand the fantasy/reality distinction.

Some time ago, I wrote about the ubiquitous eroticisation of little girls (Walkerdine, 1997). I argued that little girls stare at us from the TV and advertisements all the time, both innocent and erotic and that what this covers over is a complex eroticisation within the culture which is disavowed. I want to think in a similar way about violence. We could say that violence and the fear and admiration of it suffuses our culture. It is absolutely and utterly routine. And of course, it is a central concern for the general public about video games. However, I am not wishing to argue that video games make children violent, nor indeed in any simple sense that the media have made children violent, but I do want to think about violence as pedestrian, routine and to wonder what that means. Of course, we could easily say that this routine and pedestrian violence – the violence which we laugh at when Daffy Duck is squashed for the fourteenth time – is just the acting out of a biological aggressive drive, to be violent, to kill, to conquer, or that we all have to face death and destruction and that these humorous places for the enactment of violence present us with a way of dealing in a light way with our own mortality and the unpredictability of life. This is not unlike the argument made by Jones (2002) in his popular book, *Killing Monsters*. This is, that the communication of violent feelings through games is better than the repression of violence and that if we try to make children banish or ignore their rage, they respond by violently identifying with it. The issue for him is not whether violent media are good or bad but how to empower youth to neither dissociate from a powerful component of their own psyche nor

73

overidentify with it. He suggests that games can be used in many different ways to produce emotional complexity and maturity. While I am not totally lacking in sympathy for this argument, I want to point up his taking for granted of something called 'a powerful component of the psyche'. This approach assumes a psyche which has certain propensities which have to be understood and engaged with. If we think about Foucault's argument in the *History of Sexuality* Volume 1 (Foucault, 1981) he tells us that Victorian sexuality was not repressed but displaced as medicalised, so that it became the object of a certain kind of discourse. Sexuality became an object of scientific enquiry and medical regulation. Let us think in a similar way about violence. It too becomes the object of scientific discourses which attempt to understand it and some of these at least rely on a notion of aggression. Hence, like Jones they identify something – in his case a component of the psyche – which has to be regulated – expressed but not repressed but not over-expressed and so forth. If we follow on from this approach violence becomes an object which has to be constantly monitored and regulated both for the subject and by the subject. In particular, it has a central place in the regulation of contemporary masculinities. I want to argue that the very routinisation of violence covers over the central importance for masculinity of its regulation. I argued in Chapter 3 that many video games build upon the genre of the Western in which the hero has to work at being the conquering hero, defeated, struggling only to triumph in the end. If this is the story of the action hero, violence is absolutely central to its narrative. Both being defeated and being triumphant are the essential work of the action hero, sometimes represented as a mythic struggle of good over evil. Fighting the good fight in Christian iconography links the hero with the triumph of God over the devil, or indeed God or the devil inside the man himself. Other more modern narratives present this struggle as the human or cultured over the animal or beast, as in Social Darwinism or indeed Freud,[1] who sometimes presents us with a struggle of drives versus civilisation. So masculinity is presented as in a tension – life and death, good and evil, animal and human, rational and irrational, masculine and feminine. It could be argued that fighting is absolutely essential to the grand narratives of masculinity – the stories which over long periods of historical time come to define social difference, for example between masculinity and femininity. So, I am not saying that men are naturally bestial and this has to be tamed but that this is a central aspect of the classification, governance and regulation of masculinity and femininity.[2] This chapter argues that the current ways of thinking about the relation of violence to young children's video game play are mistaken. The two main arguments put forward are that on the one hand, video games cause children to be violent (usually referred to as 'effects research') and that conversely video games can be understood as allowing safe expression for violent emotions and can therefore be understood as cathartic. Rather, this chapter argues that both positions start from an unhelpful premise. Video games, it is argued, offer sites for the performance of masculinity and provide a space in which masculinity can be practised and managed. They therefore neither cause violence nor contain it in any simple sense. The expression and containment of violence is essential to contemporary masculinity and the complex rules by which violence is considered part of masculinity which must be expressed (e.g. physical violence in war, on the football field) but also must be curtailed (physical violence against others for example), while verbal violence is still often sanctioned (e.g. workplace bullying, macho posturing) or occluded (e.g. rational modes of argument), these practices of the self have to be learnt and managed. I use the idea of self-management in the sense that Michel Foucault talks of the necessity for liberalism of what Nikolas Rose calls 'practices of freedom' in which individuals are governed through a number of techniques which mean that effectively they govern themselves by managing their behaviour. In this sense then we could say that video games are one site where self-management practices around violence in relation to masculinity are learnt.

Today, we are surrounded by violence and yet apparently abhore it. We are terrified of its appearance everywhere but we still expect our heroes to embody this dualism, this fight. But we have to know when to fight, what to fight for. If action is a central aspect of a performing masculininity, don't video games provide a splendid vehicle for practising action, for fighting evil, for facing defeat and not giving up, for doing this through brains (rational calculation) and not brawn and for learning to be a man when the action required is in a knowledge economy?

God forbid then when men get it wrong and become addicted to action heroes; when they can't distinguish between fantasy and reality. We have a whole lot of accounts to do with mothers to explain that one. This has been a central aspect of the argument put forward to explain killings carried out by boys. Both the Columbine High School Massacre in the USA and the James Bulger murder in Liverpool contained accounts like this. In the case of Columbine, the boys were supposed to have played video games and in the James Bulger case, watched violent videos, such as 'Child's Play 3'. The issue in these accounts is not that they played or watched – the violent acting out came from a failure to be able to distinguish between fantasy and reality, itself taken to have been produced through poor socialisation. Violence in this scenario is pathologised – it is a failure of bonding leading to a psychological problem. Children should learn that the boundaries between violence in a game and violence in the playground are fixed. Indeed, all children in the research were articulate about the clear distinctions they saw. We specifically asked children in our interviews if they thought that playing games made children violent.

Children's responses

What becomes clear from the children's responses is that the narratives of children committing violence following game play are well known cultural narratives, circulating from parents, the media and so forth, as in Francesca's interview narrative:

> **Interviewer**: Okay. Now we're almost towards the end a couple of last questions. Some people think that computer games and, video games can be bad for children and they give different reasons why they think it's bad. Do you think they could be bad?
> **Francesca**: I think maybe shooting games could be bad because I seen lately that they could make people more like shooting a gun without caring. Or maybe I don't know. I think like games like Mario and all that are fine.

And Maria:

> **Interviewer**: Now some people say that computer games can be bad for you, that they can cause you to be violent, or not very friendly to other people. Do you think that there is any truth in what they say?
> **Maria**: Yeah I think there is. Well it depends. I do, but sometimes they tell lies and you just don't believe them, and they tell the truth and you just believe them because they show you what happened to the person . . . and they start playing computer games for a couple of years and then what happened to them and you just believe them.
> **Interviewer**: What story is that one? Can you tell me more about that because I don't know that story.
> **Maria**: Well it was on TV once on the news, a kid had a gun game and the kid was . . . and then . . . playing violence games after. It was a long time ago.

Notice how, in these girls' accounts, these are apocryphal stories which seem to suggest a danger lurking within masculinity. This is often countered by the boys with a strong statement about boundaries, where children recognise that violence inside and outside the game are different and the rules of different practices must be acknowledged. In addition boys are more likely to be specific about characteristics of games, set in a discourse of realism as in realist graphics or an assertion that their imagination about guns is harmless because it is simply imagination.

Boys therefore seem more likely to resist being positioned in relation to violence within the games. I suppose that this resistance is inevitable since many games are intrinsically violent (you have to kill or destroy something to improve your skill/game and win) and this violence is invisible. Interest and investment are therefore signified in terms other than violence (which is ever present and invisible.)

There is some sense in which the games are presented by many children as 'not violent' (because its not real) and even when they can describe something as violent they say they like the game because the graphics are realistic or cool (or for the girls cute). They never take up the position that the game is good *because* of the fighting/violence – though they may concede that they like the fighting. But their enjoyment of fighting is strictly limited to the game and connected to mastery and winning. I think there is a significant distinction to be made between 'fighting' and 'violence'. I think fighting is a softer term and a daily event that signifies squabbling, arguing and minor fisticuffs dependent on context. It does not seem to be collapsed into the term 'violence' which signifies something more severe. Again, I think this is connected to the positioning of violence as about the Other and can therefore be understood as a disavowal.

Interviewer: Tell me about fighting games, do you like them?

Dan: Yeah.

Interviewer: And what sort of things did you fight?

Dan: The robots, like you choose a robot and you have to fight against it.

Interviewer: Okay. Now some people say that games, like fighting games are bad for kids because they turn kids into . . .

Dan: Monsters.

Interviewer: . . . So if you learn how to fight on a video game it means that you are going to go out on the street and fight people in the street. Do you believe that?

Dan: No.

Interviewer: What happens when you are playing fighting games? Do you get worked up or do you think oh I could be like this?

Dan: When I lose, um, I get a little bit frustrated yeah.

Interviewer: But you don't think it makes . . .

Dan: No.

Interviewer: . . . you want to be a person who fights other people?

Dan: No.

Interviewer: So what would you say to those people then who say the other thing?

Dan: I don't think it is true that if you play a fighting game that it will affect you in a way and stuff like that.

Interviewer: Um, do you think if kids go around playing games where you have to shoot people and they see blood and stuff everywhere do you think that might turn them into people who could end up shooting people on the street?

Dan: Um, it might, I don't know about that one. It depends how graphic it is and stuff like that.

Interviewer: Okay, so you think that maybe if the game is more real, more realistic and the graphics are really good it might actually affect you?

Dan: Like there is a game called Resident Evil, you have got a gun and you are walking around killing zombies.

Interviewer: Yeah.

Dan: It is really graphic.

Interviewer: Have you played that?

Dan: Yeah we have it in the back room.

Interviewer: Alright. Do you like playing that?

Dan: I play it occasionally.

Interviewer: Yeah.

Dan: But it is very gruesome.

Interviewer: So how do you feel about the gruesome? Do you actually, when you see the gruesome things happening are you happy because you have actually killed the zombie or um and do you like seeing the gruesome stuff there?

Dan: I don't actually like seein' it, um, I am glad that I killed them and that, that I am getting further and further into the game.

Interviewer: Right. And does that have different levels or is it . . .?

Dan: Yeah there is lots of different levels and areas to go through.

It is interesting to note here how ambivalent Dan is about the realist graphics. On the one hand it is good, but on the other the Resident Evil graphics appear to him too gruesome to watch, which suggests that the realism is quite troubling. But in order to progress through the game, as he says, he is 'glad' he 'killed them'.

And Andrew:

Interviewer: So what about those kids in America they said they have played all these violent games and that gave them the idea to go out and shoot up all their friends?

Andrew: That's kind of like the people, that's only some people who think only certain people, the game doesn't affect them, they think that whatever they see they can do. For example they could even read a book about someone for example they read a book about Hannibal Lecter, they think they can go out and do what he did.

Interviewer: So it is not the games themselves, they could just find that anywhere, actually watching a movie or reading a book or . . .

Andrew: Watching the news what's happened and do the same thing.

Interviewer: Why do you think people are like that?

Andrew: I don't know.

Interviewer: That is just the way they are?

Andrew: Mm they just want to think, they think well they are in public things, maybe if I do the same I can get that famous and all that.

So, Andrew has taken on board a notion of copycat violence.

Interviewer: Do you think it might be rather than bad for your thumb, do you think it might be bad for you as a person to play some of the games?

James: Well it depends on how you think, because if it was shoot 'em up game and you didn't think properly you could get your hands on a gun and just go around shooting people thinking it was a game.

Interviewer: So you think that happens?

James: Yeah it has. I've seen it on the news.

Interviewer: So are you scared about that or scared about becoming like that?

James: No.

Interviewer: Why is that?

James: Because I don't think I will.

Interviewer: So why don't you think you will, what makes you special?

James: Because I don't think about guns much and I don't like them.

James again implies the difference set out by Dan, that there is a difference between having to kill to progress in a game and liking guns. William seems to be able to reproduce a discourse about violence but not actually engage with it, or sustain a position that requires him to engage with it.

William: Well Playstation because there is this boy who played a lot of shooting games and in America he killed all these people that . . . like boom, boom, boom, boom.

Interviewer: Yeah.

William: So it is bad, shooting games, if you have got the shooting controller because like you play the game, anyone who pops up, boom, boom.

Interviewer: So you are a bit concerned about playing with a gun controller?

William: Yeah. That is what they said on TV.

And later in the same interview:

Interviewer: So how much is too much? You are scratching your head now. I mean what I am saying is say someone gave you a lot of money and say you spent $20 today and play that shooting up game in the arcade for two hours. Would you be worried that it would do you some harm?

William: Um, no. But it does if you pick up a real gun and think you are playing the game.

Interviewer: Alright, so you think because you play the game make believe, if you had access to a gun and you would pick the gun up and think it was a game? Is that what you are saying?

William: Yes that is what they did in America, they said that is what they did before the War they would get just these gun games for practising.

Interviewer: Right, so it trains people.

William: Yeah like they were getting these games for police officers and so instead of using them as targets, they can just use an ordinary screen.

Interviewer: So do you think, what does it do to a person if they play those games? What do you think the games do to the person?

William: Um, just make them better shooters.

Interviewer: Does it stop them from . . . about what they are shooting at?

William: No, they just think they are playing the game.

Interviewer: It sounds like you are talking about brainwashing. Do you think that is what he is talking about Mum? He is talking about, he is saying if you play computer shoot 'em up games, arcade games with a gun, when you have access to a gun, you would pick up the gun and think you were playing a game. Is that what you are talking about?

William: Yeah that is what they said on the news. That is what the boy did.

William equally is trying to make a distinction between being a good shooter and being violent, which seems to trouble him.

Interviewer: Sometimes people say computer games are bad, what do you think overall what we have talked about today?

Sam: Um, for some people it is bad, because I saw a show on what do you call it, News, and I saw kids they played 007 I think or a shoot 'em up game and then they went outside and they started being aggressive and really kicking each other. Not just pretend, real kicking.

Interviewer: Do you think that was real?

Sam: Well it looked like they were fighting. They were on the trampoline with . . . like they were playing a shooting game. The first session they were playing quiet and then they . . . 64s and playstations and all that. They started playing and then maybe 30 minutes later they got out their biggest water pistols they could find and then they started shooting each other out the back.

Interviewer: You don't think the adults made them do that or suggested they do that?

Sam: No it was the game because it gave them a bad imagination piece and then they made their imagination bigger.

Interviewer: So you think, why doesn't that happen to you? Or does it happen to you? You said you played 007.

Sam: I have but it is a bit boring going outside and just going bang, bang.

Interviewer: Why do you think kids do that then?

Sam: I have no idea.

Interviewer: So do you think Sam would be affected by 007?

Sam: No. He is not into guns. I don't know. I am not into normal guns. All I am into, the only guns that are in my imagination is about bazookas, plasma guns and sometimes . . . guns and machine guns but that's about it.

Interviewer: So which are the bad guns do you think?

Sam: I don't like hand guns because they are too puny and not dangerous enough. I like explosions, that's what I like.

Interviewer: You like the special effects?

Sam: Yeah. I like boom. I don't like . . . shoot something bang. I like the bazooka. You shoot it and you see smoke coming out of a missile and you see this fire cloud go everywhere.

Interviewer: So it is the special effect rather than the idea of shooting someone?

Sam: Yeah.

Interviewer: So do you think some kids like shooting people? Do you think that's exciting?

Sam: Well I don't like blood. I don't like looking at blood in games.

Interviewer: Have you played any games with blood and guts?

Sam: No all I have played is blood.

Interviewer: What?

Sam: All I have played is games with blood. Like little specks of blood.

Interviewer: So do you know about the rating of games. Do you know G8 games . . . what sort of games do you play?

Sam: Any game. 15+ anything. Like sometimes I think they rate it wrong. Because I have played this game and it said MA15+ on it and I went home and played it right. And all it is cars with missiles on the side, that shoot other cars. And I don't see how violent that is. And the explosions don't even look real. They are little puffs of smoke and the enemy goes flying back.

Interviewer: Any other things you think might happen by playing too many computer games?

Joshua: . . . if you are playing too many computers you might . . . playing them and you might get hurt a lot.

Interviewer: What do you mean by hurt a lot playing . . .

Joshua: Like . . . if it is an action movie or somethin' and you get swords and that like when you have a sword fight or something, if they really hit you hard in the leg or somethin' could break your leg.

Interviewer: Yeah but computer games are only imagination, so what do you mean by get hurt?

Joshua: 'Cause if you play it heaps of times then you go: Mum can you make me this uniform?

Interviewer: So you think you might want to play the computer games . . . real life is that what you are saying?

Joshua: Mm.

Interviewer: So you think some people . . . play the computer games in the playground or they try and play the same character in the computer game?

Joshua: . . . most of the kids do but some of 'em don't.

Interviewer: Do you play some of the characters in the computer games in the playground?

Joshua: Sometimes.

Interviewer: So what character do you play?

Joshua: I play um in the army ones I play the sergeant.

Interviewer: So do they do special things, they do special punches or kicks or things?

Joshua: Mm.

Interviewer: And do you go that in the playground?

Joshua: Yeah . . . if I am excited I play one of 'em, like I play the second sergeant. And the . . . all the army men.

Interviewer: But do you do the same thing in the game, do you actually hit people?

Joshua: You don't actually hit them, you just run around and that.

Interviewer: You told me before that you came up with one of the rules in the game didn't you, that . . . not supposed to hit anyone.

Interviewer: Alright. Um, so what do you think might be the bad things about computer games? Or are there no bad things about the computer games?

Felix: None.

Interviewer: What about the violence, some people say the violence is really bad for you.

Felix: Nope.

Interviewer: You think the violence is not bad for you?

Felix: 'Cause it is only a video game.

Interviewer: So you know it is not real?

Felix: Yeah.

I have given so many examples, because there is in them a clear and strong cultural narrative on the part of these boys. That is, that America is the site of gun crime in which game players have killed, that this was a news item, and that despite their assertions that game violence is not a problem, there appears to be some anxiety about it. And I feel that these boys attempt to make a split between fighting and violence in games and actual offscreen killing, especially with guns. Yet, they are clearly troubled by this violence. When we come to the example of Melissa talking about this issue, her anxieties come into sharper focus:

Melissa: Yeah, no, I think there is a game like a party cake, like a ball game, um, I would like ooh, I forgot what I was going to say. I'd make it so you wouldn't have to fight a lot because violence is bad and we watch TV, we watch the news and they say games like even games makes kids want to kill each other or something and make them go into violence. I think I can make it like Banjo Kazooie or something finding something to get to another level and you get like poker balls and chuck it at people and that.

Interviewer: So it is a fun sort of thing, not really hurting people. Do you think when you hear those things on TV about games making kids violent, do you think that is true?

Melissa: Yeah, I sort of do because on the TV they said in America a 6 year old boy killed a 6 year old girl in class and an 11 year old boy shot 80 children, his classmates. But that was in America, it is not here. But what I think is when there is a whole lot of violence, I get worried that I might actually turn into that, and I don't really want to because I am kind and I like the kindies, I love playing with them. They are so cute, but I don't want to turn into someone mean when I grow up.

For Melissa there is some sense of something dangerous potentially lurking within her, which could turn her in to a murderer. Is this anxiety present all the time she enjoys playing games? Does it act as a break on her playing? Interestingly, Melissa is one girl who affects exaggerated squeamishness and is terribly afraid of being killed. Might we imagine that she is terrified of the potential of her own murderous feelings, which she is keeping at bay with the squeamishness? Such oppositions are relatively easy to understand on the basis of a psychoanalytic theory of the defences. However, I want here to concentrate on the relationship between the complex kinaesthetics of the games and the embodied performance Melissa displays. On the one hand, we have the kinaesthetics of the killing in the games. On the other, we have the stories of child murderers. These relate to embodied practices in that Melissa affects to let others do her violence for her when playing games and expresses a fear of being killed which manifests as poor prowess in the game and leads other girls to become protective towards her. In other words, a whole ensemble of practices is mobilised, which contain complex inter-relations. In addition to this, we have an embodied and expressed anxiety – that she will turn into a murderer, an anxiety which is held at bay by the practices of squeamishness. In this account, while we have not traced the complex path of her anxieties, we have demonstrated how they are manifest as patterns within practices and intertextualities. Melissa is the only child who expresses an anxiety that she could be a murderer, though the narrative of children in America killing others in relation to game play is clearly well known. What seems to be the case is that there are conventions such as realism which allow certainly some of the boys or perhaps cuddly characters for the girls, which serve to remove violence from the 'real'. But for some children, the defences against this violence affecting you have to be quite strong, as with Melissa, and Dan finds gruesome graphics difficult to watch.

If we think about cartoons, the graphics, the fact that characters get resurrected, that we laugh at their pain, all serve as distancing devices. The distancing device that Melissa uses is to be squeamish so that she never positions herself as someone who could possibly be violent. This suggests to me that we could read the anxieties, displacements and disavowals as evidence of a much more complex relation to violence than has hitherto been presented in either pro or anti effects arguments.

The way in which violence is understood as the Other of femininity is exemplified by Felix's exaggerated performance of violence to shock his mother:

> **Interviewer**: Alright. Have you ever played one part of the game over and over again?
> **Felix**: Yeah.
> **Interviewer**: So what parts of the game do you like to play over and over again?
> **Felix**: Most of the interesting parts.
> **Interviewer**: What are they?
> **Felix**: Like the violent parts.
> **Interviewer**: Violent . . . your Mum has her head in her arms here, the violent parts. What are the violent parts in Crash Bandicoot?
> **Felix**: Not really much.
> **Interviewer**: Which games do you think are violent then?
> **Felix**: Aah, James Bond.
> **Interviewer**: James Bond that you play down the road at your friend's place?
> **Felix**: Yeah.
> **Interviewer**: Alright.
> **Felix**: Um . . .
> **Interviewer**: But you like playing the other games as well?
> **Felix**: Yep.
> **Interviewer**: I think you just keep saying violent because you want to see your mother do something . . .
> **Felix**: No.
> **Interviewer**: No!
> **Felix**: I like violence.

This serves to establish his distance as not feminine and not a mother's boy. We can see Melissa's exaggerated squeamishness as equally an attempt to instate a binary – boys are violent while girls hate violence and are afraid of having violence done to them. The establishment of this binary through embodied practices understood through certain embodied and kinaesthetic relations in this case in games, apparently cements a gender difference which is fluid and unstable and which must be cemented in the life world in order to minimise anxiety about not inhabiting an unacceptable gender category.

But, the pathologisation of the acting out of violence occludes something, and that something is that this is not a simple problem of something going wrong but is a central aspect of the management and regulation of masculinity. We should not be surprised therefore if central problems of how to negotiate and manage the complexities of when and how to act and not to act and desires to act in unsanctioned ways are around. It is a problem of the outside, as it were, but it can become a problem of the inside.

As I discussed in Chapter 3, Tyrone, one of the fathers, says he is addicted to playing the avatar Snake in the game Metal Gear Solid. What becomes clear is that Tyrone could understand his position as feminised: a single father and as not enough of a man – poorly paid. The game is where he gets to practice action masculinity and also to do violence, to kill his opponents. He uses the discourse of addiction, which suggests that he worries about his constant desire to play this game. But if we look at what the game gives him in the light of the demands of contemporary masculinity, it is possible to argue that the game both provides solace for a feeling of a lack of masculinity but is also a constant reminder of failure to live this out in the real world. This is why I think that the idea of violent games as either a pathological media effect or a cathartic containment of violence is far too simplistic as a dichotomy. I suggest we would get further by attempting to understand the regulation and performance of contemporary masculinity.

It could be argued then that some video games present us with one site, among many, for practising the regulation of violence for men, for knowing both when and how to act and to be violent and knowing when to stop it. So, to be clear, I am *not* saying that playing games causes masculine violence. Far from it. I am simply saying that some games are one site amongst many in which contemporary masculinity, action heroics, which involves violence done to the hero and violence acted out, is managed and regulated. Doesn't this knowledge form a central part of how contemporary masculinity is regulated and performed?

If so, how is it embodied? How do men and women live that regulation? Tyrone lives it by using the game to create a space in which he embodies action masculinity. We can speculate that this is related to his feminisation as a single parent and carer of a child with learning difficulties. It also creates a possibility of a space for him that is his own while not having to leave the house and therefore the children, or pay for entertainment outside the home – he has a low income. I suggest that we can see how the three fold approach to affect works – regulation, self management and the creation of the fantasy scenario for acting out link self management practices, a kinaesthetically configured virtual environment and the embodied affective engagement with it. Meanings and actions within the environment or between the space for the computer and the virtual environment, between the meanings in the game and the meanings, performances, affectivities in which Tyrone is already operating, provide a complex site for the production of action masculinity and its associated meanings. Because we only have Tyrone's report at interview and no sense of his engagement with the space itself, we cannot take that example any further, but we have many examples of children playing games which contain violence. I explore more fully how to analyse these examples in Chapters 8 and 9.

Disavowing violence

I want to suggest that there are two other discourses and practices worthy of consideration in relation to violence. I want to explore the ways in which violence is rendered as Other, indeed something which has to be managed. Of course the idea that violence is a threat to civilised masculinity is hardly new. It could be considered part of the very animal primitivism which must be civilised for the enlightenment project to work. Thus civilised masculinity is rational and irrationality is Othered as both feminine and primitive (the location of instincts, drives). It is this Otherness, I would argue, that has to be constantly managed in order to produce an action masculinity in which enough masculinity is established not to be seen as feminine but not too much to be brutish. It is a hard act. Games allow you to have rational control according to some parents, which denies violence.

The other way of disavowing and keeping violence at bay is a femininity which claims to abhor and be the opposite of violence. Girls also render violence harmless by infantalising it as in cute and cuddly characters. This allows them a position of power as mothers but still splits off violence as something they would not want to do and yet they do! This was clearly exemplified in Chapter 4 by the choice of cute and cuddly characters in their nurturant relation to them and yet the performativity of killing in games.

I argue that girls must display this abhorrence of violence to maintain a soft femininity. This means that violence cannot be allowed to be safely expressed for girls at all, except through a more recent discourse of girl power and the idea of active girls, and is moreover highly regulated (Ringrose, 2006). Destruction is often synonymous with progress in the game and so children have to learn the skills necessary for competent game play and therefore competent destruction to avoid being destroyed themselves and thus losing. Moreover, as with cartoons, such violence can be funny as Sam says:

'I like games that are funny. Like they are in combat but they are funny. I played this game with my friend and we were in the toilets fighting

people and you picked up a toilet and threw it at the enemy. And people
come out of the bathroom and they fight you, and all they have got,
they have got no clothes on except their towel.'

It can also be very pleasurable, as in the numerous examples of children
getting excited about killing, as in 'come on, let's kill!' or the myriad
cries of 'kill him!' or Gina's 'I love killing!' – the power to kill and therefore have control, manage a defeat that signals progress in the game,
power, control, is, of course pleasurable. However, the ubiquitousness of
violence means that there is an issue about its disavowal: that is, the idea
that the routine violence in video games is not really violence or not
really important. This split has characterised the debate about violence
in that many media theorists have tried to counter effects research by
arguing that this routine violence is of no consequence (Gauntlett,
1998). However, conversely, effects researchers tend to blame video
games (along with other media such as violent films and videos) for
social violence, especially murder committed by boys and, as I have
indicated, it is clear that the children know this discourse and are anxious about the split. Thus, the debate becomes polarised, which has the
effect of making it difficult to discuss the routine violence I am talking
about without being attacked from both sides of the debate. I am therefore trying to argue that both positions are unhelpful. What I want to
suggest is that routinised violence must have a place in the production
of masculinity and that games have a place in this. I am certainly *not*
proposing any kind of cause and effect model. Far from it. In Chapter 1,
I made a point of critiquing the standard opposition between activity
and passivity when it comes to debates about violence. I suggest that
there is what we might term a disavowal of this routine violence
amongst both the children and their parents. It becomes clear that part
of the way in which this violence is learnt and managed is to make various separations between what is and is not understood as routine and
serious violence and this involves a denial that the routine violence is of
any consequence. Statements such as 'its only a game' serve to shift the
focus away from this as violence to an area of 'real life' in which violence
cannot be tolerated and which therefore counts as the site of 'real violence', but that doesn't take away anxiety about it as the boys make
clear. Thus, I suggest that the self-management of violence involves a
number of discursive manoeuvres which render certain violence understood as harmless and the other as harmful. I want to argue that routine
violence in games is disavowed as harmless because it is part of a game
and therefore fun, not serious and also because competence in games

requires 'strategic thinking' which disavows the violence at the heart of the Cogito.

In order to unpick this statement, I want to think about what is meant by there being violence at the heart of the Cogito. The Cogito is the idea that rationality is the central component of selfhood, an idea enshrined in liberal government. Many scholars have understood this as doing violence in the sense that it implies control over nature by culture, of femininity by masculinity, of the irrational by the rational (Walkerdine, 1989). This means that the Cogito implies a binary in which the other term is suppressed or pathologised or disavowed. It implies that civilised rationality must conquer the irrational, the primitive, the feminine, which are rendered as Other. I argue that action masculinity in its early twenty-first-century variant demands heroics, action, being quick on the draw but produced mainly through a knowledge economy in which fast computer skills are essential. This means that action masculinity must be simultaneously displayed and denied. This dualism is at the heart of the self management practices demanded for masculinity. So, we could say that the violence of killing in game play is always in a struggle to control and rationalise it, from which it must always escape or exceed. Violence has to be there and equally rationalising and containing violence has to be there. There is no essential opposition, but a dualism manufactured to contain the subject of liberalism. This is why it is both presented as harmless, containable and potentially harmful. This is why the failure to contain the violence to games is pathologised as faulty socialisation, the failure to separate fantasy and reality, as in the James Bulger killers. A person who cannot contain the impossible contradiction and acts it out has broken the binary. This 'breakdown', understood as psychological and internal, is actually a central binary of liberal masculinity. Can the boundaries be broken? Of course. What is demanded is a difficult if not impossible task. Would this not be lived through attempts to exist only in that part of the binary which makes one feel truly a man or a woman, pushing away any Otherness? My examples of Melissa and Felix could be said to exemplify this.

Parents' views about violence

Let us now turn to a closer look at the interviews with parents. Here, reference to violence is exclusively a concern about boys: parents' discussions often slip from talking about children to 'he'. No parent of a girl discusses violence in games as an issue for girls. Conversely, while several parents of boys talk about violence, there is a great deal of concern about boys becoming violent. Violence is an issue for masculinity, not femininity. This has a particular effect in relation to girls' displays of violence in game playing in relation to the disavowal of violence in both their and parental accounts. However, even in relation to parents of boys, violence is what is perpetrated by others, not their son. There is a very clear discourse of regulation amongst the parents in which many parents understand violence and addiction as problems caused by lack of effective regulation of children's (boys') game play. It is striking that this is largely attributed to poor families in which lack of effective regulation is itself understood as the cause of violence. Thus, violence is othered – it belongs to poor boys and is caused by their families. As one parent says:

> 'You can pick the kids who are a bit more violent generally, more physical. They are the ones who tend to be watching the M-rated movies and they have got the video games that are M+. Like there is no supervision.'

If the poor boys without supervision are the ones who are potentially violent, there is a strong belief that games are not a problem for their own sons and indeed that games can actually be helpful. No one accepted that games made their own son violent, yet male violence in others was clearly understood as a problem according to this father:

> 'So, I think you have to weigh these things up too, like if he is not going to sit at home playing a computer game, he is going to sit at home and think I have nothing to do, I will go out in the street and out in the street he is going to think I still have nothing to do, I'll break into this car or I will rob this shop or I will knock over this elderly person or I'll drag a branch off a tree. You know, so where I am not there to supervise them in what they are doing, I would rather they were home playing computer games than wandering the streets and shopping centres.
>
> I don't really have a problem with them (games). I don't think they are some sort of big threat to society or anything like that. I think that some of the games, with some of the violence, and I can't sort of name what they are, but the ones with lots and lots of killing and shooting and mutilation and all sorts of crap – I think I will always object to those no matter how old he is. But otherwise I think it is enjoyable entertainment. I am happy if he enjoys it. I don't particularly get into it myself. And you know it probably gives him a few skills around problem solving.'

Violence according to these views is produced by lack of supervision, inadequate regulative strategies. Children who play videogames are not out in the street and therefore are not being violent and getting into crime. They may be having fun and even learning a few skills. Thus, it could be argued that parents strongly support an analysis of the place of games in the production of violence in contemporary masculinity which focuses on games as an aspect of the practices through which the management of violence is learnt as part of contemporary masculinity. In making a distinction between supervision of game playing, play in the home and crime on the street, violence as danger versus games as fun and skillful, they stress the ways in which boys can learn to both display and regulate their own violence – that is, they learn places in which violence is just a bit of fun and which actually involves the learning of a cognitive skill and where violence is unacceptable – the playground and the street being the two places mentioned by parents. Indeed, Jenkins (1998) points to he way in which middle-class American children are now expected to play in the home not on the street, park or fields. Video games in the home become a safe form of play in which physical activity is abandoned in favour of manual and intellectual skill, thus providing for the rational self management of violence – always the middle-class way (Bourdieu, 1991).

Can we think of violence in terms of a binary of violence as pleasure and violence as danger? That is, violence slides around discursively depending on what aspect of violence and whose violence is being pointed out. Since masculinity has to include the self regulation of violence then this sliding is hardly surprising. What I am trying to point out is that the parental discourses differentiate between both types of violence and practices for the production of violence. Not all violence is bad in their accounts. Indeed, we could say that the disavowal of violence in games as anything more than a bit of fun, a fantasy not impinging on reality, is something which has to be learned by boys.

The failure of this distinction is what is understood by many parents as a failure of parenting – lack of supervision which leads to pathology. It is these boys and only these 'disturbed' 'psychopathic' (in parents' terms), boys who are understood as constituting a danger because they have not been able to recognise the boundaries between fantasy and reality and between sites for acceptable and unacceptable violence. This is because they were from 'deprived' homes and have been poorly supervised. As a result what in one discourse is the 'natural propensity to violence of boys' (Walkerdine and Lucey, 1989) is turned into anti social violence and crime. In this way, violence as a central issue for masculinity and the complex ways in which violence is both desired and abhorred for men, is completely elided.

While I am certainly not wanting to suggest support for effects research, I would suggest that there is indeed a problem in the disavowal of this as violence, which seems to characterise parents and children and which also characterises some opponents to effects research. In particular, it denies that we are constituted as subjects within the demands of regulation as well as the centrality of affectivity in which a split between fantasy and reality is irrelevant. However, let us look more closely at what this split achieves in relation to masculinity, violence and games. I would suggest that this split is a site of a key distinction in the management of violence, that is, that there is play or fantasy violence which does not count or which can be encouraged, which is to be distinguished from 'real' violence, that is, violence enacted outside play settings. The performance of violence within games, whether they be video games or football, is then not understood as being 'real violence'. It is by distinctions such as these that the complex distinctions necessary to embody contemporary masculinity are learnt.

While boys do talk a lot about fighting and, as we saw in Chapter 3, certainly express anger and frustration about not being able to play well enough, there is not a huge amount of fighting in the videos. Almost all fighting offscreen is about how to play or who will get a turn – that is, who will be dominant. Yet there is little discussion of frustration by girls and none by their parents, so girls are simply not presented as being angry or frustrated if they cannot do something. What happens then? Yet they fight in the sense of arguing offscreen a similar amount to boys – 27 male instances versus 31 female ones. Yet, still we continue a discourse of violence as masculine.

If violence is a discourse of masculinity, it is not difficult to recognise that the girls do not present themselves as violent within interviews. It is common for the girls to present a femininity which abhors violence and which is its opposite. In particular, as we saw in Chapter 4, they like to present themselves as liking cute and cuddly characters, as embodying a femininity which is antithetical to violence and yet they are no less enthusiastic at killing than the boys. However, if we take the view that the narratives presented by participants relate to and often elide Other narratives, we could note a certain defensiveness in the girls' protestations about violence. Of course, this is hardly to say that violence is not something which is most often perpetrated by men against women, who are its victims. But there is something strange about the way in which many of the girls present a kind of cuddly femininity (liking for cuddly characters, etc., ones that can be mothered and looked after) and therefore disavow any interest in the violence of games. I say this because when it comes to thinking about girls actually playing the games, they engage in delight about killing an opponent with plenty of vigour, though this has to be qualified (see later section). What I have argued in Chapter 4 is that the girls have a different set of self management practices from boys. That is – to perform well in the games they must embody a masculinised game playing subject, but this threatens a femininity which must also be displayed to maintain their position as feminine with other girls and indeed with boys.

This becomes much clearer when we look at the actual play of boys and girls. Both girls and boys display an enjoyment of routine violence in that they engage in attempts to win, to kill, to avoid being killed, etc. However, there is a complex gendered performance of violence produced, as it is as a dichotomy of killing and being killed in relation to skill levels in the game. Violence is enacted as a gendered performance of skill at game playing. For many boys, the embodiment of this skill is a mark of considerable status and so friendship is performed by means of it. Boys will go out of their way to practise at game playing until they are in a position to win, as I discussed in Chapter 3. Such boys are admired and become heroes to their friends, according to some parents.

Within Australian culture, male friendship is embodied in the myth ology of 'mateship', a term which has particular resonances with the huge loss of Australian life in the ANZAC campaign at Gallipoli in the First World War. In this context, a combination of male friendship, bravery, bravado in the face of violence and war is the 'best of times within the worst of times'. Of course, Australia is hardly the only country in which male friendship is nurtured and lived in relation to violence – we might think of the place of the physical contact and pain of team sports (especially the various codes of football) within western cultures, as well as its association with British public schools and the brutality involved in the making of upper class men. And of course, the endurance of physical brutality is hardly a stranger to lives of poor men and those engaged in forms of manual labour. Thus, the competent male player is one who can kill more times than he is killed in a game and who therefore takes up a position as the fantasised possessor of power/knowledge. So, in the following exchange, Sam defers to Rob during a game of 'It's a bug's life', and Rob displays his knowledge, which allows him to beat his opponent, which brings Sam's deferring and subservience to Rob.

> **Rob:** Go on, stop jumping and go. Get that, that's something, I think. Chuck that on that. Chuck it on.
> **Sam:** I can't.

Rob: Don't worry about that, just keep it, come on, come on. You're goin' backwards.

Sam: No, I'm not. [*inaud.*]

Rob: Cause you're gonna just bump into that. What are you doing?

Sam: I just don't know where I'm going or how I'm doing it.

Rob: You're going to the Ant hill. You have to find the Ant Hill.

Sam: Oh, so you just go across the town to find it? Ant Hill.

Rob: Go that way, you're going backwards, not that way, down there [*Pointing to the screen*]

Sam: Where? Oh there it is, I thought this way.

Rob: You have to get that, you have to jump on that. You have to jump on that, get [*inaud.*] You're dead, my turn.

Sam: You have my turn [*Rob now playing*] Got to get to Ant Hill.

Rob: Down here.

For many girls, the situation is very different. No girl admits to practising on her own at games in order to be able to win, as many of the boys do. This is not to say, however, that girls do not like to win. There is ample evidence within the data that they can be very competitive. However, if winning and therefore killing for boys brings the kudos of an admired masculinity, it represents a threat to girls that in winning they have moved too far onto the side of the masculine. No girl uses competence in games as a marker of status which brings female friendship. Rather female friendship is produced through elaborate performances of a complex dance of winning and losing in which winning too much appears to engender a competitiveness which appears to threaten female friendships. I would argue that this is produced not because of any intrinsic lack on the part of girls, but because the technologies and practices of self-management are much more complex for today's girls. They have to display performances regarded as masculine while also displaying femininity, for example as in winning without losing female friendships. Obviously, different girls manage this very difficult task in different ways. In addition to this, masculinity is taken to embody action, activity (violence, killing, winning), while femininity is taken to embody passivity (losing, being killed, being the victim of violence). Girls struggle to embody both activity and passivity, killing and being killed, winning and losing. These are not intrinsic positions, but rather the discursive binaries through which gender difference is produced (Butler, 1990). So, for example, a girl can take up the position of knower even when playing with a boy. In the following extract in which Liam and Julie are playing Rugrats, Julie certainly manages to take a dominant position of authority in relation to how killing is to be accomplished.

Liam: The Mysterious Mr Friend.
Julie: I know, you got to kill Mr Friend, I watch Rugrats.
Liam: Who's Mr Friend?
Julie: He's an alien doll, you gotta kill him. There's a lot more.
Liam: Is there?
Julie: Yes
Liam: Did it hurt him? Where are they?
Julie: You gotta find them, they'll come behind you, go up stairs and run from it, go jump, forward press forward, you'll get away from them, then they can't get you. Go, don't stop, don't stop, turn, you gotta turn, ok. My turn, you've been on it long enough.
Liam: How do you bring the screen with it?
Julie: I know exactly how many steps there are.

However, when it comes to her preference for games and characters, etc., she finds the question too difficult to answer and isn't able to name any favourite game characters. Instead she chooses a cartoon character, 'Tweetie Pie'. In another example of play between a boy and a girl, the less skilled player, Ginny, defers to the more skilled Wyatt.

Ginny: Can we play a two player game?
Wyatt: That's a bit like a two player game, but I bet you won't like it. It's a bit violent.
Ginny: What?
Wyatt: It's a bit violent.
Ginny: What does that mean?
Wyatt: There is fighting. [*Researcher asks why does he think that Ginny won't like fighting?*] I don't think she'll like being a boy. Cause at the first stage your going to be a boy.
Ginny: [*Researcher asks Ginny if she minds playing a boy character*] No. Put two player in.
Wyatt: It is, but as long as I find Barrett [?]. There's a nutbell [?] there. This is analogue. I wish you could use that analogue.
Ginny: I think you gotta watch that star thing.
Wyatt: Yeah, you do. But I don't like it, it takes long.
Ginny: Or do you have to go to continue, I think you do.
Wyatt: Are those meteors or stars? Ah, there's the girl.
Ginny: Did she die of something?
Wyatt: She dies on this part. No that's a girl, she's shopping, there she is. This is what happened to her, she was paralysed. Hello Loveless [*Points to it on screen*] Final Fantasy seven

Ginny: She didn't die.
Wyatt: Yeah, she was just paralysed.
Ginny: What does paralysed mean?
Wyatt: You can't move that much. Oh there that's my start. This is gonna be hard against these baddies. Where am I? Oh there's Barrett [?] That's me.
Ginny: How do you know it's you?
Wyatt: I wish they call your name out ready.
Ginny: I think I'm the purple one, I think I'm the purple one.
Wyatt: No I can control, see, Oh I have no barrier, Aww ice.
Ginny: Did you even get it into two player?
Wyatt: Yeah, it is, I'm doing ice.
Ginny: Who am I? Who am I? The police guys? Am I the police guys? Could I be that guy?
Wyatt: Oh, I go up a level
Ginny: Did you even do it into two player?
Wyatt: Yeah. Yep, that's my name.
Ginny: Is that you're name there? How did they know it was your name.
Wyatt: Because it's my ID, Oh there you are. That's you, Barrett.
Ginny: Where am I?
Wyatt: You're hiding somewhere, that's why I didn't follow you. Uh, oh, I'm fading. I gotta find out a weakness. Huh [*inaud*] oh easy.
Ginny: Who am I am I those bad guys?
Wyatt: Yeah, you need [*inaud*] first. Ice I killed all your people. Oh what? I'm using my magic on you.
Ginny: How do you use the magic and stuff?
Wyatt: Yours was bite and [*inaud*]

This extract is noteworthy for several reasons: Wyatt positions Ginny as a girl who will not like violence. This way, he is able both to present his own position of unquestioned masculinity in liking violence and her as Other, an Other who he knows and can speak for. He knows she won't like violence or playing a boy. She answers that she doesn't mind playing a boy or object to violence, but we witness a further twist when she is forced to play a boy character but the girl character they refer to is called Loveless (can you believe this?) and doesn't die but is paralysed. This is such a classic melodrama twist, that we are confronted by the complexities of the positions that Ginny has to negotiate and the complex practices, emotions, discourses that they produce.

Notice that in the following extract, Paul consistently attempts to put down Gina's attempts to play skillfully (now I'm flying), by saying 'who cares if you fly?' And later 'you can't even hurt anybody cause you're too tiny'. This is a reference to the avatar, Kirby, that Gina is playing. Kirby is a big favourite for the girls. They refer to 'her'[3] as 'cute with a poison tongue'. It kills by sucking victims in.

Gina: What did I press to fly. How did I fly before?
Aisha: Well, I don't know
Paul: [*Continues roaring noise*]
Gina: But I can fly. Usually I can fly and now I'm killing myself. Ohhh, now I'm flying
Paul: Who cares if you fly?
Aisha: [*Laughs*]
Jim: Not me
Gina: Me
Paul: You can't even hurt anybody cause you're too tiny
Aisha: Me?
Gina: Kirby!
Paul: You're not hurting me. See?
Aisha: Well maybe I will
Gina: See if this attack works
Paul: [*Roars*]
Aisha: Oh. Lifesaver
Jim: Oh, he just fell of the edge and I had a very good [*inaud.*]
Gina: What does this attack do?
Aisha: No! Go away, I don't want to lose this. Lifesaver. Oh, it was caught
Paul: I just grabbed you
Gina: Hey . . .
Jim: Remember, Paul
Gina: . . .who did that?
Jim: Me
Aisha: Hiya, you sucked me in
Gina: Opps
Jim: Sorry. Donkey Kong, we're together
Paul: [*Roar*] Bad
Gina: Ah, I spat you out
Aisha: Good
Gina: I'll suck you in
Aisha: No, don't, don't. It loses points for me
Paul: Throw it at me
Aisha: Stop sucking me in
Gina: [*At the same time*] Oh it's such a good . . .

It is interesting that it is a character who manages both femininity and violence that is favoured by Gina as with many other girls. But more than this, with this character, Gina is able to get her own back on Paul by sticking out her avatar's tongue and sucking his avatar in! What is interesting about this is the form that the violence takes – incorporation, consumption. Is that not the very power that is projected onto women – the vagina dentata that will swallow, suck men into the vagina and therefore annihilate men through their sexuality? It is possible that this avatar's tongue also has resonances of the phallic mother? In any event, this character can hardly be said to be neutral in terms of fantasy and sexuality.

Kill or be killed

There is a striking difference in the ways that many of the girls and boys relate to killing and being killed. There are many examples of girls apparently attempting to avoid being killed rather than actively seeking to kill, as I demonstrated in Chapter 4.

Repeated entreaties to other players in the form of please such as 'don't kill me' are common especially from some girls, whereas they are much less marked in the boys' game-playing. On one level, this is explained by a clear difference in competence between all of the girls and most of the boys. They have trouble in doing more than just surviving in games where they have only basic knowledge. This does seem to lead to more attention being paid to avoiding being killed than actually actively killing and winning. But something more is going on than this I think. What the girls and boys display appears, on first sight, to conform to the active/masculine, passive/feminine dichotomy. Boys are violent – girls are the objects of violence. Yet, again and again, as I have indicated earlier, girls have no problem in actively seeking to win and to kill. What we could ask instead then is how the practices and performances of the games are at the same time performances of well rehearsed and regulated masculinities and femininities that are affectively and discursively associated with the many other sites and practices in which masculinities and femininities are produced and performed. And how do these add up to a self management for girls which can cope with the huge contradictions and conflicts between the positions they have to negotiate and somehow live at once? If we look at what is demanded by the games and then how some girls and boys perform what is demanded, as well as what is demanded by the relationship between the children, this should become clearer.

One of the most striking characteristics of the differences between girls' and boys' playing is the level of competence. For reasons which will be elaborated in Chapter 6, the girls in both groups simply do not play as often as the boys and do not display the apparent desire to practise to become good. As I have explained earlier, there is a huge investment in being the boy who is best at games in terms of friendships, etc. Girls do not talk of filling their spare time with game-playing, but of playing other kinds of games, such as fantasy role play with television characters (see Chapter 4). In addition, parental regulation of girls' game playing is far more strict than that of boys, meaning that girls simply do not have access to the games and practice time that boys have. Consequently, there is a marked contrast between girls with a low competence level who try not to get killed and boys who generally are more accomplished, who try to kill. I have been at pains to suggest that there are girls who are just as keen on winning as boys, but often their competence level makes that difficult. It is not uncommon to see girls struggling with the very basic features of games, so that they never actually get beyond the introductory section to games and so are frequently frustrated and give up.

However, while many girls display a desire to 'live longer', they are also much more relaxed than the boys about dying and are prepared to have fun dying, giggling about being killed one more time. In one sequence which was included in field-notes but not recorded, two girls had the most fun by actually giggling their way through being chased and killed by the dinosaur in Crash Bandicoot. They sat swinging their legs and giggling so much that several boys came to see what was going on, only to lose interest when they saw that the girls were losing the game. They intimated that they couldn't understand why any girls would want to lose! However, if femininity is situated on the side of practices that present it as cute, cuddly, nice, friendly, not violent, giggling; and masculinity on the side of winning, killing, power, strength, then no wonder girls appear ambivalent as they struggle to manage both positions if they want to do well in games. This means that sometimes, like Melanie, they project their desire to win onto others while appearing to hold onto femininity for themselves, or they choose characters which are generally reckoned not to be as powerful but are more acceptable in terms of cuteness, cuddliness or femininity, or they position themselves as implicitly masculine as Gina does when she and Melissa are playing together.

> **Melissa:** Baboom. Oh, I just got electrocuted and I'm holding a knife
> **Gina:** Yahoo. You got dead, you got dead
> **Melissa:** I don't care. I still have, some sort of life, where am I? Get it, get it. Oh, bugger. Pokaball. Pokaball
> **Gina:** I know, I'm trying ta get it. What do you think I'm trying to do?
> **Melissa:** Yes. Oh, I should have got a Pokaball

Gina: Cool. I'm gonna die you. Oh damn it, you're good
Melissa: Stop it
Gina: I can do whatever I want. I'm a grown man now, mama.

The use of the phrase 'I'm a grown man now mama' certainly recalls the style of the action hero of a Hollywood western.

Conclusion

I have argued in this chapter that violence is neither something which is produced as a bad effect of games or a good cathartic aspect of game-playing – something which allows violence to be safely expressed. Rather, I have argued that violence in games has to be understood as part of the management of contemporary masculinities and femininities. As such, the production of the ubiquitous killing in games is part of a set of practices through which masculinity expressed as the power to kill and therefore to win, is established. This means that femininity is always constituted as its Other and opposite. I have been interested in how this plays out in both parental and child interviews and in the ways that playing itself as well as the strategies for playing, become gendered. In the next chapter, I will explore the issue of parental regulation of game play.

6
Regulating Game Play: 'Clingy Sooky Mummy's Boys' and Other Personas

Introduction

It should come as no surprise to the reader by this stage in the book that I think that gender and sexuality are central to the parental regulation of the game playing of the young children in this study. The parental regulation of boys and girls as well as the ways that girls and boys describe their game playing, differs considerably. For me one of the most interesting things is that parental discourses about regulation are concerned almost exclusively with the need to regulate boys. The regulation of girls is generally suggested by parents as unnecessary. It is what is held behind this silence and apparent non problem that began to fire my own imagination and made me wonder why it is that regulation is a problem in relation to boys but not to girls. Girls' regulation was not considered a problem because girls, we were constantly told, were not interested in games. What began to emerge for me was a story in which girls are simply not given the same chance to play games as boys in part perhaps because they are understood as unfeminine and that, games are presented in relation to key regulative discourses for masculinity – around a masculinity which is about action, separation from mothers, but not addictive or violent.

Regulating children's game play so that they do not become addicted has been one of the central concerns of many parents since the games became a popular form of play. In particular, the spectre of the unsupervised and addicted boy recalls 1950s arguments about unregulated addictive television viewing amongst working-class families (Himmelweit, 1958).

I understand regulation both as active regulation by parents and the importance of the development of techniques of self regulation or self management in which the 'free' child (in Rose's sense, Rose, 1999) does not have to be actively regulated because 'he' freely chooses not to play video games to the point of addiction and therefore becomes the rational subject. Parents in the Sydney study overwhelmingly thought it unnecessary to overtly regulate girls' game-playing. According to them this was because girls chose to do other activities such as playing other kinds of games or watching television, which had to be strictly regulated. This way of framing the lack of need for regulation however could be said to cover over what we could read as the active attempts by parents to stop their daughters from having access to video games, as I will demonstrate. What may we ask was thought to be at stake in insisting that girls and video games did not go together? If games are a site for the production of contemporary masculinity, this response becomes less surprising. Parental regulation of boys shows how much regulation is understood as a contradictory practice for the production of an active masculinity, in which games should be encouraged to reflect a moderate level of rebellion, a standing up to authority, so as not to produce what one father called a 'clingy sooky mummy's boy type person', while at the same time not becoming an 'addictive personality', who never leaves their bedroom.

I want to discuss the modes of parental regulation adopted by parents as discussed in their interviews. What I want to think about is how regulative practices help to constitute the child player and how the practices help produce a gendered split in modes of regulation, with the optimum regulative strategy being understood as self regulation – the production of the classic liberal subject.

If video game regulation is constituted as a problem in relation to boys, one in which boys must have the required level of rebellion, but also must not become addicted or violent and have rational control, it becomes clear that parental regulation is a complex task aimed at producing the desired form of masculinity. Parents of boys simply talk about regulation vastly more than parents of girls. In some cases, parents of girls who had brothers talked more in the interviews about the brothers than the girls who were the participants in the study. I argue therefore that the task that games perform is hugely complex so that it is not simply a question of games being good or bad for children. To produce the rational, liberal, independent subject is a big task and an anxious and impossible one for parents. Thus, I would argue, just as I have throughout the book, that the regulative tasks in relation to girls and boys are different. The sets of binaries and discursive parameters that constitute the boy – rational, independent versus mummy's boy, violent and addicted, for example, are quite different from those through which girlhood is constituted. We should not be surprised then that the modes of regulation and concerns about regulation should be very different for the parents of boys and of girls.

In the next section I want to explore practices and techniques of parental regulation as expressed at interview and go on to think about the Other of that regulation – that is, what is guarded against.

Regulating boys: producing the masculine

The first thing to note is that expressed parental concern about the regulation of boys in relation to video games far outweighs concern about girls. The boy is understood by many parents as potentially dangerous. One way of understanding this is a discourse about boys' inherent 'violent bent'. As one mother put it:

> 'They're all shooting people and absolutely violent and I truly believe no matter how many studies are done that say that these are harmless to young boys in particular who really do have a violent bent from an early age, you know surely they're doing something, surely they're reinforcing something that is probably not conducive with society as we accept it today and yeah, young boys in particular, I worry more about boys than girls, they are into guns. Johnny's three and a half and we don't let him have guns or anything but he'll turn his drill out of his tool kit into a gun and start shooting people because he picks up at day care you know from the kids that have got elder brothers and sisters. . . . It is some male violent crime or thing that obviously is part of our human survival that we have suppressed to be in this society that we are in at the moment and I don't think it [playing video games] is a healthy release of those kind of high energy urges if you like.'

While the view of the mother above is quite typical, she prefers her son to work out his 'violent bent' as a 'healthy release of high energy' on the football field than play video games with its sense of being shut up inside and therefore the threat of addiction. Many fathers, on the other hand, understand this inherent violence as necessary and many therefore argue that boys should be allowed to 'test-drive' it, to learn to manage and regulate their 'natural' impulses through activities like 'action' and 'adventure' type video games because in a sense not to allow them to do so would be to emasculate them. The discourse of the 'sooky clingy mummy's boy' makes it clear that in some sense it is just as much a problem if the 'violent bent' is absent as if it is present. For example, one father argues that he would find it more worrying if his son meekly accepted his attempt to put time limits on his son's playing than if he resisted.

If he just meekly and just sort of said: 'Yes sir', and switched it off it would be much more worrying. So, but yeah, we try and keep it down, yeah to within I don't know sort of modest levels. You know, life is a bit more interesting than computer games and I wouldn't want him to get too caught up in it.

His wife says:

Well I guess, a) I don't really understand the games well enough and don't take enough interest to be full conversant with what being on level whatever means anyway and b) because he's so enthusiastic and it is in a sense an achievement when he gets to these levels, one doesn't want to, I think its a fine line, you don't want to let your disapproval quash the child's sense of achievement at having done something that they consider to be pretty good.

Interviewer: Does that set up a bit of a quandary for you that in one sense you're reinforcing him going different levels then at the same time you're concerned about him being addicted to the games to play to the end or spending too much time on them, so how do you feel about that?

Mother: Yeah, well I think it is a quandary and that's why we sort of set times, time limits you know and try and keep him under control, try and keep the whole thing under some sort of control. Another one of (child)'s friends, his dad is a big computer and Playstation buff and (friend) spends as far as I can work out pretty much all day everyday on school holidays when he's not at the movies playing Playstation games.

So, it seems that regulation has to walk a fine line between squashing natural impulses of masculinity, which include action and rebellion and encouraging those very qualities, especially if they lead to the development of rational practices of self control and achievement. This view of childhood masculinity is hardly new. I wrote about it in relation to mathematics education in 1989/98 (Walkerdine, 1989, 1998). The idea that natural childhood involves action, naughtiness and rebellion and that therefore somehow girls were already defined as pathological children by being well behaved, was enshrined in English primary education from the 1960s. However, of course, the discourses which underpin this are far older and build at least upon Greek views of masculinity built into a post-Enlightenment scientific rationalism that underpins liberalism.

In this sense, the regulation of boys' play has to have two faces: it must simultaneously encourage activity, rationality, self management, rebellion and prohibit excess. This could take the form of encouragement or reward on the one hand and prohibition, denying access to games, censorship, taking games away as a form of punishment, on the other. The spectre of the addicted child is also presented as the unhealthy pastiness and over-weight of someone who has spent too much time indoors and in front of a console, as this mother says of her son's friend:

> 'No I don't know him well enough for that, I mean something I do, one does observe is that and this sounds dreadful, I mean he's actually a bit overweight and its probably because he's spent, and he's sort of pasty faced and a bit overweight, which is probably because all his times indoors playing Playstation.'

The idea is that games only become addictive if you let children play them too long or they'd play all day if you let them, so parents have to limit their time:

> 'Well I think they are only addictive if you let your kids play hour after hour.
>
> I think they have a place and I think that it is okay but I don't think it is something kids should be allowed to do all the time. I think they are addictive and I think that kids get quite obsessed with them. And I know that Jack does. And I know that there are some games that I really don't like.
>
> But I think it is only what you allow to happen. I don't think the games themselves are addictive, it is just easier for the kids to play that than be involved in other things. There is not enough emphasis put on family type things.
>
> I guess I would probably say addiction is to some degree about expo-sure and that is about how you expose kids to the environment, so I would probably say addiction is probably as much a parental responsi-bility as it is in . . . the video game. As for the violence in video games again it depends on the video games that children are playing. There is no doubt that some of them are incredibly violent. And if that doesn't have an effect on the child I would be quite surprised depending on the age. I certainly see, for example, our three and a half year old when we started buying him a Batman video versus a Thomas the Tank Engine video. He suddenly took on the . . . would go and punch other kids.'

William is only allowed to play on the computer for a maximum of an hour a day or not at all if there is a lot of homework ('there is just too much else to do'). Another mother expresses the idea that her son's desire to play games is so great that it would dominate his life, but that if you regulate his games-playing (do deals that the pay off for doing certain tasks is to have time on the computer to play games) he will be motivated to do the tasks, like a training in deferred gratification/training desire, so that games-playing (his overwhelming desire) doesn't dominate his life, according to Kylie. This leads to the problem of disciplining expressed by other parents in the idea that unrestricted access to games leads to addiction so that children wouldn't do other things the mother would prefer them to do, as the mother of Wayne says. This can be avoided for some parents by having 'a good mix of activities', as Martin suggests. Bianca wasn't going to get a Playstation initially because she had heard they were addictive (but then the whole family was addicted to the computer and Internet when they first got it). The idea that wanting to finish a game when called to dinner, and resisting coming when called, constitutes 'addiction', according to Pamela.

We could argue that regulating children's time spent playing games as well as attending to the type of games that they play constitutes part of the attempt to produce civilised masculinity. The regulated player is not addicted and can manage to cope with the desire to play enough to leave it alone. I suggest that this is a lesson that has to be learnt and many parents either explicitly or implicitly see it as their job to teach this. In this sense, addiction, like violence, is a spectre. It is sits there as an excess, as that which has to be avoided while allowing the 'untrammelled desire' to be expressed in a regulated way. So what is the desire and why is it presented as so threatening and alluring? Addiction is understood as what Jude presents as 'that they really love it and it gets them going'; to love the object of affection, to be immersed in a fantasy and not be able to leave and go back into the real world. These seem to be some of the fears expressed by the term 'addiction'. On the one hand we can, following Foucault, understand it as a medicalisation of a certain set of feelings and desires (Foucault, 1973). This is why it has to be presented as unhealthy to be addicted and yet the skills of masculinity are those which have to be practised. Perhaps we can find some clues in the discourse of masculine rationality in which excess itself is regarded as animal and has to be avoided in order to produce the rational subject in control of their own destiny, master of their emotions, of their nature. If that nature is the primitive, the uncivilised, just as with violence it threatens to break through the surface of the rational. To desire to only exist in the world of games to the exclusion of everything else is an expression of a longing. How might we look at that longing? One way of thinking about it is in relation to the father, Tyrone, who we met in Chapter 3. For him, playing Metal Gear Solid took him to both a space and to a position within that space, the controller of his avatar Snake, which meant that he could inhabit a masculinity which he could not in life outside games, as he was a single father of a learning disabled boy and in a low paid job. I suggest that to understand this we have to think about the contrast between the positions that are presented – the feminised low paid father versus the action hero who saves the world through his daring deeds. Of course, such a juxtaposition is not new – Hollywood has given us such heroes for some time. Popular fiction presents them to us – they surround us. A Lacanian reading would stress the importance of the fantasy of having and being the phallus and the necessary but elusive search of masculinity for it. He presents us with an Imaginary world in which we can inhabit this position, in which all dreams come true. But here, I want to develop this in a different way. I want to think about how the two positions oscillate around the possibility of embodying the positions accorded to masculinity in the present. Inhabiting the character of the avatar, Snake, allows him to manage better his position in other practices – low paid worker, single father, practices in which perhaps he fears he is not really a man. After all, the low paid worker has little status, little consuming power and the single father, apart from some small romantic cachet, has little claim on a heroic masculinity. Could we say then that in a moment in which traditional divisions of labour are breaking down and in which there is little manual work left in the West to convey a heroic masculinity, this space provides a context in which the man might fantasise feeling whole, complete, adding a side of him which he has lost, a place where he longs to be. If we were to develop this in terms of my three-fold approach to affect, we can see how the affectivities circulate throughout the life world and catch him up into them.

In Chapter 2, I argued that boys who were successful were more likely to be able to practise until they had the skills to win, whereas boys who were less successful were more likely to rely on a 'magical' strategy of invoking power through a powerful character, just as Sam unsuccessfully invokes the power of the Jedi in Star Wars Racer. I would suggest that whether it be the desire to practise or the desire to inhabit a character or a scenario, it is a desire for power, the power of masculinity. In any event, the imagination to want to win or be someone or somewhere has to be invoked and is a prerequisite of change. Is it the problem of the fantasy/reality distinction? I would suggest that this is a spurious distinction. Our current world is absolutely saturated with fantasy scenarios and the distinction between these and something called 'reality' is untenable.

But we do have here certain affectivities working together. We have parental anxiety about a normal and well adjusted masculinity set against the longing to inhabit it totally, perhaps without failure. This gets played out in particular practices and in this case, modes of regulation. So, parents have a number of practices and technologies designed both to prevent excess and to punish it. For example, Caroline bought a console but describes it as hers, so that her children are only allowed to play if she thinks that they deserve it. Some parents refuse to buy consoles both on the grounds of cost but also because of concerns about video games taking time away from other activities. Some parents will only allow computer rather than video games as they feel these have a higher educational content. Another strategy is to censor and police game play in terms of not allowing certain kinds of games (mostly those considered too violent) and only allowing appropriately classified games rather than those allocated to a higher age group.

Placing time limits on play is perhaps the commonest form of regulation for boys. Daniel is restricted to half an hour per day, whereas William is to have one hour. Others have time limits or days in the week when they are allowed to play. Some have rules like homework first. This is the cause of frequent disputes between boys and parents. Another strategy adopted by some families is to hide the console or to keep it in a public space in which play can be monitored rather than in a child's bedroom. Quite a few parents use a strategy of taking access to games away as a punishment for misbehaviour.

On the other hand, children are invited to participate in game playing in a 'well-adjusted' way. Particularly with middle-class parents, this is accomplished through a discourse of rational argument. Walter says 'they are not unmanageable, they listen to reason', 'we find that if we explain things to the kids then they go along with it, they understand . . . and they don't give us a hard time and they certainly don't make my life a misery'. Julie explains to her son why she hates certain games and why he isn't allowed to have higher rated games. Helen says that when she thinks a game demands more maturity you have to spend a bit more time explaining to the children what it's about, asking how they see it and what they think about it. Susan explains to her son that force should be used for the good of society and how violence is not OK, in order to attempt stop him thinking it's 'so cool'. Finn tells his son that the blood and guts are not real, while Susan tells her son when he forgets to save Final Fantasy and is in tears, that this happens all the time throughout life and you can't do anything about it and have to come to terms with it. She and her partner make their son save up his own money to buy a game and when it fails to live up to his expectations, explain to him that packaging is designed to make you compulsively buy something that may not be particularly good. They now insist that games are rented first to avoid this. In that sense, part of the regulation and disciplining is in the art of consumption.

Given the way that class practices are regulated in terms of power (Walkerdine and Lucey, 1989) it is perhaps unsurprising that some of the working-class families are more likely to use a discourse of what they do or do not allow rather than an explanatory rational strategy. Caroline simply tells her son what is and is not allowed by her. Finally, a common technique is to steer children away from games and towards other activities, especially sport and reading.

I want to end this section by thinking in more detail about the production of one child, Bill, who is apparently disinterested in or gets easily bored with games. I want to suggest that this Bill is carefully produced through the intersection of a number of practices designed to produce a certain relation to games, thus a certain relationality.

There are a number of practices or kinds of training which 'predispose' Bill to a particular relationship with games. For example, Bill's parents choose to send him to a Catholic school because there is a certain supervision of his activities, a certain moral framework, his father's treatment of him as a little adult ('we don't treat them as children so much, more as equals'). They also instil certain values and manners, such as being thoughtful to other people and thanking people for looking after him. This has to be explained rather than simply ordered. These are then naturalised as part of Bill's character. His mother says that he 'just likes to do the right thing' while the interviewer notes in his fieldnotes that Bill seemed very polite and helpful. There are only two entertainment video games in the house and all other games are educational computer games. Yet, his mother says that Bill would play all day in the street or watch TV all day if allowed. What I am arguing here is that the naturally helpful Bill who doesn't care much for games is carefully crafted and is produced relationally at the intersection of a number of practices even if what emerges as a result is what is presented as a 'natural' set of personality characteristics or a disinterest in video games.

I shall now go on to think about the regulation of girls' game playing and the production of the antithesis between femininity and games.

Regulating girls

The story that girls are not interested in video games and therefore do not need regulation as opposed to television where much regulation has to take place, forms part of a narrative which assumes girls and video games simply do not go together. Girls are not interested in video games – period. However, if we probe this a little further, we can see that the story of masculine rebellion, but not addiction and rational control simply cannot be a story which applies to girls. Does this narrative of lack of interest therefore elide another story, one in which there is a concern not to produce girls who are too masculine? Or perhaps girls who insufficiently feminine? Is there another aspect of a complex denial, just like the cuddly characters we met in Chapter 4 who elide and disavow the complex relation to violence on the part of the girls? Is this also another site of denial in which femininity *must* be presented as antithetical to the masculinity implied in games and in which girls do not rebel, are not overly rational and do not become addicted? Is the rebellious girl or the over-masculine girl more of a threat? Does the spectre of girl gangs or Riot Girls provide an image at once too butch and too sexual? The protestations of lack of interest in games are particularly strong among the parents of the middle-class girls, who want their daughters to play 'educational games' on the computer. I was left wondering in fact if, despite the evidence to the contrary, there was more concern about girls than there was about boys and whether the silence about girls was itself full of meaning.

As I have said, the regulation of children with respect to video game play is presented by parents as a problem for boys. This is easy to understand because the concerns about violence and addiction link primarily to discourses about masculinity. But is this precisely the reason why again and again parents in the study simply claimed that girls and games didn't go together? For example, Bianca says that her daughter is not really interested in the Nintendo so there is no need to regulate her play and will not be interested in the Playstation her brother is being bought for Christmas. Bianca imagines having much more trouble regulating her son's play. Again and again, mothers and fathers claim their daughters are not interested. Paul says:

> I don't impose any rules because there has been no reason to. I mean she hardly ever goes. Sometimes she does, when she has friends over, they play a computer game that you've got to get over obstacles but no, I mean it just doesn't occur.

Jim says:

> Well I don't really, there is no point, I don't need to regulate that because she doesn't overdo it anyway.

This is a very typical story, repeated many times over by many parents. Girls are disinterested or show a little interest and do not need to be regulated because they stop playing and move on without any overt regulation. Steven says of his daughter:

> 'She will jump on the computer every so often and get really bored but then she will come around and she will say you know, from time to time, "I am bored." And we will say, "Well the computer's upstairs if you like." "Oh I don't want to do that." She will ride her bike around the streets but it is a bit hard around here because of the traffic. But she will ride it around. She likes doing anything artistic so lately she is into doing things with candles and making patterns and that type of thing. Anything artistic that is her main interest.
>   No she doesn't want to play that sort of game (violent games), she would rather play . . . I mean if we had a boy it might be different, but she would rather race cars, or race trucks or play this World Rescue game.'

Steven sums it up for us nicely – it is boys who are interested in violence, in speed (car racing) and girls would rather do other things – in the case of his daughter, anything artistic.

Parent after parent tells us that no regulation for girls is needed, they easily get bored and stop playing. On the other hand, as I said earlier, elaborate rules are put in place to regulate girls' TV viewing. Girls, it seems, can't get enough television and have to be given strict rules about watching it. This suggests that a simple explanation in terms of girls being more docile, well behaved and rule following would not make any sense at all, since this would mean that girls would be equally said to be placid about television watching, which is not the case.

I want to suggest a different form of explanation. That is, that girls' disinterest and lack of need for regulation is produced in a complex set of relations. It does not have a simple explanation or cause but is produced out of a number of relationalities working together. There is little doubt that many girls like playing games. They joined the video game clubs and were keen to play. They also can get excited about killing and violence as the boys. However, I suggest that their skill level is rarely as good as that of the boys. The boys report that 'you have to practice, practice, practice' to be a successful game player. The girls in the club are most often in the position of novices who cannot even master the most simple rules of many games. This leads them to give up easily as they are often 'killed'. So why don't they go back to their bedrooms to practise like the boys?

If, as I have argued throughout this volume, games are one site for the production of contemporary masculinity, it would not be surprising that many girls might not want to practice. I wonder though if, in some way, this is also a reason for girls not to be bought consoles or games ('she wouldn't be interested'), to be only given computers and educational games and to be directed towards more gender appropriate pursuits. Could the lack of regulation and the insistence that girls are not so keen on games, elide a set of concerns and anxieties about femininity? Of girls being too masculine or not feminine enough? Remember that many girls when playing games seemed to have to manage both masculinity and femininity at the same time, often with difficult consequences. Does a set of anxieties about femininity mean that while boys' play has to be regulated to produce a balanced masculinity, girls' play has almost to be disavowed to guard against the possibility of an over-masculinisation? Middle-class parents certainly encourage their daughters to play 'educational' games on the computer. This fits with a discourse of girls' educational attainment, which must be encouraged, but console games perhaps signify masculinity in a different way, in that they signify characteristics of masculine action heroism, violence, which have no place in the rationality of female educational success.

Some parents refuse to buy consoles for girls because they are too expensive, antisocial or because girls are not sufficiently interested. I have included below a long sequence of an interview with one mother, whose daughter was part of the study. She has an older brother, Kyle, who has recently moved on from games to guitars. It is interesting to note that although the daughter, Michelle is said to be really keen on games, this interest does not appear to have been approached in the same way as that of her older brother:

Interviewer: Yeah. Um now have any of them nagged you about getting particular games or getting a play station or . . . sort of things?
Pamela: Yes. Kyle is nagging me at the moment, he wants more memory on our hard drive, because it is, well it is fairly slow, well compared to sort of like my one at work and you know, when you are on the Internet it is fairly slow and when you are downloading things and all that sort of thing. So he is really nagging me about that at the moment and I am sort of looking into it but um, as for computer games and things, no. Not really. I mean Kyle has had all the games. He

has had a Sony Playstation and he has had a Nintendo and he has had all that and um he sold it all a while ago.

Interviewer: Oh right.

Pamela: And then he bought a guitar. Oh sorry, he plays the bass guitar. So now he has given away all of those things to play his . . .

Interviewer: . . . moved onto something . . .

Pamela: Yeah he has moved onto something else. Yeah, so he plays the bass guitar now and he is in a band.

Interviewer: Oh excellent.

Pamela: Which is really good and I was glad that he got rid of them you know because, I don't know, they sort of get stuck in their room and you know sitting there playing these silly games and . . . you know, so um I was glad he got out of that and um and yeah so he plays that now but with the computer that was a sort of new interest for him as well with the updated one because the old one was really just an old thing for games really. Um . . .

Interviewer: Did Michelle ever want to use the Playstation? Or was she disappointed . . .?

Pamela: Oh she was too little then, oh she was only about, I mean that was like, how long has Kyle been playing the guitar now, for four years.

Interviewer: Oh okay.

Pamela: Yeah so she was a bit too young to play those sort of things. No she doesn't really nag me for games and things like that. She hasn't sort of specifically asked me to buy her a game for the computer or you know, no.

Interviewer: Now just a minute ago you said that some of the games are a bit silly.

Pamela: Yeah.

Interviewer: Would you consider actually getting Playstation again for Michelle and letting her play those sort of games?

Pamela: No. No.

Interviewer: Why? This is really important . . .

Pamela: Yeah. Because I just think it, it just takes away all their social and family time sort of thing, you know they are stuck in the room playing you know a Nintendo or Sony Playstation or whatever they are and um I don't know most of the games, I mean there are a lot of girlie games that are you know sort of pretty good and there are a lot of educational ones as well but you can get all that off the net and get it all off the computer.

Interviewer: Yeah. So you are much happier . . .

Pamela: Um, besides that they are expensive to buy the games for those things as well and yeah I just, I am glad we don't have one any more. Yeah.

Interviewer: So you have got the computer and you are happy for . . . on the computer and . . .

Pamela: Yeah. Yeah I would rather buy a game for the computer or an educational CD rather than you know, one of those game things.

Interviewer: So were you concerned that Kyle was spending too much time in his room just playing games and not coming out?

Pamela: Yeah. At the time, yeah. It was like, oh well I guess it like anything when they first get it, you know, it is a novelty sort of thing and the novelty wears off after a while but you know it is like . . .

Interviewer: . . . for him . . . natural . . .

Pamela: . . . rather than studying they are sitting there playing you know their games and all that sort of thing, and you know, I was really glad that he decided he didn't want it any more, you know. And that was good.

Interviewer: Rules about playing the computer. Did I ask you that already?

Pamela: No.

Interviewer: No, okay. Do you have any particular rules about how long they are allowed to spend, or what times of the day . . .?

Pamela: It just depends. Well Kyle doesn't get on the computer until usually after dinner, sometimes he is on it when I get home, it depends, you know on what he is doing. If he is doing something for school he will be on it before I get home or whatever. There is no real time period it is just that when Michelle wants to have a go it's usually when Kyle is on it and he has been on it for a while so I will sort of say to him, you know, let Michelle have a go or whatever. Or Michelle waits till Kyle finishes what he is doing, depending on what it is. Um but there is no real, um, time limit of you know, as long as they sort of share it and be fair about it and um, you know, then it's okay.

Interviewer: Have there ever been any times or instances where um like they have spent five or six hours and you have suddenly had to tell them to get off the computer because they have been on there too long?

Pamela: Sometimes Kyle will be on it until ten at night, just you know on the ICQ talking with his mates, you know, and he is talking with his mates that he sees at school every day and it is like I am going to bed at ten o'clock and he might be still on there. You know, that was when we first got the net on and that has sort of worn off a little bit now as well although he still chats every night but not as late. That used to sort of annoy me a little bit. But um, um, no not really, apart from that you know he wouldn't be on it for longer than you know a few hours or whatever, you know.

Interviewer: Yeah. Well let's get back to Michelle. Out of all of the things that she is really passionate about, she told me some of the things that she really likes to do, where would you say that playing games on the computer or emailing, or using the computer, where would that fall into the scale of things for her?

Pamela: Um, probably, I mean she really loves playing on the computer, like it sort of makes her feel important I think, you know, when she sort of gets on it and plays, especially if she has got a friend over and that, you know, she will show them how to play the Winnie the Pooh one, you know, and so it is like she can show somebody how to do something on it. Um, I think it would probably fall about third.

Note here that Michelle is said to love video games, yet unlike for her brother, her mother will not buy her a console and in addition, she has to wait her turn behind her brother to go onto the computer. There seems to be no sense that because Kyle has now moved on to guitars, it is now Michelle's turn to have priority on the computer or to play games. Indeed, there is not even the suggestion that just as Kyle was indulged by buying him many games and allowing him to spend hours playing them, this would also be a stage that Michelle might go through too.

There are many other accounts of brothers hogging the console or computer and brothers actively attempting to stop their sisters playing, such as turning off the computer or resetting the machine so the brother can win or by being so competitive as to put the sister off playing the game. Of course, this is not the first time this has come to light. Many times during the club sessions, boys would disavow girls' competence or stop them winning in underhand ways. In other words, female high performance in games is a threat because it seems to mean that girls are exhibiting something that doesn't belong to them, something that should by rights belong to masculinity – as though in fact girls who are good at games actively take something away from boys – the fantasy of possession of the Phallus perhaps? Being beaten by a girl is threatening just as liking girls' games like Barbie is simply not admissible.

If masculinity and femininity are natural opposites, then girls and 'sooky clinging mummies' boys' are skating on thin ice. They are always in danger of crossing over a border, one that must be carefully policed. Girls' educational attainment appears then to come from another discourse, one which is already well established, so that girls can be allowed access to computers to do educational work but not to play games.

According to parents, girls spend a great deal of time watching TV. The shows most often cited by them are *Charmed*, *Sabrina* and *Seventh Heaven*. Each of these shows stars powerful women with magical powers. They are dreams of power which it seems are at least more ambivalently expressed in games, or perhaps the desire to be like these heroines is more socially acceptable if expressed in television shows. The women in *Charmed* and *Sabrina* do not kill – they cast spells and they are determinedly heterosexual. The shows have a very careful blending of traditional feminine power and heterosexual attractiveness.

Regulating Prudence

In the rest of the chapter, I want focus on a case study of the parental regulation of one middle-class girl, Prudence. We will begin with her as seen through the interview with her father, Jonathan:

> **Jonathan**: But Sarah [Prudence's mother] and Prudence, the game they play on the computer here called Hokus which is an old, in the good old days when Apege made computer games you know that sort of old Apege sort of VGA?
>
> **Interviewer**: I am not sure if I can remember that.
>
> **Jonathan**: Well Hokus is the one where you have this sort of man and he walks along and he shoots all the bad dragons and he gets potions and stuff it's quite a good game, it is a bit of a shoot 'em up game. And they became, the two of them, Sarah and Prudence became obsessed by it, you know. And Sarah was sort of obsessed by it and she was playing it all the time, Prudence sort of watched and then Prudence would have a long go and they would sort of be competitive about the levels and getting up to different levels and that was quite interesting to watch. And then like with all these things, the thrill wears off, you know, and you need a new game to play. One of the things that I have noticed about computer games is you actually, they all have a sort of a um, you know, it just wears off. I guess in a way it is like re-reading a book you know, it is like a multi layered complex book, you might read it a hundred times you know in that respect, but you know what I mean and sooner or later it gets to the point where it becomes, despite the fact that you know, I guess you just explore all the levels, or all the possibilities of the game.

It seems that Prudence and her mother have been playing an old 'shoot 'em up' game together and been rather competitive about it. But note how carefully Jonathan goes on to tell the interviewer that Prudence is not just a competitive game player – she has an empathic side, a point which he makes when the interviewer suggest that Prudence is more animated when she plays video games with boys. He seems to accept the possibility of girls liking 'rough and tumble', only to add that Prudence has an empathic side.

Interviewer: One thing I did notice about her she would be more animated when she played with a group of boys, because we deliberately mixed boys and girls up and did all sorts of things just to see what would happen. When it was girls only she would kind of play but take a bit of quieter role, but when she was playing with the boys she seemed to get more involved and playing more excitedly.

Jonathan: Well I think, you know, I think to put it bluntly she just becomes more boyish, you know, because at her age she is not really like that kind of discriminated you know what I mean. And I think in the company of boys she becomes more boyish and quite enjoys a bit of rough, you know, she quite enjoys quite a bit of you know, I think she quite enjoys boys' play to an extent and I am sure that is common for a lot of girls. I mean I don't know about your own experience, but anyway, you know, you obviously go through periods with this sort of thing. Is that the same with other female, other female kids?

Interviewer: A few of them, and particularly the same in my experience actually. So I really related to Prudence because I don't really know why even, but maybe because you can swap and change, and I just don't know.

Jonathan: Anyway another thing that Prudence has, she does have a very, she has a very strong empathic quality in her, she is a person who is very easy to relate to, she, I have noticed this since she was a baby, she has a very high degree of what I would call companionability, you know, she is somebody, there aren't, I suppose there are probably a lot of eight year olds who you could just sit down and spend the whole day talking to. But I noticed with her years ago when she was four or five I sort of thought this is a four or five year old I am talking to, you know, and I had been just talking to her as if she was an adult, you know what I mean, so she definitely has a good ability to relate to people in that respect.

So there are things called 'boys' enthusiasms'. Why does Jonathan tell the interviewer that Prudence has an empathic side? Could it be that she seems to have strayed too far onto the side of masculinity, which has to be corrected by an assertion of a feminine characteristic, such as empathy? Is the interviewer to be left in no doubt that Prudence is a 'real girl'? According to her father, Prudence

> 'is probably happiest if she is sitting down and having a game of Junior Monopoly or playing cards, do you know what I mean? playing cards or playing . . . I think we have thrashed Ludo and Snakes and Ladders to death and she has had a few games of chess and she has a bit of aptitude for that but I am not pushing that, because I think she is a bit young for chess, she actually takes an adult concept of strategy in a way, she can play and with a little bit of help she can you know, she can beat me, you know with a bit of help. But so yeah, so I don't know, so computer games are a funny sort of thing. I wish they were more, I wish in a way they were more didactic and less, because it is driven by the market economy they're just basically they're like everything, they are just appealing to people's lowest instincts, do you know what I mean, they are appealing to the instincts for thrills and for adventure and for simulation of doing horribly illicit things like shooting thousands of people and leaving gory you know corpses all over the floor, you know. I mean I don't think they are very noble kind of qualities to be doing, and if I had my way all that stuff would be totally you know, banned, you know what I mean? But in actual fact because it is market driven that stuff is 90 per cent of it, isn't it really, at least 90 per cent of it, probably more. And of course it is aimed at boys again and that still reinforces that same thing you know, because it does appeal to boys' enjoyment of violence and . . . you know . . .'

So, Prudence is left with Snakes and Ladders and Ludo! But the interviewer does not give up. She points out that Prudence likes a strategy game called Zoom Beanies:

> **Interviewer:** It sounds like one of Prudence's favourite games is really a strategy thinking game. She was describing it to me and it sounded extremely complex.
> **Jonathan:** Oh Zoom Beanies . . . Oh yeah, that is a very interesting one because that is extremely didactic, not only is it didactic it is like one of these old fashioned sort of learning programme type of thing where, when you complete one level, you know the thing gets harder, and it sort of does that and the programme just adjusts itself and it gets harder as you get more and more through and I think it must time

the time it takes you to do a thing and then if you are doing them quickly suddenly new hazards or new difficulties come into the game. But that is basically, it can be boiled down to one simple phrase which is simply boolean algebra, you know, it is just about the, and, or, if, you know, it is basically all the kind of concepts of boolean algebra, but like wrapped up in a cute little package with these little creatures and stuff. It is just about, you know, conditionals and about thinking about, you know . . .

Interviewer: Logic skills are coming . . . being developed here.

Jonathan: Well it is definitely helping them. Yeah. I think so. I think in that case, that's what I mean, I think games could be, you know that is the only one I have found, I mean we have bought other things like Scale and Mysteries by Edmark and Thinking Things, you are probably familiar with those are you?

Interviewer: Not Thinking Things.

Jonathan: Oh that's, they are quite good, they are the same type of thing, they are sort of teaching, but as usual for the Americans, they have sort of lost it, the later versions that have come out haven't really improved the basic kind of conceptual thing, they simply put glamorous backgrounds you know, better animation you know, but that's not, they've missed the point you know what I mean? Instead of increasing the sort of teaching quality or the usefulness of it they are just increasing the saleability of it so there you go . . .

Interviewer: Oh.

Jonathan: You know, just, you know gave her a bad attitude watching Channel 10 in the morning. I think, you know, you would have to be mad to let your kids watch Channel 10 before they went to school, you know. But even so I've kind of got rules with her about the ads and stuff, you know, she skips through the ads and stuff like that.

Interviewer: I was going to ask you about rules, mainly in terms of playing on the computer, but in general in TV as well because Sarah brought it up as well, what sort of rules, or how do you regulate Prudence's playing games or interaction with the media in general?

Jonathan: Um, we don't regulate the playing of games because she is allowed to do that whenever she likes on the computer, within reasonable limits. I mean I don't really care if she wakes up first thing in the morning and goes into the room and does, you know, and plays on the computer, but that doesn't happen that often. She might wake up in the morning and play her game boy for a bit. Or she is more likely to wake up in the morning strap on her head phones and listen to the Pokemon CD, the soundtrack from the film, right.

Interviewer: Yeah.

Jonathan: That's what I sort of meant about the merchandising stuff, you know, in other words the game itself has become subsumed to this whole sort of fantasy world created by the television series and by the film and by the merchandising. The friends . . .

Interviewer: Which came first?

Jonathan: The game came first. The friends, her and her friends, they have all got little figurines and when they meet they take their figurines around in their backpacks, you know, and sort of have, you know, it is like Perky Pat, you probably don't know what that is an allusion to, it is like a sort of game you play, a bit like dolls but with more . . .

Interviewer: Yeah little action figures.

Jonathan: Little actions figures, or like boys with little action figures, but they are playing action games, they are not playing sort of dolly things, you know. They are actually Pokemon trainers and they are getting in battles and they you know, stuff like that . . .

Interviewer: Yeah that is pretty amazing.

Jonathan: So I think it is quite good in that respect, (a) that the girls love it for some reason, I mean all the little girls, all her friends, I don't know if it has just been her, whether she has sort of influenced them all, or if it is generally, but all her friends are all completely mad about Pokemon and probably think about nothing else, as often as they can, except when they are made to concentrate at school or something like that. So in terms of computer games just in the sense of what plays on the computer, well there is . . . Beanies and there are a couple of other bits and pieces which she plays. Well I don't really, there is no point, I don't need to regulate that because she doesn't overdo it anyway. In terms of television she would watch television far more than she should if she was allowed. So she is not allowed, basically. I mean we don't want television during the week at all, oh except when she does the wet dressings because of her eczema, you know, that has become a kind of obviously a Pavlovian kind of thing, you know, she is conditioned, at least it means she sits down and puts the ointment on and stuff which is an unpleasant thing for her to have to do and it gives her a little bit of a reward you know for doing that. Plus there is the interesting thing, as I said, the training and sort of planning in advance for you know recording something so that you can watch it that night.

Interviewer: Yeah. Yeah.

Jonathan: So that's it, really, half an hour a day during the week, and on the weekend she can watch whenever she likes but it is sort of negotiated, like if she has crashed in front of the tele I will tell her to turn it off basically, and say 'Come on you don't want to watch television all day, you have got other things to do. Let's go for a walk around the block' is always a good circuit breaker you know what I mean? But in fact on the weekend I wouldn't think she would watch more than in total maybe 4 hours of TV, total on a weekend, maybe 6, no probably 4.

Interviewer: Compared to how much time would she probably play on the computer?

Jonathan: That comes and goes in phases for some reason. She is on a Pokemon thing now. On a Beanie thing now which is related to the Pokemon thing, because like you know we have made a deal that I will buy her the Pokemon film on video if she gets another hundred of the Zoom Beanies home. So there is like five hundred of them. There is five hundred . . .

Interviewer: Yes she was telling me . . .

Jonathan: She has 250. I mean she has had it for two years. It is the sort of game, as I say, as it changes as you get, you know, you can't really get sick of something that gets harder as . . . and it is quite good, the only problem is that you have to run it in 256 colour.

Interviewer: She was complaining about that too.

Jonathan: Yeah, and it is really boring, and obviously they haven't upgraded the game or anything and I mean the game is actually about 3 or 4 years old. But anyway, that's fine. But apart from that and when she had the Hokus craze and there has been another craze on something and very occasionally she will go on the Internet but I don't think she really understands the . . . I don't think she really understands the kind of connectivity of that, she doesn't really realise that it is actually out, you know, an avenue on the world whereas some people, I am sure there are plenty of people her age who do, and again I am sure there are plenty of boys who find it as a good way of you know getting on there and trying to get free things or do you know what I mean?

Interviewer: Yeah.

Jonathan: So that's basically it. So I think in terms of the number of hours per week on the computer probably only a few and with the game boy as well perhaps a few more. So you know, I don't know, hard to tell.

Interviewer: Now do you play any games with her?

Jonathan: . . .

Interviewer: On the computer, I mean you have mentioned that you do all sorts of outside and other things apart from the computer with her, but what about playing?

Jonathan: Well I help with the Zoom Beanies a bit.

Interviewer: Yeah.

Jonathan: But there is no actual game where I play, where I hold one set of handles and she holds the other and we sort of play against one another in that way. But if she is playing I will sometimes just watch her and say, well what about you know – oh I . . . Dad, watch this, and I say oh isn't that . . . oh yeah that's right. That's the thing. But apart from that, no we don't play against one another.

Interviewer: Do you play games yourself as she watches?

Jonathan: Not really.

So it seems that Prudence is very keen on Pokemon and plays Zoom Beanies a great deal, as it is one of the educational games she is allowed to play. Her father doesn't help her or play with her, but it is actually her mother who played Hokus with her while they had their joint 'obsession' with it.

Yet it turns out that Jonathan appears to have obsessions of his own. For the rest of the interview he spends a great deal of time talking about his interest in and knowledge of the latest computer software.

Jonathan: And also of course there is another thing that is happening is the technological push because I mean, you know, processing power, more is law, what is it processing power is doubling every three years and I mean the same things are applying to all the technologies not just computers, really because of the trickle down now into other devices like, I mean, I wouldn't go out without my Palm V now, you know, that's only, and that is now obsolete, it is only a crappy old 1 meg of Ram, now they have got eight, you know what I mean?

Interviewer: I have still got my little old Filofax.

Jonathan: Oh right. Well yeah. No the Palm V is an excellent thing. I don't know how . . . you should get yourself one because they are an extremely useful tool. I mean I was using things like Microsoft Outlook on the computer, but I don't use Outlook any more because I don't like Microsoft stuff very much. That particular one, especially Outlook because if you try and use it over a small home network a Land, you know, it . . . says it is only a one user thing you have to get Microsoft Exchange if you want to do, you know, and I found a thing called Organiser which does the same, exactly the same sort of thing but will run, you can actually have it open on one computer and open on the other and the person who shuts it last is the one who saves you know, the sensible way for a thing to do. Anyway, apropos all that, that has got all our phone numbers and all our kind of contacts and notes about this that and everything and every morning you just update it to the Palm so you have got a complete list of phone numbers, all your appointments you have made in the last 2 years, people's names and addresses I mean, because text takes hardly any information storage at all so, 1 meg, you know that, even with 1 meg of Ram I have got about two years of data, solid and it is not even half full, that part of it anyway. So apropos that so getting back to the games, you know the computer game that you were playing this time last year is actually a bit old fashioned by now, do you know what I mean? So a game that you were playing a year ago you might go back and have a look at you know, a reminiscent sort of play on it, but in actual fact what's out now will probably be faster, more colourful, more action, or more layers or more complex player, or whatever the other things are that people are finding in games. As I say, I don't actually play computer games very much.

Interviewer: Or do you use the computer just for work and other things.

Jonathan: I just use it for work and other things, yeah. Fairly broad use. I use it mostly for work. I am becoming more and more of a graphic artist actually.

Interviewer: Right.

Jonathan: I used to be a set builder, but I am quite proficient in CAD drafting and stuff so I am doing a bit of 3-D work at the moment and using . . . doing virtual modelling and stuff like that, you mean, I am having fun anyway, and she can see that, you know what I mean? I mean she watches what I am doing and says what's this? Oh it is a model of this set we are going to build for blah, blah or something like that, you know. So yeah.

Interviewer: Maybe that is why she is telling me she wants to be an artist when she grows up.

Jonathan: I think she, yeah, I don't know I think she guesses that it's an easy life. She is, she shows a reasonable aptitude for art but she definitely doesn't show the kind of you know, to be an artist takes a lot of dedication, I don't think she will be . . . you know the thing is that the, I mean it is like what is happening to me, I think the boundaries between being an artist and being something else become very blurred. I mean at the moment I have stuff on my computer, on Friday I burned a CD right, of all the, I did all the photos of stuff I have built over the last 15 years. I scanned in 270 photos, this took a while to scan in and then I took them into Photo Paint and squared them up and cleaned them up and made them sharper, and got the contrast right and did all that and then I did them all in PowerPoint and it is unusual for me to be nice about Microsoft but that is a lovely easy program to use. It is very easy to use to get something together quickly and I did it, it worked really well. And I burned a few copies of the CD and I did the cover art, you know, I did the cover art, and I did all the sort of text panels and stuff and the document, I mean you know, I mean and a finished product that five years ago would have cost me $10,000 to have done by some, you know, do you know what I mean?

Interviewer: Yeah I do. Yeah.

Jonathan: It would cost ten grand to have that done, you know what I mean and I did it for you know for free, well I mean it took my time, but you know what I mean? So you sort of realise so gosh you know this computer isn't just a thing for playing games or, well I don't even use it for playing games, but it really is an extremely important tool for enhancing your kind of, well not, yeah enhancing your abilities or perhaps for giving a vehicle for your latent abilities, you know what I mean, like I am reasonably artistically inclined, you know.

Interviewer: Yeah.

Jonathan: But I have always never been a bit like her, I have never really wanted to sit down and spend all my time doing paintings or drawings or something like that but I find when I am starting to use these programs like Photo Paint and Photo Shop and Corel Draw and you know, and these 3-D modelling programs, Studio Max and stuff like that I have found that I am actually you know, actually seem to be good at it, you know what I mean?

Interviewer: Mm.

Jonathan: So the thing is when Prudence grows up, which after all is still a good ten years away at least, I mean at this rate of change, I mean I don't know exactly what artist, being an artist will mean. It could have quite a lot to do with doing videos on a computer or something, do you know what I mean?

Interviewer: Yeah. Well it is really interesting because one of the reasons we were asking people to draw diaries is to see the different range of technologies or uses of computers that go on in the house that the child can observe because it is just really interesting to try and track where the child is coming from and what sort of background they have had and how much exposure they have had to different technologies.

Jonathan: Well a few people . . . use statistics don't we, but I just, there was on I think it was on JJJ last week saying now something like, 80% of all households have got a computer, it can't be that much. It was high though. It was 70 or 80 percent. Australians have always been early adopters of technology. We have always been straight into it. It obviously comes from the old tyranny of distance or something you know and it is the best way to keep in touch. The Internet is beautiful. I have a friend, my best friend lives impossibly far away, which is on Flinders Island in Bass Strait, right. I mean we get to actually physically see one another once every couple of years, but we are e-mailing two or three times a week, you know, sending pictures and you know, we have sort of running jokes and writing stories, and you know what I mean?

Interviewer: Yeah . . .

Jonathan: So anything else you want on?

Interviewer: Well basically I just wanted to get your attitudes, the things that you thought were good about games and . . .

Jonathan: Well the good side, you know what I think the good side is the didactic side. You know where it is a teaching or learning tool. And I mean there is an element of that even in games that involve you know hand to eye co-ordination and so. I presume there is a learning in that but it is probably a learning that is specifically oriented towards hand to eye co-ordination for computer games rather than for anything out in the big world really, maybe it might be useful for driving a car later on, I am not sure.

Interviewer: It was interesting, something Prudence said that because she was saying that one game really helped her reflexes and it helped her playing on the soccer ground and I thought how can it help you on the soccer ground when the reflexes are only small. She said that there is a part of your brain that is to do with reflexes and if you can use your reflexes quickly there part of the brain has been working for a while and it knows how to work in the use of . . .

Jonathan: Yes and there is also another thing . . . the spatial sense also, I mean you know because you are working on a computer screen you are having to visualise an exaggerated spatial reality so that sort of again can probably extend to the outside world. So no there is definitely benefits of . . .

So, there we have it. Jonathan has a considerable knowledge of new technologies, recognises their importance for the future of work, yet he rarely helps his daughter with them. And Prudence and her mother are consigned to old technologies, old games, old obsessions. We could say that Jonathan even seems to be showing off his technological prowess to the female interviewer as though it were an aspect of kudos for masculinity to be so knowledgeable about the latest 50 megabites of RAM.

I want to end this chapter by thinking about the different practices through which Prudence's regulation is accomplished. In this analysis, I will think about the general regulative strategies employed in order to help produce Prudence as a particular kind of subject in order to demonstrate the way that regulation in relation to games is part of a larger picture. Her parents employ a number of positive practices which have the effect of steering her in a particular direction, that is the production of a cultured and fully rounded person. I will enumerate these below:

- Full diary syndrome: this is a strategy very common amongst middle-class families in the Sydney study. It involves the family having a very complicated diary for after-school activities, in which the child is given so many things to do that video games have to be limited to a small time window.
- ABC-FM (the high culture station) on radio in background of interviews, general atmosphere of 'culture' and disdain for commercialism, etc. Learning to play chess from her father, mother reading 'short-listed' books, and making judgements about what books should have been short-listed. Goes to art galleries.
- Rewards for getting a certain number of zoom beanies (father).
- Father: getting Prudence to tape Pokemon and then play it later is a 'training thing', training in planning in advance, according to him, but can also be seen as a training in deferral of pleasure/desire, in harnessing impulse, necessary to the construction of cultured middle-class girls.

In addition to the above, we noted a number of negative practices designed to censor, prohibit or limit access:

- Prohibition: commercial TV banned.
- Limiting access: ABC-TV viewing highly regulated (no viewing during the week though tapes Pokemon (commercial) every morning and is allowed to watch it while tending to eczema treatment at night). Game-playing regulated by there being no games at home (except a newly

acquired 'Gameboy' and Zoom Beanies game). Prudence's use of computer being regulated by it being located in the office rather than her bedroom ('we decided consciously not to put the computer in her room because we felt that she might spend too much time on it if it were in her room' and so that she and her father would have company when using their individual computers). This is to stave off addiction/not being on the computer all the time.

- On computer for about an hour and a half per day though sometimes none (this time is not regulated except for windows of opportunity in other activities, i.e. various activities regulated through full-diary). Is not allowed to wake parents until 7 a.m. so Prudence plays with her Gameboy or computer or reads or draws until then.
- Censorship: father vets the games, though mother agrees – researches them, wants to trial them before buying (but can't, sometimes it isn't what they want), downloads them, and 'investigates' the hardware technology (reviews in magazines). They tend to buy the educational games like they have at school: reading blasters, maths blasters, paint brush. She has some shoot 'em ups, so she occasionally plays them. Hokus is OK because it is not life-like and is always shooting a monster to protect the good one. Mother doesn't like real life shoot 'em ups with blood splatters, though the baddie still gets killed so it is OK 'but we have made a conscious decision to try and steer towards the more educational ones, the ones that are more interesting, keep away from the shoot 'em dead ones' and M enjoys the educational games. Though mother says this is probably because she hasn't got older brothers and sisters saying oh, don't do educational ones, lets do the more exciting ones.
- The Internet is connected to Prudence's bedroom but she won't be allowed to put a computer in the room until she gets to high school (when she is old enough) when she will need Internet connection. The Internet is seen as a site of potential future danger which father will regulate through electronic blocking.

What is the problem with TV?

The parents don't like the effect it has on Prudence because they believe it creates a problem in relation to disciplining her ('behaviour problems'). They say that Prudence would want to watch TV rather than do homework or piano practice, which would interfere with the development of social skills, sitting alone in front of a TV and being an only child. Her father says that when Prudence watched commercial TV in the morning before school it made her really moody with a bad attitude.

What is the problem specifically with commercial TV?

The commercials – they can't stand them, no further specification, though mother does later say that if Prudence does see things advertised on commercial TV, there is pressure to get it from Prudence. Her father's response is 'no we are not getting it, it is advertising. It is aimed at your age group. No, they are manipulating your mind, we are not going to get it.' Her mother is more amenable and will buy some advertised products that Prudence asks for, such as health foods and art things.

What is the problem with video games?

Addiction: When her father first downloaded Pokemon Blue, Prudence was on the computer all the time and they had to say, let's go for a bike ride or let's play Cluedo or something but 'once she has worked out the game and will play it and then she will have a break, so it hasn't become a problem yet which is great'. Sometimes they had the same sorts of behavioural problems that were encountered with TV viewing – hard to get her off the computer to come to have breakfast.

Her father says that boys become obsessed and spend far too much time on video games. He says he used to be an egalitarian, used to believe in socialisation theory, but now believes there is a fundamental difference between girls and boys. Boys may have some 'home qualities' but generally grow up and turn into little 'shits'; they like to go around bashing things up and blowing things up, whereas girls are more inward looking and tend to do things that don't involve shooting, racing cars and shooting up aliens. Prudence has a bit of a competitive streak in her and can become obsessed with games, though not as much as the boys she plays with. Prudence probably becomes more boyish when she plays with boys and enjoys boys' rough play.

Cultural contamination: her mother can't stand the American accents on video games and the idea of kids starting to talk with am American accent. According to her, Prudence has started to talk with an American accent after spending too much time at school on educational games.

Violence: her mother sees games and TV generally as dangerous because of depictions of violence. Controlling who you kill on a computer is no different than watching someone else do it. Her father argues that games appeal to people's lowest instincts for thrills and adventure and for simulation of horrible things like shooting people. Most games don't convey very noble qualities and are marketed to boys because they appeal to boys' enjoyment of violence. In addition, her father suggests that games are frivolous as compared to using computers for 'real' things like art and writing.

He can be amused at Prudence and mother's obsession with (frivolous) computer games at times while *his* obsession with 'real' computer work goes unremarked on and is subsumed in notions of taste and culture. He says that computers are an important tool for enhancing your abilities and for giving a vehicle for latent abilities, not just a thing for playing games.

What is good about video games?

Her mother thinks that educational ones (maths and reading blasters) help increase literacy through having to read games instructions (Pokemon Gameboy game); fine motor skill development and hand–eye co-ordination (mother and father); and are teaching and learning tools (father). Unlike TV, computer games are interactive and so it is possible to control what is happening. Father argues that educational/didactic ones (Zoom Beanies) help develop mathematical logic; they are logic/thinking games. Prudence herself says that after spending ages on a computer game (Zoom Beanies), she did her homework and knew nearly every answer herself because she had just done lots of thinking and had got her brain going, and Hokus helps develop reflexes which carries over to a game of soccer in the park where she was really good at catching the ball. 'So it gets your hands moving for catching and stuff.'

Self-regulation: father might watch the news, nature programmes, space programmes. Father is on the computer most of the time doing work-related stuff (CAD). Mother will watch 'interesting' programmes but doesn't specify. He certainly isn't addicted to or obsessed by games, though he reports that mother and Prudence have been, on occasions. *His* obsession with computer technology doesn't require regulation (his interest is real and serious).

Friends: when friends come to Prudence's house or she goes to theirs, they all have to have a play on the computer for a little while – new games, different games, etc. Prudence has a particular friend (boy) that she plays a lot with, gets competitive with (Pokemon on Gameboy).

Pedagogy: Father's practice is to read computer manuals before even turning on a new computer programme, so Prudence is familiar with that practice (and actually does read manuals several times in the club sessions). Prudence often fiddles around with things herself first, but usually has to read the manual first to figure it out. Father is also heavily into self-education and has taught himself everything about computers, including building them. Prudence is habituated to figuring out things by herself too. So you could say that these (middle class, but particularly the father's) family practices of self-education, full diary, possible severest regulation of sample, culture, high literacy, in reading, are producing Prudence as the middle-class girl. It is a type of femininity that is not into girlie things.

Gender-wise, Prudence 'is not into dolls or anything like that because we've never really been into that' (mother) and Prudence obviously disdains 'girly girls'. Prudence is interested in the things that her father is interested in (Space). What is encouraged and cultivated and rewarded (sometimes literally) is cultural activity like reading art music (and 'serious media' consumption), computer activity such as educational games, learning to touch type, and physical activity like swimming and ice-skating. What is discouraged is commercial TV (through strict regulation).

There are a variety of ways to understand Prudence's engagement with video and computer games. The meanings she brings to the club from home are very middle class: computers as educational and self-development/expression tools, computer games are disdained if commercialised entertainment only (as is commercial media) except for educational games. Her games playing at home is regulated in accordance with taken for granted assumptions about the dangers of media. So Prudence could be ambivalent about engaging with games and becoming proficient in them in the club, just for fun: there has to be a 'task'. Her emotional investment in this position as proper middle-class girl can partially be explained by her obvious identification with her father's dominant authoritative position (in his interests and values, etc., to some extent shared by the mother) as arbiter of the family's consumption of media/culture. Yet she obviously also identifies with the position of 'brat' (her interest in the book *Elaine* – bad girl – and wanting to go on a roller coaster with a friend, not her father, so she can scream and not be embarrassed: she can't tell whether she would be embarrassed by her father 'snoozing' on the ride or by her being 'childish' in front of him – her parents' story of her is of 'adult/advanced child').

What can we make of all this? What sort of analysis/discursive production should we embark on? Do we analyse the narratives of Prudence as productions from positions, for example, that parents constitute themselves as 'good parents' through stories of their 'good child', the teacher constitutes themselves as a 'good teacher', possessing professional expertise/competence through stories of their assessment of the child's progress, level of development, skills, etc. That is, these stories are more about the tellers than Prudence. So where is Prudence? Prudence tells a story about herself which is no less a 'construct' of who she is. How does she construct herself and in relation to what, through what sorts of discourses and investments? She is highly invested in the relation to her father. She spends a lot of time with him. She is interested in what he is interested in. He himself takes up the position of primary knower in his capacity of arbiter of the family's practices of media and other consumption. She is the sophisticated, brainy, cultured, proto-adult girl, not a 'girly girl' or a childish 'brat' who exercises her 'brattishness' away from the father – she has learnt to subjugate her brattishness to the requirements of a good performance of rational, cultured middle classness. We could, therefore, rework this analysis through its engagement with a set of affective relations through which the relations between the participants and their engagement with the practices of video games are affectively organised within a complex dynamic. What I have described as Jonathan's investment in a particular narrative of his daughter is precisely both his mode of regulating her, and that which is constituted in an embodied affective way in and through that relation. This way of thinking about things is lost if we think only about these as different or even competing narratives, or if we think of them simply as positions produced through rational regulative calculations.

What we recognise as Prudence is constituted in a myriad different ways, which already configure what she brings to her games playing practice in the club. For example, certain understandings of computer games playing imbricated in her production as a middle-class girl, through her family's complex investments in producing her through certain regulatory practices and practices of affection or affective relation.

We need to add to this mix her family's (mainly her father's) general disdain for games playing because he sees it as commercialised, marketed (i.e. corrupt, manipulative, culturally contaminating), an 'entertainment'/'serious' dualism where, at best, games are harmful (though probably a waste of time) and, at worst, contribute to the development of undesirable traits (e.g. violence, aggressiveness, competitiveness). Games are understood as most often appealing to people's (mainly boys) lowest instincts for thrills and adventure and not conveying very noble qualities. Games playing (including board games like chess, Cluedo, Scrabble) are given a positive value when they are serious/educational – educational games are seen as contributing to developing computer literacy, hand–eye co-ordination, fine motor skills and cognitive skills. These are the 'real' things that computers should be used for, to enhance abilities or as a vehicle for people's latest abilities (father). His own heavy engagement with computers is unproblematised because he uses it for these 'real' things – work, creativity, education. So, Prudence generally approaches video and computer games as a serious intellectual task (figuring them out, mastering them, etc.), though the club experience subsequently offers other meanings and experiences and subjectivities to do with games playing (excitement, competitiveness/winning as well as losing).

Her 'comportment' as a middle-class girl

Her parents' understanding of Prudence's TV viewing as a site of production of problematic behaviour (defiance, resistance to homework, agitation) underpins their regulation of her TV viewing (even though Prudence likes watching TV). Prudence's taping of a TV programme for later viewing is seen as training Prudence to 'plan ahead' (father). Her father's practice of conversing with her as if she were a empathetic, understanding and therefore emotionally mature adult (rather than as a child) and the full diary syndrome leaves little space at home for Prudence to take another position (e.g. silly, immature). The highly regulated access to media (through both prohibition/censorhip and provision/reward) is based on what is good for her (educational rather than 'exciting' games, and a sense that commercial TV makes her moody and gives her a 'bad attitude'). The upshot is that she is being produced as a quiet, discerning (judging that a book should be short-listed), cultured (art, art galleries, ABC as the only media allowed), emotionally well-regulated (not excitable or defiant), self-regulating middle-class girl. And, perhaps through these same trainings, trained as a particular girl/woman, as empathetic, understanding, entering into the world of others (i.e. men mainly) – not a centre in and of herself (the perfect 'wife' for the father). Prudence's 'brattishness' and 'irrational' excitement (e.g. fear, competitiveness) has to be performed in another space – with friends playing games, or in spaces like 'Wonderland' or in fantasy (books like *Elaine* or even video and computer games). It is also possible that there might be a certain collusion between the mother and Prudence in sharing prohibited pleasures (e.g. exciting and frivolous video and computer games playing). In the father's story of her as a proto-adult, possessing an innate ability to relate to other people, of being 'companionable', as of girls being innately more inward looking and responsive – excitement, competitiveness, self-centredness, etc. can't be *in* Prudence, they must come from *outside* her and influence her. Hence the 'contamination' approach to media, games, etc. and why their consumption (incorporation) must be regulated. And hence also why he understands *her* excitement in games playing with the boys in the club to actually be the boys' excitement that she has simply entered into (empathy, 'companionability' or 'becoming more boyish') when playing with boys (his words): it is not her own nature, bringing its clear distinction between masculine and feminine modes of being and performance. Her nature therefore must be guarded through the regulation of these influences. Yet Prudence is not a 'girly girl', by her own, her mother's and the staff's account . She is 'not into dolls or anything like that because we've never really been into that' (mother). So Prudence is presented as having a nature, a character, which can be the basis of intellectual training, not a girly girl, though the desired femininity also incorporates physical culture (the full diary also includes swimming, ice-skating and football). Yet Prudence wants to be an artist like her father (designer) rather than an intellectual at this point. Her father says 'she likes me', her mother says that Prudence likes what father likes because he talks about what he's interested in all the time. Given her investment in him, his approval and disapproval of what she does, and of the behaviours she displays, is the dominant factor in her self-regulation/production. Her father hates video racing games and beat-'em-ups and says that girls don't like being involved in racing cars down fantasy streets and shooting things. Given this, how does this set of regulative strategies and affective relations prepare the entry into club game playing practices? We could say that Prudence generally approaches video and computer games as a serious intellectual task (figuring them out, mastering them, etc.). Prudence likes playing alone (is also an only child) and 'figuring things out for herself', and often is not very co-operative and communicative with other children. Perhaps she positions herself as proto-adult (autonomous, rational) in relation to the other children? Though in other games she gets excited. Perhaps because of home practices and often playing alone (no other children in the house, plays with parents) and autodidacticism, etc. she prefers the one-player games where she is not competing with other children. I wonder also if this position particularly in its stressing of strict rationality, lack of girliness and excitement, jouissance, deliberately elides and avoids a femininity which is other than the nurturant/ rational mix demanded in contemporary practices. This Other femininity is that which has not only been disavowed, but which has been presented as working class, excessive and ladette. These practices must therefore aim to produce her as Other to this kind of femininity, in some ways presented as dangerous to the possibility of a secure adulthood for her, I would suggest, both culturally and in terms of her market potential as a neoliberal subject.

   Let us briefly follow what this actually means for how she plays games at the club. She hates racing games (father hates racing games because of aggression, competitiveness, mindlessness) and is no good at them. She is spatially disoriented in the racing games, can't tell what directions she is going in, visibly loses interest and 'deflates', sometimes asking the other child to swap consoles/cars out of a sense that the competitor has a better car, and sometimes even stops playing and says 'I hate this game' etc. as the car keeps crashing. But she shows no interest in competing (she says she doesn't like playing against others) or mastering the moves unless the other player is disadvantaged (the other players are always more proficient than her at playing racing games) e.g. by their console not working. In that case, Prudence takes full advantage of the situation, e.g. pinching another player's chosen character when that player can't control the character choice. In this way Prudence becomes 'the cheat', and wins only through others' disadvantage. She likes games where she has to figure out what to do (platform-type games). In all games she positions herself as 'a knower' in specific things: she says promptly on several occasions 'so can I' when the other child makes a comment to the effect that they are able to figure something out (e.g. how to play the game) or find where something hard/valuable is (hidden tunnel in Pokemon).

She positions herself as 'not-knower' in other things: not knowing how to play the game, regularly says 'this is difficult', 'this is too hard', 'I don't know how to play this' and in this case often asks the other player to do it for her (take over the console), to finish the game for her, or the other player offers to do this (not necessarily to help Prudence but to get the game over quickly so that they can move on). In platform games, when she is not playing (1-person games) she quite happily directs the other player on what they should be doing, what moves to make.

In her relationships with other players, she operates differently depending on who she is playing with. For example, with Aisha she has a complex relationship of competitiveness, but is also co-operative in playing, and collusive in terrifying themselves in Boneyard in Crash Bandicoot. Aisha the pretty girl, who is aware of her performance as a female (putting on eye-shadow before being videoed), is the competent player who other girls (Gina) want to have on their 'team' playing games. However, Prudence is better at Under Pressure in Crash Bandicoot than Aisha, and Aisha concedes this. This game can be played slowly and involves manoeuvering and avoiding obstacles. When Aisha indicates that she is afraid ('girls shouldn't be playing this') or doesn't want to go in to Boneyard, Prudence dares her over and over again and Prudence wants to play it over and over again. Neither of them play it well but get pleasure out of being chased by the dinosaur and being terrified. In a later video, Prudence and Aisha are playing Super Smash with two other girls. When Prudence realises that you can get the computer to play for you and that you do better and even win that way, Prudence gets the computer to play for her all the time from then on, as does Aisha (the researcher's notes say that she thought that Aisha did this so that Prudence wouldn't win).

With other boys and girls she acts differently again. For example, Prudence takes advantage of the situation where Maria's controls aren't working and tries to snatch the character and win from Maria, who is a better player than Prudence. They only have very brief snatches of co-operation and friendliness. With the boys she is different. When playing with Timothy, he is co-operative, friendly and helpful, but Jim doesn't include Prudence in the boys game-playing, ignoring Prudence and always directing his interest/attention and conversation to the other boys, such that William says several times to Jim that it is Prudence's turn. But Prudence responds to Jim's antics, giggling: her pleasure is his pleasure, her excitement is the boys' excitement, not her own (she doesn't play well).

In summary, there are different Prudences in different games that can be understood by the type of game being played, which in turn is inflected through family attitudes to games playing and who Prudence imagines she is (not a 'girly girl' and not wanting to play one of the Crash Bandicoot games because it is too 'girly wirly' – the character is a petite blonde female who sits on a jet ski). Girls who are invested in becoming intellectual (and/or cannot construct themselves as a pretty, attractive, girly girl) do not identify with the very feminine characters in games. Perhaps her reluctance to master games despite many weeks in the club is to do with these other investments, affectivities, positions. She likes playing thinking games with others, but other games by herself.

In conclusion

I want to conclude by suggesting that the multiplicity of practices through which Prudence's regulation is accomplished demonstrates the complexity of the regulation of girls' play, which gives us, in effect, different Prudences in different relationalities. In this sense, using the Deleuzian concept of the assemblage, we could say that Prudence is assembled out of the shifting dynamic relationalities in and through which she is constituted. The regulative practices themselves could in fact be understood as part of a parental attempt to create a stable 'Prudence' with a particular nature and particular traits and what we see as a stable Prudence in fact moves and shifts around between sites and between relations with different people. The discourse of girls not being interested in video games elides another set of discourses: those of pleasures, desires, competitiveness. The excessiveness of the regulative practices might be set against that which has to be kept at bay, that girls might derive pleasure from those practices associated with masculinity. This means that this pleasure is dangerous and is therefore difficult to address. I would suggest that this difficulty is not an essential difficulty of or for girls, but a difficulty for masculinity. That is, if some of the pleasures of masculinity rely on its difference from and opposition to as well as power over, femininity, then girls' enjoyment of the pleasures of masculinity may threaten the possibility of fantasies of 'real men' and 'action heroes'.

So, for me, the importance of the regulative practices as in some sense 'normalising' is that they seem like an attempt to produce the desired characteristics and guard against the feared ones, such as a boyish girl or an addicted or violent boy, or a sooky, clingy mummy's boy. In that sense then they attempt to create, stop, mould, but in order to understand their force we must acknowledge what anxieties lie at their heart – the Other which is guarded against. Such attempts to create something in the face of the possibility of the eruption of a feared or desired Other has enormous affective force or energy – both in terms of its production and the energy required at keeping something else at bay. In this sense, they cannot be understood as simply rational calculative strategies of power but of complex affectivities, dynamics, entanglements, which flow both through bodies, through the dynamics of the life world and through those of the family and club within it. While this chapter has not been able to pursue this in any great detail, I have tried to sketch out how we might begin to develop and deepen our mode of engagement with these complex issues.

My argument is that regulation operates through the interconnectedness of many different sites and practices, in which affective processes and the production of fantasy have to be understood as a key constituent. We could therefore call this regulation part of a complex relationality.

In the next chapter, I attempt to take these insights further by presenting an engagement with the complexities of video games in relation both to a global economic market and to what it means to learn and to play games. In this way, I am trying to go beyond the sets of oppositions I set out in Chapter 1, to think about subjectivity and new technologies in a different way.

7
Video Games in a Global Market

At the beginning of the book I set out the issue of the ways in which we normally see children playing games, that is, as subjects interacting with an object world. I pointed out that I wanted to engage with this in a different way, one which emphasised the complex relationalities rather than subjects, objects and interaction. I am not suggesting that I have been able to follow my own advice very well as it is incredibly difficult to even begin to look and think in a different way. However, I pointed to work which understood video game play as embodied and kinaesthetic, using the sense that we feel our way around virtual space, so privileging the role of sensation and affect. I argued for a three-fold approach to affect which looked not only at sensation but also at ideation and at the ways that these work together through a notion of the unconscious. I argued that the games embody complex fantasies of masculinity through their engagement with the ways in which the player is both inside and outside the game at the same time, allowing both for what Ryan called internal and external interaction with its ego containment or controlling 'god-trick'. This made them both pleasurable and powerful. I have explored just how this relates to issues of both playing and regulation in relation to masculinity and femininity and to the ubiquitous debates about violence. I also used the Deleuzian concept of the assemblage to understand how affective relations and regulative practices might work together to create shifting subjectivities. I now want to cast my net more broadly.

It is a central claim of this chapter and the work which follows that the competent player is an embodied social and cultural fantasy which is at the very centre of global economies, multinational profits and the practices of playing, which are linked together as different sites. It is my claim that in order to understand game playing practices we need to understand how that relation is produced and lived. To do this, I want to extend my three-fold notion of affect to point towards ways of under-standing how the fantasy operates within the different sites as well as the links between them.

I want to suggest that economic relations and embodied relations of game playing should be considered not as separate levels but as different sites which are connected and flow into each other in complex ways. It is the circulation of the economy in practices and fantasies of game play-ing that it is important to understand, rather than it simply being a macro level separated from the subjective by a layer called ideology which operates in the realm of ideas and therefore of thought. This is because in the approach to subjectivity which I raised in the beginning of the book, I understood subjectivity as a layer produced through ideo-logical processes which were semiotic in nature and therefore separated from the economy (in the last instance). We have seen that games require a kinaesthetic component and are not about a level of ideology that works through language or thought, but about complex relations which are both embodied and affective. This different way of thinking allows us to think about economic relations not as in a last instance and as being completely separate from subjectivity and signifying activity, but deeply and closely related and in fact intertwined in complex ways. It is my claim that economic relations are happening while children play and that these relations flow through games and game play, while fan-tasies of the player and playing are built into games in such a way as to maximise profit. There are no separate layers or levels at all because everything is mixed up with everything else.

Some work in science studies and sociology (e.g. Latour, 2005; Urry, 2003) understands the whole Cartesian approach as separating aspects of the life world through which the work of the social, the economy and the subject is achieved. I want to suggest that the relationship between fantasies, ideas and economic processes might better be understood as interlinked practices and sites through which fantasies of masculinity are conveyed or flow in such a way as to apparently provide practices for the work of masculinity. I suggest that the marketing of such fantasies is a central constituent of the flows of capital and therefore the economics of game production and consumption. Indeed, some authors argue that marketing is the essential component of late modern capitalism. I want to understand this as part of a relational approach which I am attempt-ing to piece together.

Practices are at once local and global, minute in their detail and enor-mous in their reach. The space of the club, the living room, the bedroom is also *at the same time* a global space. This is hardly at question. The issue rather is to understand how that relation actually operates relationally to produce playing and players, products, services, workers.

I suggest that we need to rethink the ways in which we think about what are usually considered the micro aspects of social interactions and the production of psychic relations and the so-called macro aspects of the economy. The idea that these operate in different spheres and at different levels, simply does not make sense in relation to a close reading of video game practices. For example, when a player practises capital accumulation in a game by gathering rupees as in Zelda, Ocharina of Time, is this simply an ideological shadow of economic relations in which the player practises a capitalism that is lived out elsewhere? I suggest that the relation is not best understood in this way. I want to say rather that, for example, economic relations are contained in a number of interrelated practices, which link those of children playing a game in a Sydney after school club with the practices of game design and with the practises of capital accumulation by multinationals such as Sony. Every relation is nested inside the other or is linked with every other in complex relational connections and flows.

Perhaps I can begin by thinking about the successful player. In Chapter 3, I argued that the player recalled the hero in Hollywood Westerns. I argued that the fantasy of winning was a masculine fantasy of a latter day action hero, albeit a different kind of action. If the video game industry is to make any profits it must not only mobilise fantasies of heroism, but also create pleasurable spaces for their pursuit. We could say that without this figure, there would be no industry, no profits. This figure is produced in a number of sites – in the relations of game play, in the productions of the design team, in the company profits, to name a few. But, where Althusser and Lacan saw different spheres of activity – with the symbolic and imaginary social fantasies producing psychical relations, which were by their nature ideological, with the economy being pushed into a shadowy corner, the economy I suggest, weaves its way through all of the practices, such that the social and psychic, the economic and cultural, the interior and exterior, may be analysed as different domains, but are deeply interconnected in ways that mean that it makes no sense to separate when attempting to explain game playing practices. Indeed, I will go further to suggest that the very act of partitioning these off as though they explained game play, fails to engage with the very complexity which produces what it means to play games and therefore how we might understand game-playing practices. Moreover, the subject of video game practices is produced out of the intersection of these complex relations and is a fantasy, not an actual embodied player. Indeed, going even further, the embodied player is always constituted in shifting relations, which change from moment to moment, both solid and fluid at once.

I have argued throughout the book that video games are one site for the production of contemporary masculinity. This means that the binary of masculinity/femininity is continually presented as a central trope or fiction. I am arguing that this fiction is at the heart of the production of game playing as a complex set of global relations through which multinational capitalism produces profit. At first when thinking about this, I thought that the production of the player as a particular kind of masculinity through the three-fold approach to affect I discussed in Chapter 2, was a metaphor, but I think this was wrong. I feel that this figure is literally at the heart of the production of an empire (Hardt and Negri, 2000) and that we need to understand how this works. Again and again we have seen that masculinity is continually defined as a set of fantasies, actions, practices, tropes which are presented as the not-feminine (see Chapters 2, 3 and 5), while also being presented as a masculinity capable of crossing those very borders through the playing of female avatars. I have argued that contemporary femininity demands that girls cross that binary every day to perform both masculinity and femininity. Using the work of Derrida (1981), we can see that this binary is certainly not referring to an essentialised gender difference but one which is created and recreated endlessly in the cultural fictions and affective relations, which make up the central places in which subjectivities are created. Something can be a fiction but also have effectivity, that is, can be effective within a set of current practices and can circulate endlessly between sites to appear solid; a solidity which is then cemented into practices, a solidity which may be as solid as air, but which is very difficult to break apart. Yet, in this binary, for example in the case of boys presenting themselves as the authors of their own success and disavowing the work of mothers, we need to draw on how this practice is shorn up both by cultural fictions and fantasies, as well as actual embodied practices and affective relations. In disavowing the place of the mother in his success, the boy has to push away the work the mother does, a task made easy because the Cartesian subject is a central fiction of masculinity which circulates endlessly.

How can we think of the work of affectively, discursively occluding or disavowing a set of relations, in this case the relation between the mother and her son? The embodied mother/son relation is always related to and contained within others, which saturate it with meaning, which in turn forgets other meanings. I want to look at the complex interconnections of the practices in which particular children are themselves produced as the figure, the nodal point at the intersection of the complex practices which produce them in multiple ways. There is no economic that is not discursive. What I am saying is that there is no simple or even complex determination by the economy, not because the economy isn't important but because that's simply not how it works. There isn't a subject produced with a consciousness related to the economy by ideology. What produces subjects are practices in which economic relations enter as one aspect of the complex network of practices which produce them. I don't, however, dispute that some things may be too painful to acknowledge or indeed that capital deliberately obscures certain relations. However, I do think affectivity is contained in practices and that this is crucial. This is how I want to go beyond the binary of interiority/exteriority. The issue is to understand how subjectivities are embodied and lived as part of these complex relations.

Complex relations

To show what I mean, I want to talk about economic relations. My argument is that the economic enters the relation of game-playing and suffuses it, but not in any simple sense that acts as a determination, even in the last instance, nor that we might call economic relations 'macro'. Nor do I want to separate interactionism from the economy as though there were a contest between an examination of that which happens on the ground as determining, versus the power of macro economic forces. My aim rather is to demonstrate that in each realm the other is never absent to such an extent that approaches which separate something referred to as the 'economic', 'ideological' and 'psychic', as levels or indeed separate structure from agency, do not work at all in this context. While it is arguable that they might have worked once, what we are presented with here is the way in which complex relations flow between different sites and in which what is produced is not any simple object but profit generated from playing itself, which cannot be separated from the fantasies which it embodies.

Although I am not able to go into the details of this, a topic which would require a study in itself, we can find multiple examples of the way that the economic enters game playing practices as a relation, or perhaps better, in the plural, as a nexus of shifting relations, and, conversely we can also see that the game-player is always already identified, imagined, located as a subject within economic practices. After all, the economics of game manufacture and sale would make no sense at all without the imagined figure of the consumer, who must stalk through the economy like a ghost walks at midnight. The player who then consumes the game and plays does so as part of a position already laid out for him or her. Without the pleasure of the game player there is no profit, no industry, no economy. In the economy of the video game, there is literally no game industry without the creation of the player. This echoes recent debates about the necessity to configure the user (Woolgar, 1991; Wajcman, 1991). Let us rather therefore understand the economy as a set of practices and relations, already built into and not separate from those practices which produce the player as a relation, further connected to the other relations and practices brought to the game by the player's inscription in any number of other practices.

I want to set out in a very basic way some of the issues that arose for me when trying to think about economic relations and subjectivity in a different way, and go on to think about the kinds of work which are available to understand and analyse such phenomena. In relation to game manufacture, there are two sites of production, one in the West and the other in the Pacific Rim. In the first, games are constructed by a team which consists of a game programmer, game designer, level designer, game producer and game artists. In some games, this is actually a team of artists, each working, for example, on one character. Although, video games are a very big market, according to wikipedia.org/wiki/ Video_game_industry, only 5 per cent of games devised actually make a profit. This means that 95 per cent of games lose money and has the effect of producing a very insecure labour market in this industry. Games development teams are actually working in quite insecure positions. They might be cool young men in an industry much hyped as glamorous, but they join the huge armies of people working in cultural industries whose work is very insecure (Gill, 2006; Stephenson and Papadopoulos, 2006). In order to understand the economic relations in this sector, the practices of production and the imagined characters and consumers of the game are in a crucial relation. What is far more likely to be occluded is the other aspect of game production, that is the manufacture of the games and consoles. Indeed, most discussion I have come across of game economics fails to mention them entirely. Since few games make a profit but require huge development industries, it is hardly surprising that game manufacture is cited in the Pacific Rim countries, with the majority being in mainland China, according to a recent search of the Web. Indeed, one manufacturer has on their web page a photograph of young Chinese women assembling components. Although not an assembly line, this is clearly a factory. All the workers are women and all are young.

In what Haraway (1991) calls circuits of exchange, the figure of the young Chinese female worker is a central component in the production of the video game industry and yet she is barely even a ghostly presence. Her labour and the practices of production in her factory make the West's profits possible. Without her, there would be no profit in an industry in which only 5 per cent of games make any profit at all. If we add to this other sets of practices, which produce the possibility of this industry – the massive advertising to produce the desire for the product, the other sites like magazines such as *Game Developer* for the industry and the many magazines for consumers, such as *PC Zone, Game Revolution, The Escapist*, etc., the interlinked practices to produce and sustain this industry are enormous and the place of subjects within them are linked in very complex networks and circuits of exchange.

In addition to this, not only are game developers working in an industry with fragile profits, but the industry has spawned sweatshops of workers in Eastern Europe and Asia (mostly mainland China) playing games twelve hours a day for low pay to support players in wealthy countries. I want to explore how this works. According to articles sourced online, workers, usually referred to as farmers, work in sweatshops playing massively multiplayer games for twelve hours at a stretch. The *Observer* (13 March 2005) investigated the case of workers in Romania who were employed by a company in California. Workers play games continuously in shifts for 24 hours. The pay is very poor by the standards of North America and Western Europe, but in a situation of very high unemployment people are desperate for the work. The *Observer* argues that 'the most valuable commodity in all games is time, and this has spawned the rise of the virtual sweatshops. Every new player starts at the bottom with little virtual money and few skills. Moving up to the next level of the game involves carrying out dull, repetitive tasks such as killing thousands of virtual monsters.' The article claims that what these sweatshops do is to do this work and then sell it to players in wealthier countries who are then enabled to move quickly to a more advanced level. To get to the highest level may take months, but if a player can buy this, for around £250, they can win much more quickly. Other companies farm virtual currency which is then exchanged on the Internet for actual money. Virtual goods, such as daggers, magic potions and high-level elves are also traded on eBay. The article claims that the market is worth more than £500 million. I understand this the same way as I understand the disavowal of the use of mothers, cheats and other devices. The idea that the player progresses through his own ability is a fiction, supported and played out in a global market in a way which builds upon past patterns of exploitation, from servants supporting wealthy families to workers' labour producing commodities. However, the commodities in this case, such as a virtual dagger, some virtual currency or time on a game, are ephemeral supports to the production of the figure of the successful game player. Not only then is this a masculine fantasy, it is quite specific to wealthier countries in the global north, supported by the hidden hands of the sweatshop workers. *Game On*, an online magazine on gaming, argues that 'farmers' in mainland China typically earn $150 per month, while his employers earn $60,000 (http://w.w.w.1up.com/do/feature?cId=3141815, sourced 22 May 2006). So we can add another aspect to our complex account, that while the sweatshop workers are servicing the wealthy player in order to produce him, others are raking in huge profits from the surplus value of the workers and the omnipotent fantasies of the players. This article also claims that this has spawned a multinational criminal network in which cartels sell MMORPG gold. One of the members of the cartel claims that the cartel made $1.5 million in one year from one game alone. So, we have a worldwide array of poorly paid and insecure workers from game manufacturers to designers to sweatshop workers, and alongside them we have multinational game companies such as Nintendo, and alongside them multinational criminal cartels. My argument is that all of this complex set of interconnections feeds and supports a singular figure and a fantasy – the game player. As the Game On article aptly puts it, 'follow the money'. As I said in Chapter 1, Adam Curtis in his BBC documentary series *Century of the Self*, argues that from the 1920s Freud's nephew, Bernays, began the field of public relations, using ideas of psychoanalysis linked to marketing. He was interested in how to get the masses to buy goods in mass production. The most graphic example he gives is of selling smoking to women by tellingly promoting it in such a way that it implied that the woman smoker would be powerful (have the phallus, in effect). Marketing has moved on. However, just as selling smoking to women would not have worked unless there were an issue of women's powerlessness experienced corporeally, affectively, none of this could have worked without the demands, pleasures, pains and frustrations associated with 'becoming masculine'. I am wanting to suggest therefore that the workers and consumers in the game industry dance like bears for the Ringmaster. Without the figure of the game player, with its attendant fantasies of action heroics and godlike omnipotence, there would be no profit. Because the other side to the sweatshop workers, crime rings and capitalism is the figure of the player playing. We have plenty of stories of teenagers playing rather than come out of their rooms – discourses of addiction. We have heroics and omnipotent fantasies of control. We can map these too because the endless circulation of capital absolutely depends upon the creation of the figure of the player. I am not however, saying simply that the player is a fiction in the Foucauldian sense. It is that, but it is much more. I am suggesting that it is the fantasy of the player that is at once a fiction and affectively organised. By this I mean that Cartesian masculinity as both hero and in control, a rational, autonomous cogito, is a fantasy which circulates endlessly in the West as a central fantasy of knowledge, capital, power. This means that the work of embodying this is endless and that it circulates affectively because apart from anything else it is built into the organisation of our relationality through the position of the mother who has to produce connection and separation, as I argued in Chapter 3. The fantasy works because it works affectively through the three processes I outlined in Chapter 2 and therefore works through the need to do the affective work of masculinity, but that this is affectively transmitted across all the sites in this complex relation through the practices themselves. Creating that is what puts the show on the road. Similarly, this show would not hit the road without other fictions which circulate. For example, the Cartesian subject who is separate, who knows and who has control of an object world, is a powerful fiction which sustained the West from the rise of science in the seventeenth century and which became central to both scientific progress and imperialism. Producing this figure is something which has to be done endlessly, ceaselessly, throughout historical time as well as biographical time, from the production of a relation of connection to separation via the mother (see Chapter 10) and across globalised space.

How do we understand this? What tools are available to us? I want to make reference to several kinds of work within the social sciences. Firstly, we could say that the work of a Foucauldian genealogy would enable us to approach the video game player as a figure in much the same way as Foucault approaches 'the man of desire' in the *History of Sexuality* Vols 2 and 3 (1985 and 1986). That is, we could examine the conditions of emergence of video games as an aspect of masculine rationality and we could also explore the self management practices through which this figure is formed. I have done a little of the latter in the earlier chapters. However, a central problem is that we are left with the psychic/social split (Henriques et al., 1984). That is, self management practices do not work with a notion of unconscious fantasies and we are left with nowhere to take these. This is why I have stressed affective relations. Donna Haraway's idea of figuration (Haraway, 1997) I think is helpful in respect of the way in which a figure becomes the centre of complex circuits of exchange. I would suggest that the video game player is exactly such a figure and that the complex circuits of exchange are the circuits of capitalist production and consumption. The work of Deleuze and Guattari (1977) is also very useful because they take affect away from the realm of simply oedipalised family relations and into the life world. Their use of the idea of the assemblage helps us to think about the ways in which the player is literally assembled from the complex relations that I have outlined. So the player is a figure, a fiction, a fantasy and an assemblage. The idea of the player as an object being assembled takes us into complexity and Actor Network Theories. Complexity theory as used within sociology (Urry, 2003) serves to argue that there are no micro and macro levels but that capitalism works through complex global flows and connections. Urry uses a Deleuzian concept of flow to understand how things move around without the use of levels. Similarly Latour (2005) draws on the idea of flow but in a rather different way. He develops what he calls an associationist sociology. This serves to map the ways in which knowledge comes into being through the minutiae of relations. By understanding the associative aspects of the ways that things are put together, he seeks to understand how objects are formed in ways which are solid but are produced out of the relations themselves. This work, dependent for its genealogy on ethnomethodology, shares an affinity with conversation analytic techniques within discursive psychology (Potter, 1996). Like that tradition, it is deeply suspicious of theorising beyond the concrete associations which it maps and is deeply empiricist. However, I have some considerable difficulties with the ways that the observer, for Latour, is meant to perform what Haraway calls the god-trick (Haraway, 1992) and be affectively out of the loop of what is happening. So much work in the social sciences has already told us how enmeshed we are the in the research process (e.g. Walkerdine, Lucey and Melody, 2002; Stopford, 2005; Hollway and Jefferson, 2002). In addition, Latour makes great play of assuming that psychology can be explained by his associationist sociology. He argues that we have been 'individualised, spiritualised, interiorised', but that the circulation of the signifiers which do this is 'often difficult to track'. 'But if you search for them, you will find them all over the place: floods, rains, swarms of what could be called psycho-*morphs* because they literally lend you the shape of a psyche' (p. 212). He adds that

> what I am trying to do here is simply show how the boundaries between sociology and psychology may be reshuffled for good. For this, there is only one solution: make every single entity populating

the former inside come from the outside not as negative constraint 'limiting subjectivity' but as a positive *offer* of subjectivation. As soon as we do this, the former actor, member, agent, person, individual – whatever its name – takes the same star shaped aspect we have observed earlier when flattening the global and re-dispatching the local. It is *made to be* an individual subject or it is *made to be* a genetic non-entity by a swarm of other agencies. Every competence, deep down in the silence of your interiority, has first to come from the outside, to be slowly sunk in and deposited in some well-constructed cellar whose doors have been beautifully sealed. (p. 213)

What a pity that Latour is not familiar with the 30 years of critical work in psychology, since critical psychologists have been arguing this very thing for a long time (e.g. Henriques et al., 1984; Potter and Wetherell, 1987; see also Blackman and Walkerdine, 2001). However, it is not nearly as easy as Latour seems to make out, to do what he is talking about, and the critical psychological road has been far from straight and narrow. In fact, as Blackman and Walkerdine (2001) argue, it is very difficult to do what he is talking about without resorting to a homunculus in some way or other – that is, an agent, despite the very many attempts to avoid precisely this. However, more than this, the kind of work he envisages that is founded on associationsim, has been, in many ways, foundational for psychology, despite his implications to the contrary. Associationism was, according to Young, absolutely central for the development of European thinking (Robert Young, Association of Ideas, Dictionary of the history of ideas, sourced online at http://etext.virginia.edu/cgi-local/DHI/dhi.cgi?id=dv1-19, on 18 May 2006) , Yet associationism was actually central to the foundations of psychology, just as Latour wants to reclaim an associationist tradition from Tarde forward within sociology. Latour argues that most sociologists believe that the social is made of socialities, 'whereas associations are made of ties which are themselves non-social. They imagined that sociology is limited to a specific domain, whereas sociologists should travel wherever new associations are made. . . . the social is not a type of thing either visible or to be postulated. It is visible only by the *traces* it leaves (under trials) when a *new* association is being produced between elements which themselves are in no way "social" ' (2005, p. 8). Both behaviourism and psychoanalysis, in their different ways, develop as associationist methods: behaviourism because it associates a stimulus with a response in its crudest form, and psychoanalysis because chains of associations are what hold the complexity of meanings between events through the affective bonds of the unconscious.

They both took psychology in completely different turns, but both are equally dependent on the idea of the association, something which Robert Young argues was prevalent from the eighteenth century (Young, Association of Ideas, Dictionary of the history of ideas, sourced online at http://etext.virginia.edu/cgi-local/DHI/dhi.cgi?id=dv1-19, on 18 May 2006). He argues that

> since the middle of the eighteenth century the concept of the association of ideas has increasingly been seen as the most basic, the most fecund, and the most pervasive explanatory principle in the human and, to a lesser extent, biological sciences. The tendency to identify the association of ideas with the school of associatonist psychology which flourished in the late nineteenth century has helped obscure the fact that the principle in its most general form has played the central role in attempts to apply the methods and assumptions of science to the study of man. The principle has two aspects: (1) that complex mental phenomena are formed from simple elements derived ultimately from sensations and (2) that the mechanism by which these are formed depends on the similarity and/or repeated juxtapositions of the simple elements in space and time. The association of ideas provides a mechanism for *ordered change through experience* which complements (and plays an analogous role to) the concept of attraction (or gravity) in the physico-chemical sciences. Aside form its obvious position in empiricist epistemology and in psychological theories of learning, it has played a fundamental role in the idea of progress; in utilitarian legislative, economic and moral theory; in theories of organic evolution; in functionalist social theory; in theories of the functions of the nervous system; and in psychoanalysis. Many of these theories are themselves closely interrelated and can be seen as parts of a coherent tradition in the history of ideas.

There is nothing at all oppositional about psychoanalysis and associationist sociology. Indeed, far from assuming a simple interior that comes from somewhere separate from the outside, it can be argued that it is precisely that which is exterior which continually appears to sediment a subject, but whose subjectivity is always elusive and never a given. Like Deleuze's affect and Latour's associations, psychoanalysis starts with the very sensations to which he refers. It is outside the scope of this chapter to consider how we might think about different approaches within psychology with respect to, for example, drives, but psychoanalysis does indeed do in principle what Latour is talking about. Take it beyond the family and into the field of affect from Deleuze and Guattari and it does it in spades. However, it does mean that we need to think quite carefully about the very empiricist and functionalist tradition to which Latourian sociology belongs.

What would it mean then to bring together associationism in psychoanalysis with Deleuzian affect and Latour's associationist sociology? Could we add to this mix Arendt's idea of a web of relations creating shifting 'whos' (Studdert, 2005) and the phenomenological turn that allows us to think about the kinaesthetic which we explored in Chapter 2?

This is a big toolkit in Foucault's terms and while I am attempting to take the research on multimedia and relationality in a particular direction, this theorising was not that which I started with at the beginning of my research. It is rather a result of an attempt to bring certain sensibilities to bear on the kinds of issues that the research team was working with. While for me it is a future project to take this forward into an account of fantasy, affect, subjectivity and capital, I would like to begin to explore the implications of working in a different way for the ways in which we might approach game playing.

Embodied meanings, affective relations, link the practices/domains/sites to each other

I want to suggest that the relationship between the multinational and the creative team aiming to produce profit has to imagine a player. Could we say even has to create a player in their imagination who will want to play the games? We do not need to assume a pre-existing player; simply to understand that what the games would need to do is to semiotically invoke certain desired characteristics, such as power for the powerless, action for the inactive, active masculinity for those who can no longer embody it because of changed relations of production. In addition, we could think of empowerment for women, who can become embodied active heroes, whose special moves can sometimes defeat men.

The imagination of the creative team is crucial here but I am suggesting that it is not any imagination. It has to be the imagination that produces profit and this imagination must make people want to play the games. To want to play the games, the games must make the player desire to win, to play, to participate. I want to go further out on a limb and suggest that this imagination contains a kind of Bakhtinian carnivalesque overturning. In video games, which are played, let's not forget, predominantly by children and young people, there is a sense in which the powerless have power and are given power. If this were the case, it would make the games immensely alluring as they would create a world in which the impossible were possible if only for the duration of the game.

We are in a world which is not the one of Althusser, which separated production from consumption and made consumption the site of the production of subjects. Here, production and consumption are centrally implicated in the relations through which players and playing are made. Central to this is a circulating fantasy or indeed many circulating fantasies, which must produce the figure of the player in order for capitalism to work. In many games, points are accumulated in the style of capitalist accumulation. For example, in Zelda, Ocharina of Time, points can be bought in a shop. This can take the form of currencies for a number of cultures – in this case rupees. Semiotically, the player learns that money is power, the power to consume, and this power may be power in and over other cultures, such as that where rupees are the currency. An imagined colonial power accompanies capital accumulation, accompanies game prowess. The game Star Wars Racer, which is a game in which players choose an avatar to operate a flying racing vehicle through a number of different environments, which they also choose, involves a semiotics of empire and colonisation as well as a strong instrumental rationality.

In many games, the players have to do something called 'beating the boss'. The boss is a character put in the way which stops the player going onto the next stage or level of the game. The semiotics of the term 'boss' to describe this character are obvious. In the carnivalesque world of the game, with enough competence, we can all beat our bosses.

Of course most games involve winning at someone else's expense, which is both essential and signifies as totally non-problematic. Winning is everything.

If the games present a carnivalesque world, we could say that they work for pleasure precisely because they allow the player for a moment to overturn social and economic relations. In that sense then, they contain those desires and make them safe, allow them to generate capital, huge profits. But is this a dangerous game the multinationals are playing? Is it possible to contain desire in this way? Is the so-called addicted player a manifestation that it is so much nicer to live in that world? Why wouldn't you want to go there as often as possible? Urwin's study of superheroes mentioned in Chapter 3 reminds us that children talk about superheroes at moments at which they need a sense of omnipotence to defend against feelings of having no power at all, of being small and childlike in a world of powerful adults who can emotionally desert them.

To conclude, within global multinational capital, we can rethink the relations of activity and passivity I raised in Chapter 1. I argued that from the beginning of mass production and consumption in the 1920s USA, desire for goods had to be mobilised and yet citizens had also to curb their desires and act rationally in order to be governed as rational actors. This is a bit like the inside/outside interaction of games – the fantasy, the god-trick and the ego confirmation. Althusser thought of consumers as produced through the ideologies of consumption. Rather, I have argued that producer and consumer flow through sites and that the fantasy of the player is what makes it all work from the game designers to the farmers to the wealthy players in the global North. The fantasy of the player works for profit and it does so by working to create protagonists linked globally in complex ways through international connections. I suggested methodologically how we might move forward to take this approach further.

In the next chapter I think about what it means to learn to play games.

8
Becoming a Player

In the previous chapter I suggested that game playing can be understood as part of a global set of meanings and practices in which playing and economic relations are constantly linked through the complex relationalities in which game playing and games exist. In this chapter, I want to take this further by developing an approach to relationality within game playing practices. In a simple sense, I want to argue that we need to begin not with the learner or with learning as a set of skills or accomplishments, but to move out of a Cartesian approach which understands the world as created by the act of thought. The Cartesian individual, as I argued, is a forgetting of the Others on which it depends. This individual is the centrepiece of liberalism and is part of a global system which disavows the relations that make it possible. To take this further, we need to think about how it builds upon the western philosophical tradition in which, following Plato, we produce knowledge not through sensory experience but through contemplation. The entire western metaphysical tradition is built upon a hierarchy in which thought is given precedence over action and action itself is seen as the product of thought. In particular this involves two characteristics: abstraction and determination. This means that certain abstract qualities or characteristics are understood as being central to the way things work – 'psychology', 'learning', 'thinking', for example. Descartes elaborated this initial split following the seventeenth-century rise of science as a scientific empirical project which assumes that abstractions produced by thought could then read back onto the world as a way of observing, describing and understanding it to produce knowledge. It is this knowledge which has been shown by Foucault to be central in the regulation and management of the life world. In demonstrating its historical production, he aimed to demonstrate the fictional and historically contingent character of its truth.

I have utilised a Foucauldian approach myself (see Walkerdine, 1984, 1989, 1991; Blackman and Walkerdine, 2001, for example). The problem with it is that it is unable to explain subjectivity, as we argued in *Changing the Subject* (Henriques et al., 1984). Yet, it could also be argued that even the picking out of an abstraction called a 'subject' may be part of the problem (Studdert, op cit). Indeed, perhaps what we need is a recognition that a double process is in operation. That is, that we are produced as separate objects of liberal governance in a truly Cartesian manner, while also acknowledging that this does not have the measure of all there is to say about subjectivity. What would it mean then to develop a different ontology? How might we develop an approach which does not have recourse to the mechanistic abstractions which put boundaries around the subject that are then read back as truths? Is it possible to produce a way of working without determining abstractions? If we recognise that it is the very separation of this activity into 'learning' or 'thinking' that produces an account which separates each part from the other, then what we need is to understand how everything works together to produce that which had been solidified into the psychological subject, just as a fantasy of the player works in global capital, or that 'Prudence' is an assemblage of many different Prudences.

I want to propose that we can approach game playing differently if we aim for a relational approach which attempts to engage with the production of being/becoming as a constantly shifting accomplishment, flowing and shifting within social relations. In this chapter I want to look at preceding work which has moved in this direction and to go on to use examples from the fieldwork to demonstrate that an approach which assumes that what seems solidified as the subject is continually created through relational flows and dynamics, might look like.

Existing approaches to learning

Although traditional approaches to developmental learning, such as Piaget, do utilise a notion of activity, he utilises it only to demonstrate how activity becomes abstracted into thought in order for the child to become a western adult. And even then activity is always understood as organised according to its resemblance to, and mirroring of, underlying natural structures which are mathematical in form and which become the basis for the development of logico-mathematical structures of thinking. In other words, Piaget's account is entirely dependent on his assumptions, which separate off action and thought. Mark Hansen, whose work I introduced in Chapter 2, also like Piaget, places us in the sensori-motor realm. For Hansen our thinking in new media never leaves this realm, unlike Piaget, although like Piaget, I argued that Hansen's work lacks any engagement with social meaning.

It could be said that there have already been a number of attempts to think about the external as being folded into the internal with respect to learning, in particular the dialogic work of Volosinov/Bakhtin (1994; 1981) and the approach put forward by Shotter (1993), for example, that follows from that and the developmental psychology of Vygotsky (1978). While there is a great deal to recommend these approaches, in particular Vygotsky's insistence that what is outside in the social becomes taken inside and his radical view of learning as a zone of proximal development, a possibly literal account of enfolding, I am critical of Vygotsky's adherence to a Cartesian version of rationality and a fixed sequence of development towards a rational goal as well as his concomitant refusal of embodiment and affectivity, since he concentrates on dialogue. We could also argue that he still retains a formulation of a subject for whom the social becomes internalised, rather than understanding a being who is always created and recreated in and through the social so that we do not have an abstracted account. Using a Foucauldian framework, I have interrogated the developmentalism which underpins this approach to childhood and its lack of concern for power (Walkerdine, 1989). Equally, it is possible to think of the cognitive anthropological/cultural psychological work of Cole and Scribner (1981) and Lave (Lave, 1988; Lave and Wenger, 1991), as directly challenging Cartesian dualism. In particular, Lave's approach to apprenticeship in practices describes the tasks which have to be accomplished for a peripheral member of a group to become a full participant in the community of practice. Such work radically redirects our attention from the subject to the practices themselves. It demonstrates that learning as apprenticeship is about the gradual accomplishment of ways of being in the cultural practice, which themselves embody performances of tasks which we could think of as social practices. What is important about this approach is that it does not separate the subject from the cultural practice. It is the participation in the practices which takes the learner from an apprentice to full membership. However, the cultural practice is understood in this approach as rather static and quite unencumbered by divisions and tensions. It simply is. Such anthropological approaches have been strongly criticised from within the discipline (Clifford and Marcus, 1986) as lacking any sense of fragmentation, or power, and therefore producing a rather static view of the cultural practices. In addition, we have no sense of the ways in which the apprenticeship is accomplished. Cole and his colleagues (1999) developed this kind of mix between cultural psychology and cognitive anthropology in relation to learning in a number of ways. Firstly, they demonstrated that we can see what we take to be thinking within the laboratory but that this is not ecologically valid in the sense that this is not how thinking takes place outside the lab. In this he follows Vygotsky's reading of Wundt, who thought that 'higher psychological functions' could not be studied experimentally. When, however, we attempt to observe learning or reasoning within a specific everyday practice, we can only see the result of the thinking. Cole and his colleagues set up a number of clubs for children in which, for example, meals such as lasagne got made, but it was often difficult to 'see' thinking because what was visible was the cooking and what was cooked, rather than thinking as it could be isolated as an object in a laboratory. What they went on to demonstrate is that what we call thinking is actually achieved through the interactions and relations within the practices themselves. Perhaps their best-known example is the study of a learning disabled boy who they call Archie (Cole and Traupmann, 1981). They demonstrate how both in the situation of an IQ test and the same test made into an 'IQ bee', the tester and teacher shift the rules of what is said in order to allow Archie to succeed. In doing this the participants produce 'thinking'. This is quite similar to what Latour argues for in respect of psychology (see previous chapter). This approach also assumes that the participants are 'reading' emotional cues given by Archie and responding to them. What Cole et al. do here is to take thinking out of the head and into the social practice. In addition to this, they have examined learning by linking this approach to a developmental account using Vygotsky's (1978) zone of proximal development. In this account, the zone of proximal development is the level that the learner can reach with help. In relation to video games, Oliver and Pelletier (2004) have developed a method for analysing game play based on activity theory. This does attempt to map the minutiae of what a player does in terms of action. However, I feel that this work lacks any sense of the complexity of the relationalities of which the action is a part.

While these accounts are very important, they have certain problems for my purpose. Firstly, practices in these accounts contain no elements of power or regulation. One is simply apprenticed as a member of a community of practice. Elsewhere I have contrasted this with a model of a discursive practice taken from the work of Foucault (Foucault, 1977; Walkerdine, 1984b, 1993). Foucault's later work also adds the important concepts of self management practices which I have introduced in earlier chapters. In some earlier work I demonstrated how infant and nursery school practices produced 'the child' as an object of practice through practices which took in developmental discourse, the positioning of the teacher, the architecture of the school, the seating arrangements in the classroom, for example (Walkerdine, 1984). Here I argued that the discursive object, 'the child', was not the same as actual embodied children, who had to take up positions accorded to them within the discursive practices. I gave an example of the kinds of play presented as educational within a textbook for teachers. There were five different types of play listed and described. This assumed a teacher who could differentiate between them, who had training and could understand the pedagogic and in this case, developmental, significance of each type of play. We could say that in this practice, it was not a question of observing a naturally occurring play but of actually producing that which was being observed, in the sense that it was only by setting up the classroom as a space to play and then interpreting within a developmental framework that a particular position would be produced for a child to enter and through which he/she would be understood. Foucault's notion of a microphysics of power works to inscribe learners within the surveillant knowledge of the school.

Similarly with video games, we could examine the complex interplay of discursive practices in which 'the game playing child' becomes a figure which circulates. These would include both technophobe and technophile discourses, those which problematise video game play in relation to addiction and violence and those which praise it for its potential for learning (Gee, 2003). But, of course as we have seen, these discourses are most important when it comes to parents' regulation of their children's game play, which certainly has a profound influence on learning, not least in terms of the differentially gendered regulation of game play.

While this is important for what it means to learn, I suggest that we have to add other aspects to our understanding of practices. I am suggesting that what it means to learn in this context is what it means to become a game player. To introduce this, I want to refer back to my work on mathematics learning in a book called *The Mastery of Reason* (1988). In that book, I discussed children's understanding of 'mathematical meanings', that is, meanings of terms in school mathematical discourse, such as 'more' and 'less'. By examining the ways a group of four year old girls and their mothers used these terms in their conversations at home, I established that the meanings of the terms varied according to the practice in which they formed a relation. The term 'more' was used at home exclusively in mothers' practices of the regulation of their daughters' consumption. In examples such as a request for 'more pudding', a mother would ask the child to finish what she had on her plate. I argued that 'more' in school mathematics practices where it referred to a comparison of quantities, may be the same signifier but it was not part of the same sign. I argued that the signs were formed in the relations of the practices themselves. Those relations were also embodied in the relations between participants – the mother's regulation for example and the daughter's experience of it. I argued that learning in this case involved being able to make a meaning link between the signifier in one practice and another, not a simple transfer of understanding at all, but a task potentially fraught with the possibility for misunderstanding, as I demonstrated with mistakes made by children.

With respect to this, I demonstrated further that when attempting to teach school mathematics, teachers often produced a complex chain of signifiers to help children move from one understanding to another. In one example of a teacher teaching addition as the union of sets, she went from matchsticks to drawings of matchsticks to numerals, using her body as the link point, uniting the signifiers and signifieds in a complex chain. However, while I thought about this chain analytically using a Lacanian chain of signifiers as a chain of associations, I did not think about it affectively. After all, as the girls and their mothers could no doubt tell us, and what Oliver Twist said clearly, 'more' and 'no more' are deeply embodied and affective. So what is transferred or indeed transformed from one practice to another is not just positions and meanings, even if the relational links are embodied by the teacher. Those meanings are deeply affective, so that we carry the associations of that affective effect in the body and through the ideations which associate with it, into the new practice, where it makes another connection.

Learning to play video games is not like learning school mathematics in that it does not lead to the disembodied discourse of school mathematics but an embodied set of practices. Yet, we could argue that children equally have to make sense of video game practices through their incorporation in relations of signification which already exist in other practices and then linking those to practices of learning games or learning new games. This would be an associative method in Latour's terms (see Chapter 7), to which I would add unconscious affectivity as above.

In the video games study I did not have access to any other meanings made by the children, so I was not able to think about how they move from one practice to another. However, as in the mathematics study, we can see something when they make mistakes. Children in *The Mastery of Reason* made the mistake of spending their money in a shopping game in an infants school classroom because they confused the relations of signification in shopping practices with those in the 'shopping game' designed to teach subtraction from 10. Their mistake was that the relations of signification within shopping designate a purchaser who spends their money, whereas the game was using shopping as a foil, with the children supposed to be subtracting their purchase from 10 pence each time. In addition, this was the occasion for fantasy play in which the children made much of small prices (2p) and large items such as yachts by acting out being wealthy shoppers. At the time I noted that it was precisely their mistake which allowed the fantasy to take place, and that while they were not learning subtraction, they showed a very clear knowledge of the subject positions within shopping, its class relations, etc. If we take that example a bit further, the fantasy of being a rude and wealthy shopper, which was accompanied by changes in accent, elaborate hand movements and gestures and a clear script, was immensely pleasurable. The children inhabited a carnivalesque space in which they could embody positions usually closed to them. I am interested here in the relation between the complex embodiment, which involved speech style, discourse, bodily posture and gesture and its play on the small prices and expensive goods. What this allowed was an embodied relation between the embodied intertextuality of shopping discourses and practices, class practices and so forth, acted out as a fantasy of Otherness. There was no simple split between the meanings within the shopping fantasy and those of wider shopping practices. Nor was there any simple split between their engagement with the embodied affect and the ideations (perhaps we might call them performances) of being a wealthy person. Moreover, we could say that the fantasy of becoming Other provided a pleasurable experience of omnipotence, that is of having power over something which, in everyday life they had no power, of a kind of magical overturning of their position of relative powerlessness. Yet, as I pointed out in the book, none of this improved their competence in mathematics. They failed to learn the lessons of subtraction from 10. In the video game play, there are ample examples of similar relationships.

For example, Sam tries to use 'the force' as Annakin Skywalker in Star Wars Racer. Of course this calls on the intertextuality of Star Wars, but in this game there are no possibilities to use the force, only racing vehicles and drivers. But if we look more closely, we can see that Sam calls on the force as an attempt to get power in the face of his losing the game to Timothy, the much more competent player. But the fantasy of embodying the force does not help him to win the game. In the films, 'the force' is an object of conquering inner strength – he who uses the force wins. Why would you not want to use this in video games? Yet Sam also remembers the excitement of this power and wants it to help him to win too. As in

the maths example, it metaphorically imports something linked inter-
textually (or indeed performatively and certainly affectively) but does so in
a way which presents a magical solution. In true Cartesian fashion, magic
will not save the day. However, this does not mean that reason necessarily
triumphs. What we observed in relation to femininity, subterfuge, is quite
common among the children. One of the central methodological issues
is that it is often impossible from the talk alone to get a handle on the
elaborate ways in which the different modalities operate together. That is,
what is done can often be quite different from what is said. A co-operative
discourse can cover over attempts to win by underhand means, such as
turning off the controls.

When Sam wishes to play Annakin Skywalker it is not because the avatar
has any particular strengths or skills but because, I suggest, of what this
character signifies and embodies.

Annakin Skywalker in Star Wars is a very special boy, a boy chosen to
become a Jedi Knight. Thus, he has a powerful mentor in a father/son
relationship. He is chosen, has powers. In Cathy Urwin's (2001) sense,
we could say that the character Annakin embodies a very powerful and
perhaps omnipotent fantasy, a fantasy of a child with power over adults.
Thus, we could argue that the fantasy of *being*, *embodying* or *playing*
Annakin is a very potent one indeed. The powers of Annakin Skywalker
within the Star Wars films would indicate a boy with very special
powers. While it is an intertextual and associational mistake to assume
those powers operate within a game of a similar name, I would argue
that the mistake is of the same order as that which I explored above in
relation to subtraction. Why wouldn't a boy think that he might beat
his partner if he were Annakin Skywalker even if the avatar in this game
has no more special powers or moves than any other avatar? In other
words, there is an affective association between Annakin in the film and
the game, which is also a semiotic association and which relates further
to a desire for power and to win. In this case then, the intertextuality is
crucial, not perhaps to the outcome of the game, but to the embodied
experience of Timothy and Sam as players.

Talk: Researcher: What are your names?
Timothy
Timothy . . . and Sam
Console: Both of them are manipulating the controls as if they were
working
Screen: Game is left at an intermediate screen, and starts to play a
two player demo as they get themselves settled

Action: Boys sit down at the table and get settled

Talk: Timothy: This isn't controlling properly

Researcher: Do a restart

Console: They don't seem to be able to control what's happening onscreen with the controllers [*perhaps because it's a demo playing and they don't realise? Timothy does something to reset the game*]

Screen: Game plays several introductory screens

Action: Sam enjoys the film sequences, moving to the music

Talk: S: That one

Talk: T: Do you want to be that guy?

Console: Both players manipulating controls, only Timothy is controlling the screen

Action: Appear to be choosing characters for a two player game

Talk: Researcher: Move hands onto the table

S: Umm . . . Anakin, I want Anakin. Anakin, Anakin

Screen: Screen is showing one of the menu screens showing one of the available avatars

Talk: T: No, this is yours

The control isn't working

[*pause*]

Oh yes it is

I think this is mine

Screen: Screen is showing one of the menu screens showing one of the available avatars

Action: Sam holds console up in front of his chest and presses lots of buttons

Action: Timothy knocks Sam's hands off the buttons on Sam's console

Console: Timothy takes control of Sam's console, reaching across his body to press buttons. Sam presses a few buttons (on his own console) awkwardly over Timothy's hands.

Timothy confidently uses console

Action: Moves swiftly through selection screens

Talk: S: Anakin Anakin Anakin

Screen: Timothy cycles through several screens that aren't seen during a two player game

Talk: T: Actually, wait, we're playing one player.

[*pause*]

I forgot. We use this. You use that

Action: Timothy reaches across Sam's body to indicates a large joystick-like button in the middle of Sam's console

Console: Sam presses a few buttons on his console.

Nothing happens on screen so moves his hands away from the control buttons

Talk: S: Yea, that one. Anakin I want Anakin

Talk: T: Nah. I'm playing this. I'm playing this. Sam you don't do anything.

Console: Confidently uses his own controls

Screen: Cycling through one selection screen after another

Talk: J: [*Long pause*]

I think it's single player so I'll go first

Then we'll do double player, alright.

Screen: Timothy makes lots of selections on screen – Appears to take much longer than the later process of selecting characters and setting up the game when both boys are playing.

Talk: S: Okay.

[*Long pause while Timothy plays single player game*]

Screen: Timothy's single-player game happening on-screen

He is a very skilled player

Action: Sam watches intently Timothy's screen (for several minutes)

Timothy's wristwatch alarm goes off. He pauses the game to switch it off, then resumes play

Timothy notably makes no comment or communication to Sam

Talk: S: Use the force

Talk: T: Use the force

Talk: S: I can

Action: Sam makes large arm gesture of a floating hand in front of their bodies.

Timothy's gaze doesn't move from screen

Talk: T: You can't use the force on this

Talk: S: I can all by myself. I'm a Jedi. I'm a real Jedi

[*pause*]

Hit, um, the ground, it's so mad

Action: Sam watches screen intently, arm and console hanging limp. As he speaks he moves closer to Timothy.

Screen: Timothy's pod starts to spin out of control, bouncing against the walls and he seems to have difficulty getting it back under control properly – has several small crashes. He pauses to the menu screen and quits out of his single player game

Talk: T: I hate that part.

[*pause*]

Console: Timothy's hands are on the controls

Sam's hands are far from the controls

Screen: Long period of cycling through loads of menu screen

Action: Timothy gazes intently at the screen

Talk: [*Pause*]

T: um I don't know how to do a two player

[*pause while he works out how to set up a two player game*]

Action: Sam watches Timothy, then at the screen, then aimlessly around the room

Talk: T: two player [*triumphantly*]

Sam

[*Exclamation of glee*]

Console: Sam alters his grip on his console so that he's holding it with the controls all available for use, but still doesn't press any buttons

Screen: Intro screen for the two player game appears

Action: Sam suddenly brightens and sits up as the intro screen comes

Talk: T: I'll be, I'm player one

Console: Timothy is continuing to control the action on screen

Action: Sam watches screen and body language suggests he is going through the process of choosing a character from the menus that appear as Timothy chooses, is very animated, shifting around in his seat

Console: Sam manipulates his controls even though they don't seem to be affecting the action on screen

Screen: Cycles through screens depicting the different available avatars

Talk: S: I'll be, I am, I'll be, um, um, I'll be um . . . I wanna be . . . him [*Sam speaks in a rambling, thoughtful way, not very assertively, and as he speaks the word 'him' it appears to refer to the Anakin avatar but is more speaking-out-loud than a clear assertion of his choice, but Timothy speaks distinctly and decisively before Sam has a chance to make his wants more explicit*]

Console: Timothy is controlling (it's his turn to select a character)

Screen: The option of Annakin appears on the screen

Action: Sam points at the picture of Annakin on the screen

Talk: T: I'll be Annakin

Talk: S: I want to be Annakin too

Console: Timothy controls quickly through screens

Action: Timothy gazes at the screen intently

Talk: T: Um

Talk: S: I wanna be Annakin

Talk: T: Player two

Console: Timothy reaches over Sam's body and presses buttons on Sam's control as he speaks

Talk: S: Yes

Talk: T: You can be Annakin as well

Action: Timothy coolly stares at the screen and blandly speaks (despite Sam's excitement), Sam jiggles excitedly, and mumbles 'cool' several-times.

Talk: S: He's cool

Console: Sam selects Annakin from the menu using his own controller

Screen: The Annakin selection screen appears, Sam selects it and moves onto the next set of menus

Console: Timothy sets up all the other bits of the game, choosing a map, etc.

Talk: T: I'm on Gaza. Start race.

[Short pause as game loads]

I'm up the top

Screen: The two racers are shown each in their own section of the screen

[long pause as the race progresses]

Console: Both players are holding their controls up and making intricate movements over the controls. Timothy is very smooth, while Sam frequently lifts his hand off one set of buttons to reach the joystick or another set of buttons.

Screen: The two player race plays on screen

Timothy is obviously a far more competent player than Sam. His pod progresses smoothly round the course. Sam's pod crashes frequently, bounces from wall to wall, and scrapes along the sides of the track. It makes very little progress along the track.

Action: Both stare intently at the screen, moving their heads and bodies along with the race pods on the screen

Talk: S: *[Giggles]* Go

[Long Pause]

Console: Timothy puts down his controller on the desk

Screen: Timothy's pod has completed the race and is stationary on the ground, Sam's continues to fly round the race course (it's some distance away from the finish line)

Action: Timothy continues to watch the screen for a moment, then looks aimlessly around the room, the first time in the segment that his gaze has moved from the screen

Talk: T: Yeah, I came first

[Timothy quits game]

Talk: T: Do you wanna, um, quit?

Console: Without warning or explanation Timothy presses a button in the middle of his controller

Screen: The game ends abruptly, switching from a view of both pods with Sam still racing, to a menu screen. This screen gives the option

to either quit the race, or return to it so Sam could complete the course
Console: Timothy is using his controller,
Sam's hands are away from his controls
Screen: Cycling through menus systems
Action: As he says 'wait' Timothy knocks Sam gently on the arm, to knock his hands slightly away from the controller
Talk: T: Alright, Um. Is that you? Wait, that's player two
Talk: S: He's good
Screen: Referring to a specific character shown on the screen (not Annakin or another frequently mentioned favourite)
Talk: T: Wait, let me, don't touch anything. Don't touch anything. That's player two And you wanna be Darth Bolt? [(?)]
Console: On 'you wanna be . . .' Timothy reaches over and presses some buttons on Sam's controller (continues for the whole of Sam's selection process)
Action: On 'let me' Timothy waves his hand over Sam's controller, seems to refer to knocking Sam's hands away, or forming a barrier between Sam's hands and controller
Talk: S: No, the [*character's name unclear*] Yer that guy.
Action: Sam nods and watches as Timothy controls the action using Sam's console
Talk: T: [*still controlling Sam's console*] Alright
Console: Timothy moves his hand away and Sam takes control of Sam's console
Talk: S: No, the bigger one
Talk: T: That one?
[*pause*]
Console: Timothy moves his hands back and takes over use of the console again
Screen: Cycling through specific avatar screens, notably Annakin's screen passes without special pause, comment or body orientation by either boy
Talk: S: No
Console: Sam uses his own console to go through the selection screens

I have included a long section because I wanted to show how we need to look at the relationship between a number of complex things happening simultaneously. In particular, I am interested in the ways in which Timothy achieves dominance and Sam attempts to wrest control from him by his reference to Annakin and 'using the force', which Timothy tells him clearly is not applicable in this game.

The controls are the medium through which the game is manipulated. Playing involves handling controls in the right sequence at the right time while concentrating on the onscreen action. The player is therefore to recognise and use the controls through his or her bodily memory without the aid of sight. Where a player looks is critical. A serious player has to watch the screen intently. I suggest that this intentness is absolutely central to mastery of the game. Poorer players do not have the same control of the controls, often take their gaze from the screen and make references outside the game and have fantasies of power. While playing Star Wars Racer, Sam says 'I'm a Jedi'. The reference to being a Jedi is an intertextual and affective reference to the power of the Jedi within the Star Wars films. As his partner, Timothy, a very competent player, tells him 'you can't be a Jedi in this'. If Sam's fantasy is one of omnipotence, it defends against the fact that he is not a good player and is not winning this game. So, the poorer player has less mastery of the technology and resorts more to fantasies of power and is unable to handle the dual aspects of being both immersed in the game and controlling the game through the god trick that we explored in Chapter 2. The more competent player, in this case Timothy, refers authoritatively to the fact that you can't use the force in this. He is the knowing Cartesian subject who is in control and indeed does control the controls. He thus also displays his game knowledge and never takes his eyes off the screen. This suggests a level of co-ordination and skill which has been perfected, The competent player, who wishes to win (and this is usually a boy in this data), spends many hours practising moves alone and getting to know the game and controls before playing with others in a more social setting. Thus, we are confronted with two different bids for power, mastering the technology as Timothy does and fantasising having the force and being Annakin Skywalker, as Sam does. I am interested here then in how the attempt to embody the power of the film fantasy is utilised by a child whose game skills are poor, with the fantasy utilised like a talisman to ward off the threat of losing. The embodied fantasies of the box office neatly divide the players into the different fantasies of dominance, with Timothy's masculinity embodying more successfully the technological dream of twenty-first-century action heroism, while Sam can only dream of it and invoke its power. The point of this example is to show how these two things happen at once in small ways and therefore how affectivity in the production/consumption relationship passes through the bodies of Sam and Timothy and is then used by Sam in a bid for power, which relates to the conscious and unconscious associations held there.

Moreover, I have already explored the way in which this is used by Sam as a failed bid for power over Timothy, a play for game dominance. I have already tried to establish that in this sense, instead of thinking of this as the players learning skills, we could see it more wholistically (Bortoft, 1996) in the relational sense that I have been trying to develop, so I am questioning a cognitive version of being acculturated into a community of practice. These practices are full of power, envy, rivalry, pleasure, pain, etc. In other words, complex affectivities are contained within the practices. And one is not simply 'a member' of 'a community'.

As I said earlier, Michael Cole argued that it was only possible in everyday practices to see the results of the thinking and not the thinking itself. For this one had to take the thinking out of its everyday context and conduct a controlled laboratory experiment. The problem here though was that such an experiment was not 'ecologically valid' in that it was not possible to infer that this was actually how thinking was accomplished in everyday life. This critique, presented in the 1970s, was important, for it argued that thinking was part of the social relations of practices and did not belong inside an individual. Our thinking is always accomplished in social practices, since the laboratory is just as much a site of practice as the field, as sociologists of science have argued (Latour, 2005). Indeed, this is what led to the development of approaches to science studies like Actor Network Theory, which was attempting to understand precisely how scientific work was accomplished. However, what Cole was pointing to is how difficult it is to see how thinking in practices is accomplished and how much easier it is to see its results. This creates a problem for empirical enquiry but it also picks out 'thinking' as an activity in its own right. Perhaps here the approach is still hanging onto aspects of the psychological as separate from the social. Perhaps 'thinking' as an object brings us back to the Platonic abstractionism I have been trying to critique. It may help to recognise that, psychoanalytically, thinking could be said to be itself produced out of a relationality. Urwin (2001) cites the psychoanalyst Bion who argued that the parental containment of early anxiety was what allowed the possibility of a mental space in which the mental engagement of emotion might be possible. Although this may sound like the continuation of the Cartesian object, thinking, I would argue that what is important is the relationality in which it becomes possible to communicate feelings. For Descartes, rationality was the rebirth of the subject without the intervention of a woman. But the intervention of a woman is precisely what subjectivity is about in the psychoanalytic account. If it is the relation that makes this possible; that relationality, I would argue, is always present. Indeed, as Austin (2005) has argued, as I discussed in Chapter 4, the intervention of a woman is what makes internal space understood as possible. The forgetting of it is a Cartesian forgetting, which then continues to forget relationalities in order to create the world as a work of thought. In forgetting those relationalities, it is the intervention of a woman, the making possible of the space of this separate sphere, which is also forgotten. In its forgetting, space has been taken away from women, who have to operate as always lacking the capacity for thinking, which they have shouldered the burden of making possible in the first place. In my view, foregrounding the relationalities which have been forgotten and occluded makes possible the reinstatement of a space for the feminine. While this approach shares some similarities with other feminist work, such as the psychoanalysis of Jessica Benjamin, it differs markedly in that I do not claim that relationality begins with the mother–infant dyad, but rather, as I will argue in the next chapter, one central problem is the positioning of the mother and the feminine as the guarantor of the relational. This means that we fail to engage with other relationalities. What would it mean to move away from the object 'thinking' towards an understanding of practices as sites for the production of the accomplishment of tasks and as part of that the fleeting, flowing, shifting accomplishment of subjects? As I mentioned at the beginning of the chapter, there are many current attempts to talk about a new ontology. While this is not the place to discuss these, suffice it to say that the central part of the ontological foundation I am trying to create here is that what and who we are is produced as an aspect of constantly moving and changing relationalities. It would seem that there are two tasks at hand. We need to understand the spatial relationalities through which game playing is produced and we need to understand this as bisected by the temporal dimension which creates the sense of history, biography, continuity and fluctuations in embodied experience. I would suggest that all existing approaches from sociology tend to foreground the first at the expense of the second and those from psychology do the reverse.

Meanings in this account are entirely produced in practices. The move which the children discussed in *The Mastery of Reason* had to make from more/no more to more/less was quite a big one. I displayed how it was achieved in Latour's sense through an intersection of intercorporeality and intertextuality, the links working like an associative chain. So, $2 + 3 = 5$ is shown as an associative shift, as Latour argues. However, in that example, I was not able to demonstrate how children made meanings only from how the teacher made the meanings for them to take up. In this sense, we could argue that I was already using an associative method, using signifier/signified relations as associative chains, following Lacan. What I was not able to demonstrate was an unconscious association. For this reason, we could add the idea of the assemblage. We could say that, in Latour's terms, the teacher's body, sticks, circles drawn on paper were all 'actants'. But I was also trying to say in that work that what was produced was an omnipotent fantasy of knowledge over the world, what Rotman (n.d.) called mathematics as Reason's Dream – a dream that things once proved true would stay true forever. So, the power in this knowledge was to read the world back through it and to convey that power to the person who can do it. Video games, unlike school mathematics, present a kinaesthetics of embodied knowledge, where the competent player is both immersed as the potential hero and controlling from the outside – the god-trick. We could say that if the player is assembled this way, it is an assemblage which we can then read as though it possessed features, had intentions, were the originator of its actions, were fixed and solid and acted upon the world. So, seen this way, learning becomes this process of assembling this figure and the fantasy of embodying its affective relations.

If we think of domestic practices as the site of the first practices for children, then maternal and paternal relations and how they are contained in practices which signify is crucial. If video games are contained within the domestic, they are also a site of shifting relations between adults and children – is the computer or console in the bedroom or is it supervised on the TV in the living room? How do we understand these relations and the meanings contained within them? When the children get to the club, they are already relatively proficient in games. If we assume that the relations of practices already hold the children in a huge set of relations, what other relations are brought from other practices?

So, to recap, I am arguing that accounts of learning as development, even in the Vygotskian tradition, play into a conception of the liberal humanist subject which underpins the emergence of claims to truth within developmental and other psychologies (Henriques et al., 1984). By assuming that the adult and civilised subject is a rational being, whose rationality unfolds whether through the interaction with an object world or the dialogic process of internalisation of the social through language, I suggest that we miss the central importance of practices and their specificity. In this sense, I agree with Lave in that her model of apprenticeship recognises the specificity of what it means to be a competent participant in a practice, rather than generalising and extracting a set of structures, skills, etc. I am therefore suggesting that we can move away from notions of development to understand precisely how the practice of becoming competent is accomplished in any particular place. To specify a developmental process or indeed an object called 'development' would mean that we would revert to the problem of the psychological with context added on, without seeing the wholistic way at all. The concept of 'development' implies a psychological process, whereas what I am attempting to develop attempts to transcend the binary between outside and inside, and in doing so recognises that any particular exemplar of learning or change must operate in a specific setting, and is not separable from that setting. Thus, we can understand this work as coming out of a tradition which attempted, from the 1970s onwards, to put cognitive development in a social and cultural context (Donaldson, 1978). In moving beyond that dualism, what we are talking about is a differently configured object of study. This does not mean that we do not approach change over time and increasingly complex accomplishments and changes, but we would approach them differently.[1]

As Foucault has argued, liberalism, as a particular development of a Cartesian work of thought, attempts to fix the subject as a Cartesian subject operating according to freedom and choice within a democracy, which governs through discursive strategies, techniques and practices which place the subject as in need of constant management and self management. This is a forgetting in which what is forgotten is the very shifting relationalities which produce the social/subject, which have become understood as fixed and sedimented in the service of liberalism and global capital. To unfix them is to recognise the mutability that is ever present.

How do we develop an approach based on these principles?

While in the last chapter I explored what this might mean for the intertwining of the economic and social production of game playing, here I am thinking about game playing in the club. I am trying to demonstrate that playing involves the simultaneous operation of a number of different relationalities. I have argued that games are one site for the production of contemporary masculinities. This means that the children are already incorporated into the intextualities and performances of those meanings. In addition, however, the games demand a reading of the virtual space of the screen, its spatial relations, its discursive and narrative organisation. This has to be linked to the controls, with their spatial configuration of buttons to press, which has to be co-ordinated with the screen. Competent playing demands constant attention to the screen while simultaneously demanding rapid manipulation of controls. This embodied performance has also to be accomplished while negotiating with and talking to fellow players, if any. In addition to this, this embodied relation recalls other relations. What embodied affective relations, what unconscious meanings have become associated with those and are now recalled in the present, consciously or not?

With these issues in mind, in the next chapter, I want to illustrate these points by referring to particular examples of children playing in the club setting.

9
Playing the Game

In the previous chapter, I set out a way of understanding the complex interconnectivity of practices, so that playing could be understood as part of a complex set of relations and connections, which I have described in relation to the three-fold approach to affect developed in Chapter 2 and the Deleuzian concept of the assemblage. If, in Latour's sense, we look for the associative links, I have also argued that these associations are also brought into any game play by the temporal relations into which the participants have entered. Freud understood chains of association as producing the links of the unconscious, so that those associations are always being made. In that sense, just as Lacanians argued that the psychic work of masculinity is never accomplished and has to be ceaselessly reworked, so the affective work of masculinity is constantly invoked through the associative links in the game play. We should expect gender relations to be constantly reworked and invoked as I have shown in previous chapters.

However, putting these ideas into operation in analysing the game play is difficult. While I agree with Latour that all associations leave traces, we have to learn to read what we see and hear in a different way. Freud's clinical way of approaching associations was to understand material presented to him in a clinical setting as what he called the 'manifest content', i.e. that which we can see. The work of analysis was to pick up the links of that content to other content, what he called the 'latent content', displaced in the unconscious. It follows that in the kind of empirical approach this project adopted we cannot access the latent content, but I suggest that we can glimpse its traces as they appear in the relations of play. One example of this is that given in Chapter 4 in which one girl gets the others to tacitly agree not to kill her avatar. In principle, I think we can adapt techniques taken from more recent psychoanalytic

171

developments in which the analysis pays attention to what is described as unconscious intersubjectivity, that is the transference relations and unconscious dynamics between analyst and analysand and between members of an analytic group. However, we have to make sure that we do not separate these associations from those which operate consciously and which flow between sites, across space and time. I have not been able to fully develop this method here, as I found that the work of simply trying to look in a different way, is itself very demanding. For example, as I have remarked in previous chapters, some things are not obvious and competitive relations can be covered by co-operative talk, which misses the surreptitious work on the controls, or a boy tells the interviewer that he solves problems alone, which account is not disrupted until we talk to his mother, whose account involves her, which his does not. This in itself tells us in detail about a complex relational dynamic. The production of the boy as independent Cartesian subject, the author of his own thought and independent of his mother, was a fiction shown up by the mother's account, but also the site of a relational struggle between mothers and sons in which the son attempts to free himself of his dependence on her. The fiction carries an enormous affective charge. Similarly, it was common for some fathers to see game playing as producing an independent and action masculinity against the 'sooky clingy mummy's boy', where we have the fathers joining in with a triangular dynamic with the mothers to produce the boy as a man, who by definition is not dependent on his mother. It requires constant work and is never secure because it is always being threatened by the relationality which produced it. In the game playing we are constantly confronted by that work. I want to show how this is always a relational production. But what I am saying is that these things are often covered over to make it look as though the relations themselves have been produced by an individual. The games playing and talk about the games at interview are full of this. We are constantly confronted by what appears to be the work of one person but further analysis reveals it to be a complex production, so faint as to be almost invisible. In analysing the data, I often felt that I had to work really hard to 'see' anything. I think this is because we have become so used to recognising certain features and ignoring others that we treat some of the work of relationality as 'noise' or background. I suggest that this work involves foregrounding that which has becomes a forgotten background in order to see it. If we imagine the life world as a constant series of flowing shifting relationships, we can look at one particular series of moments and one place (Bruno Latout calls it a site, Arendt calls it the space of appearance of the 'who') as the place in which a task is accomplished – in this case a game gets played and what we see as the player is assembled (even though, as Deleuzians insist, such moments cannot easily be isolated from the continuous movement of immanence). The accomplishment of the game is hugely complex. In each case, the players often appear differently depending on what is being played and who is being played with and given my work on mathematics, discussed in previous chapters, we cannot assume a straightforward transfer from one situation to another.

Assembling Timothy

If we begin with one boy, a player called Timothy, I want to show how there is not one, but several Timothys. Assembling Timothy occurs because we fail to see how as a player Timothy is created as and in a relation in different games and with different players. Yet, even here, even if we establish what we can 'see' in micro interaction, as Latour does, I would still argue that there is something that exceeds our most ardent gaze and that we need the gaze at the associations of the unconscious, that is the place of affectivities in the assemblage, of which we can find the surface or conscious traces, as both Freud and Latour acknowledge, to understand the creation of a fantasy of a particular Timothy which must be sustained for Timothy to recognise himself as a subject. If something exceeds what is on the surface, perhaps we can invoke a forgotten relationality, that which hardens our edges so that we appear solid, while inside and outside we are created and recreated in embodied meanings, so that we can find traces of unconscious associations. Yet these meanings can be playful, pleasurable, become hardened and located in a body in Freud's sense of chains of association and fantasy. The challenge to Plato and Descartes also involves that which exceeds thinking – feeling, irrationality, the feminine.

Timothy and Sam are playing Star Wars Racer. As I discussed in the last chapter, Sam tries to use the force. Timothy's response that 'you can't use the force in this', locates him as the knower. Later, James plays with Timothy on the same game. He is not winning and attempts to present crashing as a virtue. This bid fails and he drops out and has a headache. Nothing has challenged the Timothy as dominant which emerges. In playing with William, Timothy says that William is too slow. William retorts by attempting to change the discourse – 'I want to explore'. This tries to create a Timothy who is not in control of the flow of the game. In another game, Prudence joins in and teaches Timothy an aspect of the game he doesn't know. When she has done this, she is sidelined.

All of these interactions mobilise Timothy's dominance and create it. In another session, Timothy and Jim are playing Star Wars Racer and Jim is losing.

> **Talk: Jim:** [*directed at racing pod*] Aw come on, you can go faster than that
> **Talk: Timothy:** I'm coming third, yay
> **Screen:** Pods are speeding through a snowy landscape. Jim's hits a rock and explodes
> **Talk: Jim:** Kaboo . . . m
> **Talk: Timothy:** I hate that place!
> **Talk: Jim:** Did you hear my guy? He went aa-hahaha, then he died.
> **Screen:** Jim's pod crashes into a wall and explodes
> **Talk: Timothy:** Are you coming sixth?
> **Talk: Jim:** Yea
> **Talk: Timothy:** Oh I'm coming – fifth
> **Talk: Jim:** Purposely. I keep on crashing. On Purpose
> **Screen:** Timothy's pod completes the race, comes to rest and all his stats come up on the screen
> **Talk: Timothy:** Third
> **Talk: Jim:** Kaboom! He went Awoo Awoo Kaboom
> **Talk: Timothy:** Whoa, your guy looks mad.
> **Screen:** Jim's pod crosses finish line and comes to rest shortly after Timothy's (But much farther behind than it had been for most of the race, and the camera pans round them. Lots of figures and information about the race pops up over them.
> **Talk: Timothy:** That's finished. You're sixth, I'm third. Yay I beat you.
> **Talk: Jim:** [*Directed to the researcher*] Can we change the game?

As we see, Jim insists that he is crashing on purpose. In a position in which Jim cannot mobilise the authoritative discourse and does not have enough skill to win, his statement that he is crashing on purpose could be read as a bid to change the discourse and to present his failure (crashing) as a virtue and the point of the play. However, eventually Jim gives it up, says he doesn't want to play any more and has a headache. This would suggest that competence in game playing is less pleasurable perhaps if it is not also accompanied by the social dominance of another player that his mastery affords him. At this point, another player, William, joins Timothy. Like Timothy, William too makes a bid to change the discourse and we might also conclude, a bid for power over Timothy. This begins when Timothy criticises William's slow play. William retorts that 'I want to learn to explore'.

What is interesting in these sequences is that mastery of the controls and the technology is integral to game competence and the pleasure that this affords but it is also a central plank of social dominance. The attempts to resist Timothy's dominance by introducing a different game discourse, can also be understood as bids to gain power by becoming magical (using the force), presenting crashing as a purposeful activity or playing the game slowly (exploring). We could also see these moves as resistances to the way that the technology sets the player up to play. Wanting to explore slowly subverts the logic of the game, while bringing in the force brings into the game a fantasy which is absent or could we say, occluded, within the game discourses and practices, as in the shopping game example I gave in the last chapter.

The shift out of the teacher's shopping game was a metaphorical shift – it utilised the metaphorical axis of language. I argued that mathematics discourse concentrated solely on the metonymic axis because it was metaphor which took the subject out of the relationship between mathematical signifiers and into its reference. I argued that this also presented us with the opposition of two kinds of fantasy and two kinds of power. The power of mastery of mathematics versus the power of imagination. Both embody fantasies of being powerful, but in a different way. I suggest that the metaphoric fantasies are the fantasies of the poor, in this case of those who are poor at mathematics or are poor at games. It is the imagination of being somewhere and someone else – someone who has power in the world. The fantasy embodied by Timothy is different. I would argue that this fantasy, accomplished by technical competence and mastery, lives social dominance as though it were a real possession. Hardly surprising then that like Sam, the player who wanted to use the force, many girls in this study preferred playing at fantasy play rather than video games in their leisure time. Most girls said that they preferred playing at being characters from TV shows, particularly ones with a powerful female character who gains power through magic or witchcraft, such as *Charmed*, rather than spend many hours practising video games. Of course, the position of the witch is a classic feminine one.

Such fantasy play is the play of the powerless. It fosters the imagination, it produces empathy for and understanding of being in another position, but I suggest that, unless accompanied by the god-trick, it does not lead to social or technological dominance.

Playing Pokemon Snap

I want to turn next to another example of Timothy playing a different kind of game, Pokemon Snap. This is an outline of about an hour of playing with Prudence, Timothy and Jim. Prudence is playing the game alone as the boys sit down to play, and she is asked by the researcher to teach them how to play.

In this game there are two forms of play. The first is the snapping of pictures of Pokemon characters. During this form of play the avatar moves on a buggy through a landscape, while the player controls where it looks, and focuses on and snaps Pokemon who are roaming on the landscape. When the buggy reaches the end of its track, this phase ends and the player is taken to the next phase.

The second form is taking the photos back to Professor Oak, choosing the best of the pictures, and then showing them to Professor Oak, who gives them a score for each one in turn. The player selects the photos to be shown, and then watches as they are scored in turn. The player is returned to the menu screen, and can choose to take the avatar on another snapping expedition.

The Snapping phase of the game seems to be viewed as the most significant part by the participants in this excerpt, and who has a turn at controlling it is more closely regulated.

This outline shows who has the controls as the game with these three players goes on. Some parts are described in more detail where there is conflict over who has the controls.

> **Snapping Session 1**: Timothy is handed the controls by Prudence, and takes the first turn of snapping, with her explaining to him how to use the controls. She sometimes reaches out and presses buttons on the control to indicate to him how to do it.
> **Checking Session 1**: Timothy retains the controls and checks through his own snaps with Prudence teaching him how to do it.
> **Snapping Session 2**: Timothy hands the controls to Jim at the end of the checking, keeping his hands on it to indicate several of the buttons and how to control them
> **Checking Session 2**: As the snapping turn finishes, and Jim is laughing and talking about what he's just done, he casually places the control onto the desk between Timothy's hands, and Timothy takes it up.

Halfway through the checking session Timothy finds he doesn't know what to do.

Prudence says 'I'll show you', and reaches across him to press several buttons on the control. He retains his position with the control squarely in front of his body so Prudence has to reach across, she then takes the control out of his hands.

After she has pressed one or two buttons, Timothy reaches towards the control making to take it back.

Prudence apparently doesn't notice, and continues trying to work out how to select the photos, working at the control and moving the cursor around the screen.

After a few seconds, Timothy moves his hands back into his space, resting his head on them.

Prudence spends several more seconds, and eventually finds a way of getting to the next bit, all the while speaking with Jim about that and other features of the game.

Prudence passes the control towards Timothy, until it's in her hand in front of his body.

Timothy reaches for it, and has one of his hands on the button.

Prudence pulls it back in front of her, and gazes at some problem on the screen she is engaging with. Timothy pauses a moment before moving his hands away from the buttons.

Prudence makes one more small move through the menu system, then moves the control back to Timothy. He doesn't reach to take it.

Jim asks a specific question about what Prudence has been doing, and she moves the control back in front of herself.

Prudence retains the control to have a chunk of checking play.

Timothy reaches for the control again, appearing to press a button on it, although there has been no break in play or Prudence and Jim's behaviour to suggest a change of turn is possible.

A few seconds pass while Prudence finishes a task, then she hands the control to Timothy with an exaggerated movement, moving her body away from him to allow her arm to be totally outstretched as she hands it to him.

Timothy retains the control for the rest of this phase, with Prudence having had control for about a quarter of the time.

Snapping Session 3: Timothy retains the control, with no discussion
Checking Session 3: Again, Timothy retains the control. At one point Prudence moves to press some buttons as she explains what to do, and he dodges them. Prudence and Jim are reading the manual as Timothy plays
Snapping Session 4: Timothy asks Jim quietly if he can have another turn to do the other possible landscape, and retains the controls

Checking Session 4: Jim asks Timothy for a turn, and takes the control. Prudence asks if she can have a turn next, and both boys grunt. Prudence is still reading the manual, and Timothy at one point presses some buttons to teach Jim how.

Snapping Session 5: Jim attempts to retain the controls,

As the game changes phase Prudence turns to him and says 'Can I have a go?'

Timothy backs her up, saying 'She hasn't had a go'.

Jim counters this with 'I haven't been in the tunnel', which seems to close the discussion.

Prudence turns back the manual, and Jim continues to play

Checking Session 5: As he completes the Snapping phase, Jim hands the controller to Timothy.

Timothy takes it and passes it towards Prudence saying 'your go'

Prudence takes the control, and does the final bit of that phase.

Snapping Session 6: Prudence retains the controls

Checking Session 6: Timothy takes the control out of Prudence's hands, and declares which landscape he's going to play in the next snapping session.

Snapping Session 7: At the end of the checking, Jim asks 'Can I have a go', Timothy replies in a low whine 'No . . . '. There is a short discussion, which Timothy wins and retains the controller [*He seems prepared to go further in arguing, risking spoiling the fun, than the others do – particularly Prudence, during this excerpt, gives up on a request with no argument*]. During this session, Timothy pauses the game several times so that he can take part in discussion around the manual with the others, without wasting his playing time.

Checking Session 7: Timothy unproblematically retains control. Asks the researcher several questions about the controls, beyond what Prudence appears to know.

Snapping Session 8: Before the end of the checking, Jim says clearly 'Now it's my go'. Timothy hands the control over saying 'I know'. Jim finds a new path so effectively has two turns. At the end of this phase Jim puts the controller down on the desk between the other two. Timothy picks it up, and before he's holding it properly, Prudence says 'Now it's my go', and Timothy hands it to her.

Checking Session 8: Prudence has the controls. At the end of the session Jim says 'Let Timothy have a go at this'

Prudence says 'I haven't had a go'

Timothy says 'She hasn't had a go at this one'

Jim says 'I thought you'd just had a go. Sorry'

Snapping Session 9: Prudence keeps the controls
Checking Session 9: Prudence retains the controls without much question, but halfway through the checking she hands them over to Timothy.
Snapping Session 10: Timothy retains the controls with no question. The researcher tells them it's the last go before the end, and still no question from the others.

The point here is that were we to look at either simply the children or the engagement with the controls separately we would miss the complexity of the situation and the ways that the controls act in the relation. The relation which encompasses Prudence and the two boys puts her in a different relation to them. First of all, she is designated as teacher by the researcher. This is not an uncommon position for a girl, as I have shown in previous research on primary school girls (Walkerdine, 1989). She teaches Timothy but, unlike Jim, does not appear to enter a directly competitive relation with him. My reading of this is that Prudence serves a function not unlike mothers, but that dominance is achieved through the bid to handle the controller.

Prudence does not use her superior competence to floor Timothy. Why not? A Lacanian reading would tell us that Prudence cannot ever embody the phallus and she will never be able to sustain a position of dominant in that discourse and maintain a femininity which is 'attractive' to Timothy. She is caught. The boy must forever attempt to maintain the fantasy of having and being the phallus, while the girl must forever mount a challenge that cannot succeed. However, alternatively, we could say that her social positioning as teacher or quasi mother, is a traditionally acceptable way for a female to gain power, but that it would be much harder to openly compete with the two boys for the control of the controller, thus recalling the argument which Sue Austin (2005) makes and to which I referred in Chapter 4. That is, Austin argued that the teacher Miss Baxter who was the object of aggressive chanting by two small boys would have to shift positions away from feminine nurturance to marshall what she calls aggressive fantasies to counter this. Can we think of Prudence in the same terms?

The mastery of the controls is central to social dominance, game competence and pleasure. The mastery of the controls is the mastery of the group. Morley (1986) wrote of the importance of the fact that when watching family television, the remote control was often to be sited on the arm of the father's chair, giving him the power to choose the channel to be watched by the family. The controls in video game play also take a central place in the social activity of game play. The action on the screen has to be manipulated through the control. A player who cannot work the controls effectively is not a competent player.

In the examples given above of Timothy playing with Sam and then with Jim, William and Prudence, the flows in and through the relations combine to produce an embodied temporality of Timothy which is also mapped out spatially and interrelationally. So, we can say that there are several Timothys, in that what is Timothy is constituted and reconstituted through the relationalities, which have been backgrounded by the insistence that we 'see' one consistent figure. In this the intertexual fantasies which emerge are important. The fantasies are at once both related to other texts as in Star Wars, and at the same time relate to invisible embodied histories of relations in which particular fantasies and ways of being become sedimented. It is not surprising then that Timothy is produced as dominant again and again and we see how furtively he often strives to maintain dominance and the central role of the controller as actant within this. This dominance, reinforced through other relations, for example, discourses of practice, of his father's views about boys, in the action masculinity of the games, again and again produces this dominance as necessity, pleasure, and its absence as pain or at least discomfort. It takes us back to the invisibilised mothers' part in their sons' success and to other small aspects of the interrelationality. To name some more, Sam tries for dominance through another discourse invested with fantasy; William tries by subverting the logic of the game by exploring. All of these relations in their different ways mobilise and produce Timothy's dominance. In addition, Timothy handles the controls in particular ways – that is, in Latour's terms, the controls become an actant in the production of Timothy. In the Pokemon snap game, the play looks democratic but if we focus on Timothy, we see how he surreptitiously handles the controls, turning a game on and off, for example, or moving from two to one player to ensure he plays. If we focused only on action or only on discourse we would miss the complexity of what can be seen and what is rendered invisible. We see these small moments and actions if we look for them, but the temporal dimension, that is the other small moments which make up history and biography are only to be glimpsed through this method.

These create a Timothy as dominant. Could we say that this 'who' maps onto myriad other moments and relations in which lack of dominance is the site of unpleasure. We could look to other relationalities and intertextualities that make that unpleasure difficult to tolerate. For example, his father's encouragement of game playing is precisely about the production of a dominant masculinity. The 'practice, practice, practice' of masculinity is required to allow it to appear as natural. We could say that the opposition of masculinity and femininity exists within the social, and the pushing away of the feminine as Other, repressed, forgotten, defended against, is accomplished in relation. The practices for its production create the embodiment of a fantasy that is endlessly lived out in the minutiae of the playing.

Twice, Timothy struggles with another player over who gets to play a particular avatar. The power they want to exercise in the social world is played out through the game, for example in the struggle between Timothy and Sam about who plays Annakin.

Timothy stops Sam playing Annakin. Timothy seems to choose Annakin to defy Sam. Another example, as we shall see, is when Timothy chooses Gascano, which Jim has just chosen. Jim eventually says that he hates Gascano.

For example, in one exchange, the start of the taped portion of game play shows Timothy and Jim already sitting and settled, with their controllers in hand and having started to set up a game. Timothy is Player One, while Jim is Player Two. It seems that they are already in the midst of a dispute over who plays who, and that the process of swapping back and forth between who has control has begun before the tape starts (suggested by Jim saying 'stop doing that', after the very first time that we see Timothy doing it).

They are in process of selecting avatars. This consists of a player cycling through a menu of possible avatars. As they look at each possible avatar, a screen pops up showing a picture of the avatar, its ship, and a big table full of descriptive information. To look at the next option, the player moves onto the next screen showing all the information related to the next avatar on the list.

During a two player game, Player One selects an avatar first by moving through the screens until they find the one they want. They then make the selection, and it automatically becomes Player Two's turn. When they have made their selection, the game automatically moves onto the next phase of choosing a race track.

It is possible to switch between the two player's selection processes by manipulating your control when it is not your turn. For example, after Player One has made her choice and allowed the game to automatically hand over to Player Two to make their selection, Player One can press some buttons on her controller, and disrupt her companion's choosing process by returning the game to her selection screens, and then alter her choice of avatar. This method of disrupting the usual turn-taking can become quite confusing for both players (and transcribers), as the only way of distinguishing between the two players' screens is a very small label at the top of the screen.

It is this method of disrupting your companion's choosing process that Timothy uses during this excerpt, leading to both players to become quite annoyed with each other, and apparently become confused and lose control of the game.

> **Screen**: Avatar selecting menus, each screen shows one possible avatar and it's ship, stats, etc. The screen changes from showing Gascano [*tall monster with two arms coming from each shoulder*] and Player One's turn to select, to showing Gascano's and Player two's turn to select.
>
> **Controller**: Both players have their controllers in hand and are poised to use them, so it is not clear which boy caused the screens to change. But evidence from below suggests it was Jim using his controller to gain back control of the screen.
>
> **Talk: Timothy**: [*very quietly*] Player One
>
> **Talk: Timothy**: [*whining or argumentative voice*] I wanna be Gascano
>
> **Talk: Jim**: But I just chose.
>
> **Screen/Control: Timothy**: Timothy presses a button on his controller that reverts the screen view to Player One's [*Timothy's*] selection screen, also showing Gascano and his pod.
>
> **Talk: Jim**: – Stop doing that!
>
> **Action: Jim**: Jim speaks with animation, jutting his head forward in annoyance.
>
> **Screen/Control: Jim**: Jim at once presses a button on his control and returns the screen to Player Two's selection screen – also showing Gascano as the avatar being selected
>
> **Screen/Control: Timothy**: A split second later [*The time on the Player Two screen is almost invisible*], Timothy uses his control to return to the Player One screen.
>
> **Screen**: The screen remains on Player One's for a moment, before again reverting to Player Two [*Jim's*] selection screen. It shows Gascano as the character that has been or is in the process of being selected.
>
> **Talk: Timothy**: – Yer. You've got that thing there
>
> **Action: Timothy**: Timothy raises his arm and points at the screen showing Gascano's selection screen.
>
> [*break in transcription*]
>
> **Talk: Researcher**: Who's Jim?
>
> **Action: Timothy**: Timothy points with his thumb at Jim to answer the Researcher

Action/Controller/Screen: Jim: Jim makes a very exaggerated gesture to press a button on his controller [*The screen is currently in his, Player Two's, control*]. He moves his hands holding the controller somewhat forward in front of him, and makes a downward gesture with them, to suggest the action of pressing down the button. He is trying to complete the selection process for his avatar.

Talk: Jim: [*exasperated, trying to-finalise-things tone of voice*] Yes!

Screen: The screen changes to Player One's [Timothy's] selection screen [**Note**: It appears that at this point the boys (or at least Jim who seems the most puzzled and annoyed) from one-upmanship in who has control of the menus, have become so confused about who has control, or have altered the set-up of the game so much, that they cannot return to the point they were at before it started i.e. just about to complete their avatar selection and move into the next phase of selection.

This change of the screen to Player One [Timothy's] selection screen rather than to the next phase of game set-up is, I think, the first unexpected result for the two boys.]

Action/Talk: Jim: Jim groans

Action/Controller: Jim makes another (though slightly less) exaggerated button press to get out of Player One's [Timothy's] selection screen, and another small groan.

Action: Timothy: Timothy collapses back in his chair in exasperation [a less marked gesture than any of Jim's similar ones – Timothy remains far more unaffected by all of this, and largely maintains his usual posture and facial expression throughout]

Screen: The screen changes to Player Two's [Jim's] selection screen

Action: Jim: Jim brings his hand away from his controller, and moves it in a sweeping gesture to slap against his own forehead, and tips his head slightly forward into his hand, in a gesture of exasperation.

Screen: The screen moves through several possible avatar selections for Player One [Timothy]

Talk: Jim: Player One?

Talk: Timothy: Player One

Talk: Jim: I don't think you can get to be [*inaud.*]
[very quietly] Player Two

Screen: Shows Player One, then alters to Player Two

Action: Jim: In response to the screen returning to Player One after he's pressed some buttons and expected it to move onto the next phase, Jim lets out a loud groan, and apes falling forward onto the table, with his arms outstretched in front of him across the table.

Screen: The screen shows Player Two's [Jim's] selection screen, and moves through several possible avatars, then completes, to hand control over to Player One. Timothy presses a button to return to Player Two [Jim's] control.

Action: Timothy: As Jim gains control, Timothy reaches forward and presses several buttons on Jim's controls.

Screen: Control again changes hands several times between the two boys.

[Break in Transcription: They play the game for some time. They talk as they play, about elements of the track, mentioning if they crash or have a similar scrape, and describing their position in the race in relation to each other]

Talk: Timothy: Who are you again?

Talk: Jim: I'm on the bottom

Talk: Timothy: No, but which player

Talk: Jim: I dunno. Same as you

Talk: Timothy: Oh, Gascano

Talk: Jim: I hate Gascano! He's so slow.

Talk: Timothy: He's cool

Talk: Jim: He's slow for me. I'm used to the other guy The tall skinny guy

Talk: Timothy: That's Gascano

Talk: Jim: Not the one with heaps of arms

Talk: Timothy: Oh, Gascano has heaps of arms

[Break in transcript of a few more minutes]

Talk: Jim: I wasn't trying to get this guy you know

[Pause]

Talk: Jim: I like how this guy screams

[Break in transcript till the end of the game]

Screen: Race is ending and the closing statistics come up on screen

Talk: Timothy: I don't think you were Gascano

Screen: A screen with a table showing who has won and lost each race, with a little picture of each avatar next to the table

Talk: Jim: Yea, I was. Look: Gascano, Gascano

Action: Jim: Points at the two little pictures, both of Gascano

Screen/Controller: Moves onto the screen that selects the details of the next race, Timothy is in control.

Talk: Jim: I don't want to be Gascano! No! Change character!

Action: Jim goes through and chooses a new, different character. Timothy stays with Gascano for the following race.

In this sense, the character acts as a talisman and again can be understood as a powerful actant within the relations of winning and losing and social dominance. I have included a rather large extract here to demonstrate just how detailed and complex is the creation of the shifting relation of dominance built around the choice of avatar. Not only are the two boys continually disrupting the start of the game, but by the end, Jim has attempted to say that he doesn't like the very avatar he struggled to play and contentment with the avatar Gascano seems to be related to who is winning.

This is the start of the game session that develops into Jim enjoying crashing, and eventually leaving because of a headache. During this first game of the session, Jim crashes a couple of times and states that he enjoys crashing. We could note the way in which Jim's failed bid for dominance results in his saying that he hates Gascano. Thus, 'Gascano' is a clear actant producing Jim's failure and Timothy's success.

That is, there is a clear way in which children talk about the games. That is, there are, in Potter and Wetherell's (1987) terms, some clear discursive repertoires, though I am arguing that a discursive or conversation analytic technique is not enough. This links the players into the intertextual discursive inscriptions, as with Timothy and Sam's discussion of Annakin. Of particular interest in this example, is the way in which Timothy shifts from talking about himself to being able to include Sam. This changes the dynamic of the game. I have started this extract at a point at which Timothy has been talking about himself in a superior way for some time.

> **Timothy:** I wanna be Gasgano [(?)]. Start race. Hey you're coming first. No you're not. You just smashed into a wall
> **Sam:** [*Makes excited noises*] This is fun. [*pause*] Wooo. [*unclear*]. [*long pause*] Oh this is cool. I like this game
> **Timothy:** Yes, first. I got . . . [*giggles*] You got blown to smithereens. Look [*pointing at screen*] you keep getting blown to smithereens
> **Sam:** It's cool
> **Timothy:** [*Pause*] Do you want me to quit it for you?
> **Sam:** [*Puts down consul and leans back with excited gestures*]
> **Timothy:** Do you wanna start race?
> **Sam:** Yer, cool [*giggles*]
> **Timothy:** Let's race again
> **Sam:** That is so cool
> **Timothy:** Alright?

Sam: Yer, that is so mad
Timothy: Will you remember? You use that [*points to button on Sam's console*]
Sam: Alright. I'm gonna smash twenty guys in the head. [pause] Cool
Timothy: This Podracer's so good at cornering

We can notice here how Sam's pleasure has changed through Timothy's shift to include him by creating a new or different relationality.

Another example, is the four boys playing the fighting game Final Fantasy with William, Jim and Sam. In this session, Timothy makes one bid for dominance, which is to withhold his knowledge of what button to press. In the same incident, Jim achieves dominance as 'fun'. We could add here that Jim embodies fun. That is, he embodies 'fun' for dominance. In this way, we also break the binary of interiority/exteriority. Fun is both embodied *and* in the relation between participants. We have no need to say that it is created in the relation or that conversely it is in the body/mind. Surely, it is in both places at once. In this sense too, power is distributed. Different configurations produce different modes of dominance. This is differently configured with different games, players, etc. Skill in games could be understood in relation to the mobilisation of intertextuality and intercorporeality from one relation into another (Sam's force in Star Wars Racer; Timothys's knowledge of Pokemon game discourse and narrative).

This intertextuality also involves the way that the games unfold in time and space on the television screen. Games present a complex three dimensionality that changes rapidly through time. Within the study, there were three broad types of games played: problem solving, strategy games, like Zelda, Ocharina of Time; racing games, like Star Wars Racer; and fighting games, such as Final Fantasy. These are also sub-divided into one player and multi-player games. Multi-player games all involve an element of competition, whereas problem-solving games involve an increasing level of competence. Each game involves a scenario or scenarios, with some games involving choice of scenarios, avatars and vehicles, which may have special features. Some games have a more obvious narrative, such as Zelda, in which there are clear points through a narrative which is also a journey and quest. Many have an intertextuality, which relates to other products and depends to some extend on that intertextual knowledge, such as Pokemon, but some also import characters from other games or media products.

Another aspect of the game discourses is the use of graphics. Sophisticated realist graphics are particularly appreciated by the boys as 'cool', such as Star Wars Racer, with pejorative connotations being associated with what are considered poor graphics. Many parents say that more fantasy and less realist graphics provides less danger of 'real' violence, but for boys this makes them less 'cool'. There is a blurring between character, or avatar or player in terms of identification, which is mobilised at the level of discourse. All have temporal sequences played out in a spatial location/scenario. Thus, the player has always to negotiate a relationship between time and space. Competence includes knowing what these things are – the discursive form and organisation of the game – and being ready for them to happen, either by anticipation, skills or knowledge of the game.

Social relationality

The above relationships are also contained within what we could call social relationality. By this I mean that the talented player, who is 'clever' or 'intelligent' is not produced through a simple pregiven propensity or talent but is the result of relations which are rendered invisible. In one sense, this can be understood in relation to the discursive production of the discourses of talent and that this itself can render invisible its social and historical production, as Foucault argued. In addition to this, there are other sets of practices which further is made invisible in producing the rational subject of the cogito. It is the invisibility of these micro practices which links in with the silences and disavowals of other narratives and other discourses. So, for example, Felix says that when he doesn't know something he uses the manual. Yet, his mother argues that 'he wouldn't use the manual in a pink fit'. It turns out that, according to his mother, she is the one who helps him. It is her help which is rendered invisible in a story in which the boy's talent is self-produced. This is linked to affective embodied relations and further linked to the affective exchanges and relations. Let us return to Timothy. I have noted a number of occasions in which he makes attempts to produce himself as dominant or in control, understood as produced through a number of moves, relationship to the controls and so forth. We have also seen how other boys make counter bids, sometimes with more or less success by attempting to change the discursive or narrative frame, while Prudence's superiority is sidelined by Timothy as soon as he has learnt what she has taught him. We can show how this is achieved, but how do we explain the fight over power, dominance, control by the boys? We could, of course resort to assumptions about inherent masculinity. But another way would be to relate this aspect of the relation to the subtle affective aspects that I am trying to point up. We could infer that Timothy feels something in his body which he recognises as pain or anxiety or a desire to dominate. We cannot know what on the basis of this data. I am saying therefore that affective relations are produced, so subtle as to be almost invisible (Brennan, 2004), in which a complex intertextuality and intercorporeality is invoked. That is what Freud called chains of association. I am trying to suggest that what is invoked in the relation is other moments, a whole history and biography of moments in which the same bodily sensation has been experienced. Timothy perhaps feels good when he is dominant. This feeling of the pleasure of dominance defends against its invisible Other, it opposite, and this was a central plank of Freud's account. What we have to understand is that not being dominant may cause Timothy pain, bodily discomfort, distress, which is only avoided by dominance, hence the push to produce it in every relation. We can only speculate about the pain of being small, controlled, regulated. Most psychoanalytic accounts attend to the complexities of boys' relation to their mothers, who both care for and also have power over the lives of boys. Impotence is painful. Omnipotence is a powerful fantasy. Why wouldn't Timothy want to inhabit it? I understand that what I am saying is speculative, and that it requires us to look beyond the confines of the relation to other relations, meanings, practice. But I feel that we need to do this in order to understand that not everything can be explained in *one* relation, just as the webs of relation in which subjects are produced extend hugely through space, so they also extend through time. The autonomous subject is a fiction, but a powerful and pleasurable one, who's Other and other side is pain.

Timothy as a player is situated in a number of different practices – a network of practices perhaps. In this sense, we can witness a multiplicity of positions which produce the assemblage we come to know as Timothy. Even in the relations with other players, we can sense both the continuities (Timothy's plays for dominance) and the discontinuities (Jim's dominance in the fighting game). How is Timothy constituted in other practices? We can look at the interviews with his parents, for example. Timothy's father constructs the idea of a stable, confident self in which academic knowledge gives that stability of an apparent singular subjectivity.

Interiority/exteriority

Let us begin by looking at the game in which Timothy tells Sam that he 'forgot'. It is difficult to make sense of this without assuming a complex relation between what is and is not said. Can we make sense of the forgetting in any way which does not at the same time understand it as a cover for not knowing? Billig (1999) works with the idea of the unconscious as the 'not said' of conversation, as that contained within the social-repressed. While that might be right as far as it goes, it makes no sense to think about this without also thinking that there is some work which goes on which is invisible to the social, which we have to assume is processed within the body/mind. If we think of Timothy's forgetting as a cover for not knowing, we can think of why this cover has to be presented and where it is located. We can think about why it would be so distressing for Timothy to be presented as someone who doesn't know something. Billig is correct in asserting as others have done before him (Hollway, 1984 for example), that what we have here is an example of the social categories of masculinity as containing knowledge, dominance, power. If this is constituted as a binary, with on its other side ignorance, subjugation and femininity, we can see that there would be a lot to maintain and every reason why a boy or man might not wish to cross over to the other side, as it were. Of course, the problem is the social production of binaries, but the issue here is how those binaries, those fictions functioning in truth, are lived. Lacan (1977) gives us one explanation which locates masculinity as part of the Symbolic Order, which has Timothy desiring to be 'the Law' and to possess the phallus. His explanation relates to the need of the boy to separate himself from the power of the Mother/Other and to dominate it. For Lacan this action is defensive in that it defends against its opposite, as there is no essential psychological subject. It was Freud who first formulated a theory of the defences as a way of explaining how we push away painful feelings into the place that he called the unconscious. I suggest that we need a concept of unconscious relations in order to be able to understand how this social binary is lived. I suggest that we could infer that Timothy would experience pain if his coming down on the wrong side of the binary would be threatened. For Timothy to be constituted as someone who knows, who is dominant is clearly presented in his father's interview description of him. We could also say then that his father has an investment in this Timothy – this is the Timothy he wants and likes to see. Perhaps other Timothys would not be so well received. Psychoanalysts argue that children can unconsciously take on the parental unconscious in the sense that what is affectively and unconsciously communicated is one of the ways in which relationalities constitute the whos at any moment, a moment which is never still, which always shifts and changes (e.g. Mitrani, 1993). These kinds of associations are sensed but impossible to 'see' in the strict sense of observation presented by Latour. Timothy's father too has an investment in this particular kind of masculinity. It would not be surprising if, in all kinds of subtle and not so subtle ways, he demonstrated his likes and dislikes. But this is not a simple account of interaction or roles. The idea of the defences and the unconscious is absolutely central to this account because at its heart is pain which has to be pushed away.[1]

Let us go back to the boys. We might remember that Jim complained of a headache at the very moment that he was left by himself. He doesn't get on and play by himself. There is a contradiction between what he is doing and what he says. It is necessary I think to assume something else not visible in either the action or discourse – a third space in which I want to place unconscious processes. These then are both interior and exterior, social and individual. Timothy says to Sam that they are playing a one player game. He presents it as a fact yet it is Timothy who has configured it in that way. How is it that the invisible is glimpsed, telegraphed, signalled in some way? For Freud, the unconscious was glimpsed in dreams, jokes and slips of the tongue, but we could equally argue that it is glimpsed and telegraphed within the relations of playing and indeed within narrative and discourse.[2] To conclude then, Timothy could be understood to be composed of a number of different Timothys, produced in different relations, but which embody complex affectivities. Anzieu's (1989) work on the 'skin ego', interestingly presents us with the idea that these Timothys could be held together through history and biography by the envelope of the skin, which holds the complex and affectivities together in what we then recognise as a singular subject.

Learning and teaching

I want now to turn to examples of how children teach each other to play. In the following example, Nicole teaches Sam to play.

Nicole and Sam have been playing together for a little while. Although it was Sam's turn first, Nicole took advantage of him checking the instructions to grab his control and take her turn first. As she played, he sat in silence and watched. When she died and it was Sam's turn, she begged him to allow her another go, before finally reluctantly handing over the controls. As soon as Sam started to play, she moved between ordering him about and clear frustration that he was not as skilled a player as her, and total disinterest, looking over her shoulder or playing with her hands. This incident is one that illustrates compactly several of her typical practices in 'teaching' Sam.

> **Screen**: The game takes place in a desert landscape. It's a single player game and the player controls a gecko that explores the landscape avoiding enemies and picking up items.

Control: Sam: is controlling the game and has the controller in his hands. He is using it and staring intently at the screen.

Action: Nicole: Nicole appears disinterested, she is resting her head on her hands, rubbing her cheeks and eyes, and humming along to the theme tunes of other games that are audible in the background.

Control: Nicole: Nicole's control is on the desk in front of her.

Screen: The gecko runs over a smooth area of desert, crosses some railway tracks and jumps over a ravine.

Action: Nicole: Nicole suddenly becomes very animated, she throws both her hands up, gesturing towards the screen, and her face is filled with emotion, with a wide open mouth as she shouts:

Talk: Nicole: No! Don't go there! You've gotta get the . . .

Action: Nicole: Nicole grabs her own control and starts to manipulate it. It appears that she is performing the action that would make the gecko go back the way she is instructing if she were in control of the game.

Talk: Nicole: Go back there, go back there.

Screen: Sam moves the gecko back, as Nicole is telling him to

Talk: Nicole: You've got to jump on all the rocks. Jump on all the rocks. Or die and let me do it for me. Abb, umm . . . Or die or let me do it for you.

Action: Nicole: As Nicole makes a mistake in her articulation she laughs, and when saying it again half orients herself towards Sam and wags her finger at him, in a large gesture using her whole lower arm to emphasise the words.

Talk: Nicole: You're supposed to jump across there.

Screen: The gecko jumps over a gap onto a series of very narrow clifftop platforms, with a long drop visible below.

Control: Nicole: Nicole is still holding her control loosely in her hand.

Screen: The gecko approaches the first set of gaps and jumps over.

Control: Sam: Sam is touching the controls very gingerly, pressing buttons in an elaborately careful way. It appears that if he pushes the buttons too hard the gecko will jump too far and fall off the other end of the narrow platform.

Action: Nicole: Nicole watches the screen with obvious distaste, her brows knitted.

Action: Nicole: Nicole glances at Sam's hands on his control, still frowning (Jealously? Critically?)

Screen: The gecko approaches the next gap in a series of small, jerky movements and jumps over, nearly missing the opposite side.

Talk: Sam: Yesss!

Action: Sam: Raises an arm and punches the air in celebration. Smiles broadly.

Talk: Nicole: Now go there!

Action: Nicole: Nicole doesn't respond at all to Sam's actions of triumph, but immediately speaks and raises an arm up completely to point a direction on the screen

Talk: Nicole: Go back to there.

Action: Sam: Sam watches the screen and Nicole's arm intently.

Talk: Nicole: Around! around! around! There! there! there!

Screen: The gecko runs along a narrow path of rock with a cliff face rising on one side and falling away on the other.

Action: Nicole: Nicole continues to indicate the way with her arm, in a slightly smaller gesture.

Talk: Nicole: Go my way! go my way! Now you gotta . . .

Screen: The gecko approaches a row of items arranged along the path away from it, and stops.

Talk: Nicole: Run across before it comes back.

Screen: On the path in front of the gecko a large barrier of rock moves out from the wall of rock to the side, until it completely blocks the way. Looks like something that would push the gecko off the path or squash it.

[pause]

Screen: The barrier moves back into the wall, as the path becomes visible there we can see another barrier just beyond this one, moving slightly out of sync with it.

Talk: Nicole: Now! run, run run.

Screen: The gecko moves falteringly across the area of path, not managing to pick up any of the items.

Screen: The gecko springs out of the path of the final barrier, only just avoiding getting squashed.

Talk: Sam: Pheew!

Talk: Nicole: You just made it. Good.

Control: Sam: Sam makes economical, careful stabs at his control.

Screen: The gecko springs up several shelves of rock to emerge at the top of the series of moving barriers, so that they form a temporary path in front of it. As he pauses there, they move back into the rock face.

[pause]

Screen: The barriers move back out from the rock face, forming a path again.

Talk: Nicole: Jump! jump! jump!

Screen: The gecko jumps out onto the first of the barriers/path sections

Talk: Nicole: Up on the! Up there! Back on the! Jump there!

Control: Nicole: Nicole holds her control in her hand, and distract-edly tugs at the button in the middle. This doesn't resemble the movements that Sam is making with his control to play the game.

Screen: As the gecko runs along the barriers/path sections they start to move back in.

Talk: Nicole: [*through gritted teeth*] Jump back there!

Screen: The barriers/path sections move back into the wall and the gecko falls onto the path beneath.

Action: Sam: As soon as the gecko begins to fall, Sam lets his hands with the controls drop slightly, and his intense gaze drop from the screen. Adjusts his shoulders a bit.

Screen: The gecko becomes slightly obscured behind another shelf of rock

Talk: Sam: I can't see.

Talk: Nicole: [*in a low, slightly whiney voice*] Let me, let me.

Screen: The gecko falls off the edge of the path he's fallen onto.

Action: Nicole: Nicole makes a frustrated clicking noise with her mouth, drops her shoulders a bit and covers her face with her hands.

Talk: Nicole: Just die and let me do that bit for you.

Screen: The gecko runs around the area and gets back to the bit of cliff that Nicole directed him to at the start of this excerpt.

Control: Sam: Running round less complicated bits of the environ-ment Sam uses the control much more fluently and casually.

Talk: Nicole: Yea, shouldn't you be on the can of tuna [??]

Screen: The gecko falls off the edge of the cliff at the first tricky jump.

Talk: Nicole: [*Sigh*]

Action: Nicole: Nicole is beginning to act less interested, both her hands are fiddling with her ear lobes, and she yawns and makes different shapes with her mouth.

Action: Choe: Nicole mouths something over and over again, with-out vocalising it. May be 'Let me have a go'.

Screen: Gecko runs round the map and is again at the start of the first section of difficult jumps, and falls down the second gap.

Talk: Nicole: How many lives have you got?

Action/Control: Nicole: Nicole reaches across and presses a button on Sams control without warning or permission. He doesn't resist.

Screen: Sam's game disappears from the screen instantly and a menu-type screen appears.

Talk: Nicole: [*dismayed tone*] ooh Wha-aht!

Action/Control: Nicole: Nicole reaches over and presses another button on Sam's control.

Screen: The screen changes to another, very similar, menu screen.

> **Talk: Nicole**: You've got three lives!
> **Action/Control: Nicole**: Nicole reaches over and presses another button on Sam's control.
> **Screen**: Sam's game returns to the screen.
> **Talk: Nicole**: Waste your three lives!
> **Action: Nicole**: Nicole rests her head in her hands again and plays with her eyes.

I particularly want to note here the ways in which 'teaching' is accomplished. As the better player, Nicole does not want Sam to play. Their relationship is configured through her attempted position of superiority and disdain. She varies between telling him what to do, embodying what he should be doing on her own controls, taking the controls from him or doing things for him and ignoring his pleasure in success. She also makes semiotic link with her own body, often pointing at the screen. This pointing and other gestures, such as her head in her hands or facial expressions of boredom or disgust graphically make the link relationally in a number of ways at once. That is emotionally, discursively and pedagogically. I argued that the teacher in *The Mastery of Reason* literally made the link between signifier and signified with her own body. I would suggest that in the above example, Nicole and Sam convey a huge amount through gesture and bodily movement and position. The seizing of the controls or the pointing at the screen combine with spoken words and the onscreen graphics to create a huge web of embodied intersubjective and semiotic relations through which playing is accomplished. It is this web which both creates and holds the players and creates both the possibility of playing and what it means to play. In addition, the controls and the screen both form a central part of the construction of this relationality. It is through the body that the linkages to screen and controls are made. The complex dance in which Nicole at once points, or holds her head in her hands while Sam manipulates the controls is precisely a complex relation in which the two are enmeshed. In addition, it is previous embodied knowledge of moves, embodied in other relations and through other textualities, which allows this to develop in the way that it does. So, I am pointing out the importance of the backgrounded aspects, those which are forgotten in an account which privileges what a singular subject might do. I am arguing that it is this interlinked set of relationalities, which makes possible the learning which is accomplished here and that, indeed, neither the assemblages called Nicole and Sam could be said to have accomplished anything that would exist outside of the relations, shifting as they are, in which they are assembled. We might also point to the way in which

Sam punches the air in celebration of avoiding a near miss, which is ignored by Nicole. Such air punching conveys a masculine victory and could therefore be understood as a note of triumphalism. Such triumphalism would potentially undermine the teacherly dominance in which Nicole is positioned. To maintain her power, she has to continue to position Sam as the learner and therefore as inferior. Again we note, as with Prudence, this position appears more open to girls than other ways of gaining dominance in relation to boys. In this respect then, there is no simple relationality which is not also at once invoking other relations with well sedimented ways of relating, in this case in respect of gender.

Kinaesthetics

The numerous occasions when children display that they learn to manipulate controls, follow the temporal and spatial relations on the screen, demonstrate that they most usually first try practices learnt in one game to see if it works in another.

Dan and Phoenix have been playing for some time. Dan knows a lot about the game, both the narrative and characters, and the playing skills, of how to make moves and win battles. He has been sharing the controlling with Phoenix despite his much greater game skill, and teaching Phoenix throughout. Dan gives lecture-like stretches of information, including details of what happens later in the story, and instructions for how to win battles or control the avatar, and advice for strategy related to the narrative – for example, shortly before this extract, Dan advises Phoenix to save a flower to give to a character who is later introduced, and will be his girlfriend, rather than to another named character. This extract is taken from some way into the game.

> **Action: Dan**: Dan sits upright in his chair and gestures with his hands as he speaks.
>
> **Talk: Dan**: You know how he has those square hands? You should see what it really looks like. When it doesn't have not um very good graphics like that. When it has good – really good graphic movie clips it looks really sick.
>
> **Action: Phoenix**: Phoenix looks away from the screen and adjusts his hat as Dan speaks. As he finishes speaking Phoenix returns to his position ready to play, with the control in his hands out in front of him.
>
> **Screen**: The view is the inside of the train, quite dark and indistinct. There are several passengers, not all identifiable, including Barret/Chocolate.

Talk: Dan: He's got this giant metal plate on his shoulder.

Action: Dan: [*Dan indicates his own shoulder*]. Its really good.

Action: Phoenix: Phoenix's attention has returned to the screen, rather than Dan speaking.

Screen: A rainbow box pops up, saying: [unreadable], disappears and another appears, saying: [*unreadable*], and third box says: 'Chocolate: [*unreadable*]'.

Action: Dan: Dan has his arms loosely crossed on the table, with his head resting on them, he's intently watching the screen.

Screen: A rainbow box appears saying 'Jessie: Chocolate . . . ', then disappears. For some time the view remains mostly the same, with the carriage vibrating to the movement of the train.

Talk: Phoenix: Then he comes like through the door or something?

Screen: A rainbow box appears saying: '[*unreadable*]: Say, do you think Warrior . . . ?', then disappears. Another box appears saying '[*unreadable*]: [*unreadable*] avalanches'.

Action: Dan: Dan's head is still half down on the desk.

Talk: Dan: How do you know?

Screen: Another box appears saying 'Chocolate: How would you know? [*unreadable*]'

Talk: Phoenix: Uh?

Talk: Dan: How do you know?

Action: Dan: Dan sits up slightly and moves his eyes from the screen to glance at Phoenix.

Talk: Phoenix: Wha?

Screen: Another rainbow box appears saying: '[*unreadable*]' [*These boxes seem to show a conversation between the characters inside the train, about things that will happen soon in the game*].

Talk: Phoenix: Aww . . . I just guessed.

Action: Dan: Dan looks over at Phoenix.

Screen: Another unreadable rainbow box appears and then disappears.

Action: Phoenix: Phoenix is looking intently at the screen.

Talk: Dan: Pretty hard to guess that?

Screen: Another rainbow box appears.

Control: Phoenix: It's obvious that Phoenix pressed a button on his control to make the box disappear.

Talk: Phoenix: Because like I figured like, that door. And there was no other way. Unless you.

Talk: Dan: No, he actually comes in that door.

Action: Dan: Dan stretches out his arm to point to a door on the screen, and then returns to a more upright posture, with his head fully upright.

Talk: Dan: Like
Talk: Phoenix: Like. I figured one of the doors, because there's nothing he could get though
Talk: Phoenix: Like he could get his leg through there.
Screen: Cloud, the avatar, jumps in through the door that Dan indicated, and joins the other passengers.
Talk: Dan: He jumps onto? See? See what I mean?

The relation that contains Phoenix and Dan is different from the relationalities that produced Nicole and Sam. Dan's pedagogic style involves more testing of Phoenix. But crucial to the performance of this game is embodied action that Dan brings to Phoenix. Dan knows the game and it is through his very specific embodied knowledge of just how to move in relation to just what will appear on the screen that allows him both to guide and to test Phoenix. It is as though Phoenix is brought into the embodied relationship which Dan knows through Dan's tutelage. That Dan may know this through 'practice, practice, practice' may mean that Dan is bringing Phoenix into that set of relations through which action masculinity is produced through the games. In addition, it is important to note as with Nicole, that Dan uses his body to make semiotic connections again and again, pointing, the position of his body, such as his head in his hands, or making a link to his own body as he explains about the avatar's shoulder or his hands. In addition to this, Phoenix displays how 'thinking' is achieved through an active engagement with the spatial relations on the screen understood through knowledge of screen sites. Phoenix thinks that the avatar comes through a door but Dan tells him he actually comes through a different door. Then Phoenix says that he knew it must be a door 'I figured one of the doors because there's nothing he could get through'. So we must assume that this relation is made up of the kinaesthetic knowledge of Dan's prior playing plus Phoenix's embodied knowledge of bodies and spatial openings, such as doors and windows. He uses his own embodied knowledge about how bodies can get through openings to infer what the avatar might be able to do. It is as though, in a very small amount of time, Phoenix has been able to remember what his body knows and transfer it onto the character of the avatar.

Gina and Maria

Gina and Maria's relation while playing Final Fantasy is quite different as they are both beginners. They are playing Final Fantasy, which is a single player game. It's a role-playing adventure-type game, much like an interactive film, in that the game follows one narrative through a story without much flexibility. The action is quite structured, allowing the characters to move along a small number of paths through the game world. At the beginning of the game it is particularly structured, as all the major characters are introduced and new skills built up gradually. Neither girl has played the game before, and they had some difficulty setting it up in the machine and getting through the intro. This extract is about 20 minutes into the game, after they have already had one battle scene, and been stuck in rooms having to find the single exit several times. They have just been introduced to a new major character, and chosen a name for him.

> **Screen**: The game setting is a very industrial building, surrounded by large machines and pipes. The characters are standing at a cross-roads, with four clear paths through the machinery leading away from them. Both characters are human. The player character is small, white, has large yellow spikey hair, the girls have called him 'Stach' (pronounced 'Stash') and they have just met and named a new charac-ter, who is large and carrying weapons and metal gauntlets, is older looking and black with a beard. They have just called him 'Jumbo'.
>
> **Screen**: A blue box pops up on the screen saying 'Jumbo "If you push the directional button while pushing the [CANCEL] button to run. (earlier marked X)" '
>
> **Control**: Early in the game session it was decided that Gina would play and have control of the console, but Maria has often taken hold of it, now she is holding it, having just typed in the name for the new character
>
> **Screen**: As the box disappears, Jumbo runs away down one of the paths. The camera pans close up behind Stach, making a little bit more of the path ahead visible.
>
> **Gina**: How do you go forward?
>
> **Maria**: [*Annoyed tone*] You use that Gina, all the time
>
> **Action: Maria**: Maria indicates a button on the consul, that she is still holding.
>
> **Gina**: Oh yer [*giggle*]. Oh yes . . .
>
> **Screen**: The screen goes completely black.
>
> **Maria**: That really does look like the thing in, um, 'Deep Blue Sea'
>
> **Action**: They both orient completely away from the screen as Maria speaks.
>
> **Screen**: The black fades into the game screen again, this time a view from above showing another part of the industrial interior, with sev-eral clear paths through. Stach is at the edge of the screen, and Jumbo is in at the other end, walking round a corner.

Gina: Follow that guy. What happened?

Screen: Stach (the player character) moves clumsily towards Jumbo, and Jumbo runs away.

Screen: The two characters run through a long area of the factory-like scene, and then through a door at the end. The screen goes completely black as Stach passes through the door.

Screen: The black fades away, to show a narrow bridge linking two towers of industrial building. There is a very long drop visible on either side. Jumbo is running along the bridge with Stach a few paces behind. There are some other non-player characters visible on the bridge.

Screen: As Stach reaches the centre of the bridge, all the colours on the screen blur and spiral.

Maria: That was strange.

Gina: What happened?

Action: Gina: Gina sits up much straighter away from the table as she speaks.

Controller: Maria still has the controller.

Screen: The colours resolve into a different format of screen. The backdrop is the industrial bridge from the previous scene, but everything else is arranged in a characteristic way for a very structured battle scene in this game (one from a long series of similar games). Specific battle music is playing, Stach is lined up on one side of the screen, with a massively over-sized sword in his hand, and his enemy on the other side. The bottom third of the screen is filled with two blue boxes. In one box is Stach's name, and in the other a list of statistics describing his health. The enemy is obscured behind the boxes of stats.

Maria: Now we're playing against the things again

Screen: The camera-view pulls back slightly, so that the boxes don't obscure the characters, and you can see that there are two heavily armoured guards facing Stach. There is a yellow arrow over Stach's head.

Gina: Ahh.

Screen: One at a time the guards charge forward and ram into Stach, and then move back to their formal places, creating a lot of smoke.

Action: Gina: Gina has not returned to her sitting position against the table, but is still sitting much more upright, [*perhaps kneeling on her heels?*] and watching Maria control the battle.

Control: Maria: Maria quickly presses a series of buttons.

Screen: Stach runs forward and strike widely at the enemies with his sword, then scuttles back to his own position. One of the enemies dissolves in a red glow.

Control: Maria: Maria continues to press buttons, even though it doesn't appear to be having any effect on the screen.

Screen: The word 'Machine Gun' appears in a new blue box near the top of the screen. The remaining enemy runs forward, and shoots a gun from hip height, which produces a lot of red light. Stach glows orange for a moment, and the number 4 appears over his head. The enemy then runs back to his position.

Gina: How did you do that? How did you do that? Sta-a-ash

Screen: There's a yellow arrow over Stach's head. A little menu opens up from the blue boxes, saying 'Attack Magic Item', and a little white gloved hand pointing at the items on it.

Control: Maria is pressing buttons on the control.

Gina: Sta-a-a-ash

Screen: Stach rushes forward and strikes at the enemy with his sword. The number 41 appears on the screen.

Gina: Oops. How did you do that?

Screen: The enemy rushes forward and runs into Stach. Some red light appears on Stach. The enemy returns to its place.

Gina: How did you do that?

Maria: I don't know.

Action: Maria: Maria shrugs slightly.

Maria: Oh yea now I know! No . . . no . . . cha . . . Yea.

Screen: The menu system appears again and the gloved hand makes a selection. Stach rushes forward and slices the enemy, and it disappears in a red light.

Maria: Yessss

Gina: What did you do?

Maria: You go 'Attack' and then the handle will point at him or them. So then you point to the bad guy and then it'll, Stash will kill the bad guy

Action: Maria: Maria points to the screen as she speaks and acts out some of the movements, taking both hands off the controls.

Screen: The camera view pans round Stach, quite close up, and he makes several slashes with the sword. Then that scene disappears and a menu screen comes up. It has a little picture of Stach and several stats about his health, experience points gained and his current level. All the information is in one long rectangular-shaped box, with two empty ones [space for further player characters to join later in the game].

Gina: So you go to 'Attack'?

Maria: Yer

Gina: Oh. Cool

Action: Both Maria and Gina look away from the screen as they have this brief talk.

Screen: The game beeps as several of the numbers increase to represent how Stach has improved during the battle. Then that screen disappears and a new one appears showing money and items Stach has. In this case, all the columns are empty.

Action: Gina: Gina has a stretch, with both her arms up over her head.

Maria: Uh?

Action: Maria: Maria makes a face to go with her expression of confusion.

Gina: What?

Action: Gina: Gina returns her attention to the screen.

Screen: The screen again goes totally black for a moment.

Action/Contoller: Maria loudly puts down the controller, and Gina moves back into position sitting at the desk, and picks it up.

Screen: The picture of the bridge returns to the screen. This time with only Stach standing on it

Maria: No you shouldn't play that guy again. Here,

Controller: Maria: Maria reaches in front of Gina and grabs the controller again.

Maria: I'll just get you up to there. To the ramp, Okay.

Action/Controller: Gina keeps her hands close to the controller, and as Maria uses it, she maintains its position in front of Gina, with her arms stretched out to reach it..

Screen: Stach runs along the bridge towards a large doorway at the end.

Maria: You can play, catch up to them.

Screen: The screen goes black again.

Controller: Maria hands the control over the Gina.

Screen: The picture returns, and is still in an industrial interior. Stach is at one edge of the screen. There is a short flight of stairs in front of him, and then a landing with a pattern of pipes on the floor.

Maria: The thing does look much, a lot like 'Deep Blue Sea'.

Maria: It's down there

Action: Maria: Maria points towards the screen.

Gina: What?

Maria: No. You gotta go up there

Gina: Do I?

Screen: Stach runs up the steps and onto the landing area.

Controller: Gina holds the control in her hands, as if to use it, and Maria reaches over her to press the buttons to run Stach across the screen.

Screen: A blue box appears in the screen, with some text: 'Jumbo: Yo! This is your first time in a reactor?', for a moment, then the box disappears.

Maria: Jumbo You This is your first time in a rea- rea- reactor?

Screen: A second box appears lower on the screen, with the text: 'Stach: No. After all, I did work for Shinra y'know'.

Maria: Stash No After all, I did work for Shinra y'know.

Gina: Shinra?

Action: Maria: Maria gets out a booklet and starts flipping through it, with her face oriented away from the screen and towards the book on the desk.

Maria: Yea.

Gina: Shinra

Action: Gina: Gina shifts round in her chair.

Note how different this is from the previous two extracts with pairs of boys. Neither of the girls knows how to play this game, though they have clearly played video games before as they know how to manipulate the controls and work their way through the game. They are both willing to say they don't know, which is uncommon with the boys in the club. It is here then that the 'practice, practice, practice' of the boys comes in. The complex investments, fantasies and relationalities entered into by these girls mean that their game playing is differently configured. While the same use of the body is made, this time by one girl actively taking control of the controller while the other watches, apparently unable to make the moves for herself, neither has a very clear grasp of the kinds of relations that the boys take for granted. As well as the link to the controller and the screen, the girls also use a manual (which we may remember one mother said her son would never use 'in a pink fit' because presumably it would mean admitting to 'not knowing'). This relation poses the question of just how novices come to be proficient players if they are not guided by a proficient player? If the proficient players, those who appear to be 'knowers', are mostly boys, the girls' participation within the web of relations, and thus their being assembled as competent players, will be, in Lave's sense, more peripheral (Lave and Wenger, 1991). The relationalities which allow the participation of these two girls are screen, controller, manual, some prior knowledge, trial and error. There is little intertextual reference but there is a reference to having chosen the wrong character as perhaps a way of explaining why the play is not going so well.

I will now go on to explore the play of a single player.

Sam

Sam has been playing Mario Kart by himself for some time. The researcher has been encouraging him to allow someone else to come and play with him, but Sam keeps insisting that he wants to practise, which by now we have understood as salient for masculinity. At one point Sam says that he doesn't like to lose. As he's been practising, his confidence seems to have grown, and he's more comfortable with the game. This excerpt is after the point where he agrees to play with someone else, but no one else is available to play, and is chosen as a section where he gives himself quite a lot of 'coaching' and instructions.

> **Screen**: Sam is playing a green, dragon-like character that he says is 'cute', and is racing round a snow-covered track about halfway through a race.
> **Talk: Sam**: Oh yer, I know what the cheat is. I know what the cheat is.
> **Screen: Sam**: Sam's kart shoots down a hill and overtakes several computer opponents, to bring himself into second place.
> **Talk: Sam**: This way. And, watch out for these guys. Let them get hit.
> **Screen: Sam**: Sam's kart approaches loads of little snowmen laid out over the track, and steers past them.
> **Screen: Sam**: Sam operates one of his weapons, and his kart is surrounded by three spinning turtle shells [*these act as a shield, and can hit and damage other karts*]
> **Talk: Sam**: Ye-e-es.
> **Screen: Sam**: A smoky projectile fires past Sam's kart, and hits the kart in front of him, and is able to overtake it. You can see that Peach [*a computer controlled character*] is just behind him.
> **Talk: Sam**: I need this one.
> **Screen: Sam**: Sam's kart veers to the side of the track, and Peach overtakes him. He's now second place in the race.
> **Talk: Sam**: Yes. I'm second.
> **Screen**: Sam shoots Peach, causing its kart to spin out of control, and overtakes it, bringing himself into first place. Toad [*another computer player, with a large toadstool-like head*] appears close behind him, and shoots smoky projectiles at him.
> **Talk**: I'm first.
> **Talk**: Yes, got the gill [??]. Sss.
> **Action**: Sam makes an air-punching gesture over his head, but has to make it very quick to get his hand back onto the controller.
> **Talk**: Oh man. Ohh.

Screen: Toad is still close behind, and trying to overtake Sam.

Screen: Sam rounds a bend in the road and drives over a coloured patch of road and approaches the finish line [*But it's still only lap one*]. Several opponents nearly catch up with him, and can be seen close behind.

Screen: A sign pops up saying 'second lap'.

Screen: Sam's kart continues round the track, followed closely by Peach and Toad.

Screen: They approach a row of crystals laid out along the track.

Screen: Sam's kart picks up a crystal, and is overtaken for a moment by Toad.

Screen: Sam's kart hits a single snowman, and spins up into the air in flames, then lands and bounces a couple of times, giving the computer players an opportunity to zoom past him.

Talk: Oh no!

Action: As Sam's kart flies up into the air, his whole body expresses his cry of dismay, jerking backwards and throwing his head slightly back.

Screen: The kart wobbles a bit as it gets up to speed, and he's now in third place.

Screen: Sam passes several more snowmen by the edge of the road.

Screen: Sam carries on round the track, avoiding a banana and picking up a crystal.

Screen: Only one of the two computer opponents ahead of him can be seen in the distance, a long way away.

Screen: Sam picks up another crystal from a row laid out across the track.

Talk: Now this is the cheat to the lady.

Screen: Sam hits a banana skin in the road, and spins for a while but doesn't seem to lose speed.

Talk: Yes

Screen: Sam overtakes Peach, and is now in second place.

Talk: See? That's, that's it.

Screen: Sam negotiates past a large number of snowmen scattered all over the track.

Talk: Cause I'm the first. Now the cheat is here.

Screen: Sam avoids several more snowmen, and rounds a bend.

Screen: Peach shoots him with a firey missile, and zooms past, so Sam's back in third place.

Talk: Nah well . . . I forgot where the cheat is.

Talk: But I'm gonna keep it to my mind.

I have included this extract because, firstly, Sam wants to practise before playing with other players. Secondly, however, even though Sam is alone he talks to himself as though there were another there encouraging him. This is fascinating because it suggests that one of the ways in which relationality becomes embodied as part of the self and then forgotten is that it is contained in the imagination of the player, thus apparently becoming understood as a part of the self (this is quite dialogic in the Bahktinian (1981) sense and in other ways, quite Vygotskian – this seems literally a precurser to inner speech: Vygotsky, 1978). This also relates directly to the issues raised by the work of Urwin (2001) in her reference to psychoanalysis in relation to an embodied relationality in which thinking can take place through the other's containment of anxiety, a position which can be then taken by the self – in talking to himself, Sam is supporting himself and we could see this as his attempt to take the position of his mother for himself and so contain his anxiety. If this were the case, inner speech would have a central affective component. Sam shows us literally what it means to practice, that is, to embody in fantasy within one body, the relations which have been on the outside in order to operate as a Cartesian subject who can display skills in future interactions with others. In that sense and in a way consonant with the zone of proximal development (Cole, 1996; Vygotsky, 1978), children do help each other to follow the game practices. However, this is not a straightforward matter. When one boy helps Prudence and Aisha to get beyond a stage of Crash Bandicoot, a Boneyard scenario in which they have been giggling at being chased by the dinosaur, the relation is one of a boy helping the helpless females. In doing so, he also takes away an aspect of their pleasure. In that sense then, relationalities are always already informed by the embodied relations and intertextualities which are profoundly gendered. As we have seen from the example of Gina and Maria above, it is apparently easier for girls to present themselves as not knowing than for boys to do so. Of course, this is hardly surprising, since the history of western thought has placed femininity on the side of nature, irrationality and unknowing, and has actively suppressed wisdom, intuition and other bewitching practices associated with the feminine. This is enacted in both the minutiae of these relations and within the wider intertextual relations in which participants are produced.

When Joe and Sam help each other in Banjo Kazooey, they enact a triumphant masculinity, as I explored in Chapter 3. That extract demonstrated how the relationalities which produce the players also link them to other relations of masculinity through their reference to the accoutrements of buddies together, with their constant invoking of high fives and so forth and in this case, masculine dominance. We might also remember from Chapter 4 that when four girls, Gina, Bronwyn, Melanie and Melissa, played Super Smash, the dynamic operated to produce an unspoken agreement not to kill Melanie's avatar. There was no attempt within the group to teach Melanie, who appeared not to be able to operate the controls well, but simply what appeared in action rather than speech as an agreement not to exclude her by killing her avatar. So, just as the boys Joe and Sam perform masculinity so the group of girls manages to have a competitive fighting game while protecting one of the group members against defeat. This could also be understood through the performativity of femininity lived in relation to a complex affective dynamic as I explored. Neither Lave's nor Cole's resolutely cognitive explanations, important as they are, engage with these issues and the way in which there is no one simple move from apprentice to competent member, that is not at the same time deeply contested, deeply inscribed with the binaries of power and containing that through embodied affective relations, through which difference (such as gender) is played out.

Parents, cheats and other learning devices

Another aspect of learning is the way in which learning is accomplished by aid of a number of non-human actants, as we have seen in many of the examples in this chapter. That is knowledge of how to play is contained in a variety of settings and sources: friendship networks, cheats on the Internet, magazines, manuals and parents or siblings, for example. If the controls, screen, game and player form an assemblage, these other actants often go unnoticed in producing the competent player. In Chapter 2 I explored the way in which the place of mothers as sources of knowledge and support were often disavowed by boys. We could perhaps establish an affective geography (Thrift, 2004) through which, in this case for example, the boy practises, meets a block that cannot be solved, and which punctures his sense of being the Cartesian author of himself. He looks to his mother, who attends to the dependent small child, which then while helping restore the fiction of the self authoring male, also punctures it and must be disavowed and distanced from. Conversely, learning from a magazine or another boy, may bring quite another sense, perhaps a membership of the group of competent players, with its fictions of cool competent masculinity.

We could say therefore that the competent player is a position, an assemblage, a figure, a fantasy, a who, which is lived and created through the flows of a number of discourses and practices. If we understand the competent player as an aspiration, we could also understand it as an always elusive fiction, lived through wish fulfilment, and the constant work of playing. Just as the hero in a Western has to be beaten many times to emerge as the hero, so the player must hone 'his' playing until the fiction of never being able to be beaten can be lived out with some semblance of veracity. This means that all of the myriad ways in which the competent player is embodied operate as a cultural and psychic fantasy through which the imagined position of competent player, or perhaps, winner, can be claimed. This fantasy is supported by the many relational networks and economies which depend upon that fantasy for their existence. We could say then that embodying this fantasy is absolutely central to practices from intersubjective relations to global multinational company profits. I would argue then that fiction and fantasy which create assemblages are absolutely central to what it means to learn to be a video game player and that these assemblages are the Cartesian fictions through which we see the person as foreground and ignore the backgrounded relations through which this fiction of autonomous selfhood is accomplished.

In the final chapter I will summarise my arguments and draw out some further issues towards a relational approach.

10
Conclusion

In the conclusion to the book, I want to bring together the arguments made throughout and to look beyond them towards an understanding of the place of video game play within a wider understanding of relationality. I will begin by summarising the arguments made within each of the preceding chapters.

Chapter 1 set out the scene for the book and placed it in the context of debates about ideology and economy and active and passive subjects. I argued that the traditional split between passive consumption and active makers of meaning is a false dichotomy.

Production and consumption and with them the identities of workers and consumers are both directly related to capitalism's need to produce a mass market through working on affect and at the same time having rational citizens who would accept the moral and political order. The idea that games appeal only to the rational and the active is simply to accept one side of the dichotomy that leaves ample room for effects. I argue for affective relations in a different way and for the necessity to understand game playing as a complex relational and interrelational accomplishment. I also argued for an understanding as game playing as embodied. One thing I want to remember is that both affect and cognition, rational and irrational are needed by liberal government and capitalism. I think this relation is what we find again and again in the elements which make up game play.

Chapter 2 dealt with video game research and examined the idea that we are not spectators as in film but experience games in an embodied way. It explored research which suggested that game playing requires being inside and outside the game at the same time – internal – the fantasy of being in a space and – external – the god-trick of controlling it which brings ego confirmation. I explored this in relation to the work of Mark

Hansen who uses Bergson's theory of affect to develop an idea of kinaesthetics – feeling your way around virtual space. While I found Hansen's
work enormously important, I felt that it did not go far enough because
it was not able to explain Ryan's two kinds of interaction. I felt that in
order to approach this we needed to bring in other approaches to the
centrality of sensation and affect and so I introduced the work of Wilhelm
Wundt who argued that affect was sensation plus ideation. I then took
up Freud's use of Wundt, which further divided affect into three parts –
sensation, ideation and unconscious fantasy. I argued that this three-fold
approach to affect was absolutely central to explaining how video game
play involved not only sensation and therefore the kinaesthetic, but also
fantasy.

Chapter 3 explored the central claim that many video games are one
site for the production of contemporary masculinity. In doing this, it
sought to go beyond Neale's analysis of the Hollywood Western by arguing
that the inside/outside dynamic, the kinaesthetic and the three-fold affect
make it enormously important as a site for producing fantasies of action
heroics, the cogito and the ego confirmation of the omnipotent god-trick.
The triumph of pleasure over pain and the sense of skill and control.
Players who simply fantasise a magical power but do not manage the
other two affective aspects, I suggest, have difficulty in becoming good
players. Several defences are necessary to make the assemblage of masculinity: a defence against femininity, against dependency – understood
as omnipotence – and the fantasy of control. The self-made hero and the
rational subject of the cogito come as a pair – the idea of the self made
through hard work and practice is both affective work and the achievement of the fantasy of masculinity and the denial of its impossibility.

Chapter 4 dealt with the complex positioning of girls with respect to
games. I argued that the self management practices of girls were different
from those of boys because the management of contemporary femininity
demands both femininity as support, caring, sensitivity, nurturance and
a masculinity as competition, rationality. This is what girls play out in
their game playing, taking complex and different positions in resolution to
the dilemmas set them. We saw several girls managing different positions from the abhorring of violence in interviews to spirited attempts to
kill while playing, we saw girls who wanted others to do their killing for
them and girls with poor levels of competence. I understood all this
through the complexities of self management and therefore the complexities of fantasies in the work of becoming woman, different from
those of man. This meant that work on girls and games was often mis-
directed and misunderstood as about content while failing to engage

with these central issues. I argued that Sue Austin's work on women's aggressive fantasies was helpful in thinking about woman as space and container which meant she couldn't take space for herself – the space to stand up and fight. This was often directed at self and disavowed in the space that makes masculinity possible.

Chapter 5 argued that current ways of thinking about violence with respect to children's video game play fail to engage with a set of issues about the management of masculinity and so tend to get polarised into claims that games cause violent effects or are purely positive – the active and passive dichotomy reworked. I suggested that issues around violence are much more complicated. Masculinity involves knowing when to act, fight, not act, not fight. This is a central plank of the management and regulation of contemporary masculinity. This issue about when to fight and the relation of games to violence was the site of some anxiety for all children in the study as revealed in interviews, and boys in particular tended to deal with this by the maintenance of an inside/outside dichotomy. That is, they argued that they could understand the difference between legitimate spaces for violence inside games and the illegitimate ones outside. However, the anxiety that they could become perpetrators of violence was displayed openly by some children and many were able to cite a clear cultural narrative about children killing and relate it to video games. Perhaps this was best expressed by the girl who was afraid that there was a violent person lurking inside her over which she had no control. Equally we could find anxiety amongst parents, who are cast through discourses and practices of socialisation, with the clear responsibility of producing normal children. Such anxiety about parental responsibility was dealt with by most parents by a number of regulative strategies. The idea that it is faulty parenting that is to blame for violence is a central narrative of liberalism, masculinity and the Cogito. A disavowal of violence is one way to manage anxiety. There is also a strong separation between action masculinity and a femininity which abhors violence and therefore is its other and the object of violence. This means that, for boys, to fear violence is to be sissy. Girls do act out killing in games, though it is never presented as unproblematic.

Chapter 6 discussed parental regulation. I argued that this was strongly gendered. For parents of boys, it walks a line between curbing aggression and allowing achievement, being outgoing and stopping clinginess. It is presented as a non-problem for girls, but in fact girls are strongly regulated against game playing, which has consequences for their competence level. The regulation concentrates on the middle-class production of educational pursuits as good for girls. This is explored in some detail with respect to the case study of one middle-class girl, Prudence. This revealed a complex organisation of regulative strategies in which oppositions between femininity and masculinity, educational merit and non educational play, loom large. It also demonstrated the complex ways in which relations between Prudence and her father and mother link into and are part of the complex affective relations which flow through and relate to video game play. That is, regulation operates through the interconnectedness of different sites and practices in which the unconscious, fantasy and imaginary processes are a key constituent, but not an essentialist causality as in standard liberal discourses about violence, addiction and parental socialisation.

Chapter 7 placed video game play within the global flows of multinational capitalism. I argued that, from the beginnings of mass production and consumption in 1920s USA, the processes of mass production and mass consumption brought together worker and consumer, with a central issue being how to produce desire for the goods on sale. With globalisation this has developed in a much more complex way in that I argued that it is fantasy – the fantasy of the figure of the player – which is mobilised as the central component in a vast and complex set of interrelations. In particular, I argued in Chapter 1, that a central component of the management of the American population in the age of mass manufacture and consumption, was both the production of a desire for goods and the containment of that desire inside a rationality that produced a well regulated active citizen. This gets refigured as a concern for activity and passivity in children's game play and can also be found in the idea that players are simultaneously within and outside the game, producing the fantasy of being in the game at the same time as the fantasy of controlling it. This dual form of acting out and controlling is, I would argue a central component of the regulation of the neoliberal citizen who must regulate themselves through choosing and self production. This hard act to achieve is related also to the work of masculinity, the sense of becoming an action hero, who can muster the skills to win. This fantasy is what circulates from the design of the game to the sweatshops of 'farmers' who play the games to sell points and therefore allow players to progress. We could see this as a development of service in which the gentleman is assembled through the hidden work of servants. Here, the fantasy of the player is lived out through the help of farmers, cheats and other devices. But the point of this is that this fantasy must be sustained not simply to create the player but to produce profit. The profit is what this whole complex of relations works to achieve. I therefore argued that oppositions between active and passive modes of engagement with popular culture completely miss the point. It is as though, by presenting the fiction of the active and creative subject, we evade our participation within cap-italist social relations and the production of profit. And in any event, what was understood in these accounts as passive, is also itself more akin to the idea of brain washing than the active unconscious of psycho-analysis, or the affectivity of Bergson or Deleuze.

Chapter 8 began to develop a way of thinking about the production or assembling of the figure of the game player and the activity of learning to play games. Looking back to the work of my earlier book, *The Mastery of Reason* (1988), I argued that this work already used an associationist method which was in some ways linked to the kinds of proposals made by Latour (2005) for an associative sociology. However, I argued that there is along tradition of associationist psychology which Latour seems unaware of, from behaviourism to psychoanalysis and that the kinds of issues he proposes have been the object of some considerable work in critical work in psychology for the last 30 years. In going back to *The Mastery of Reason*, I wanted to look at the way that mistakes made by children allowed us to see how the relations of a practice and relations between practices, worked. Lave and Cole work in a long tradition which has attempted to understand how thinking is accomplished in cultural practices in such a way that it cannot easily be seen. However, I suggested that Cole's assertion that we can only see the results of thinking, rather than thinking itself, might be an issue with respect to the singling out of thought as a separate object. Rather, indeed as Cole was suggesting perhaps, what we call thought itself is assembled, and so objects such as thinking and learning are pro-duced as part of the relations of playing. In this sense, I invoked the idea of the player as an assemblage and discussed how we might understand playing as a means for assembling the player, without imagining an object called learning in any simple sense. In order to understand this, we need to engage with how affectivity is mobilised to produce before our eyes the effect of seeing a player who appears to be the author and origin of their actions upon an object world. In this sense, we can understand playing as the simultaneous operation of a number of different relationalities, from the production of the fantasies of masculinity and the affective work that this involves, to the complexities of the relations between players, controllers, screens, avatars, etc. How does affectivity flow through the kinaesthetic relations both temporally and spatially to produce playing and players? The relations we witness when watching the children play also recall other moments, other relations, that are tied up in those which are present, both semiotically, kinaesthetically and affectively.

In Chapter 9 I took this further by illustrating the argument I was try-ing to develop with examples of game play. I explored the assembling of one player, Timothy, to understand that there was, in effect, not one simple Timothy, but many Timothys, produced differently in different relations. However, all of those Timothys were held together through history and biography and through the boundary of the skin (Anzieu, 1989). I showed how controllers, screens, avatars, all became actants in the process of assembly. In addition to this, I also looked at the ways in which the dual engagement with inside and outside the game, was managed by different children and how this was manipulated to produce social dominance within a group of players. I showed how the semiotics of masculinity was invoked and how the relations were differently worked between girls and boys. In the groups of players, I also demonstrated how affective relations were distributed within the group so that, for example, Melanie and her co-players entered into a tacit agreement for them not to kill her avatar, which meant that they held her fear of being killed for her and distributed it affectively through an unspoken but strongly present dynamic within the group. In that sense then, I argued that we cannot examine the processes of assembly without understanding the complex place of fantasy within it.

Throughout the book, I have argued for the centrality of affect to understanding a relational approach in which the assembling of players and the assembling of profit might be understood as part of a complex set of interrelationalities. While I have only begun to gesture towards this approach, I have sought to begin by bringing together my previous work using post-structuralism and psychoanalysis with work on affect, flows and associations. I have tried to demonstrate how we would need to develop this work to produce a relational account.[1] The work of developing this account is for my next book.

Finally, here I want to end by pointing to the centrality of issues around masculinity and femininity, which are underdeveloped in the affective turn. I have made a strong argument throughout the book that the relationalities I am working with are profoundly gendered. That is, it is the figure of the game player as male that sits at the heart of a multinational empire. I have argued how important the three-fold approach to affect is, to show just how complex are the processes through which masculinity is worked through as both a fantasised entry into virtual space while also controlling it from the outside. I have argued that such processes are central to the ways in which the work of masculinity endlessly circulates to keep both the Cogito and capitalism going. Thus, any account of relationality and how it works must engage with the fact that some relations are highlighted and others occluded, and that not all relations are understood within our contemporary present as being as important as others.

I want to argue that the various forms of domination, domination of nature by culture, of women by men, of colonial subjects by the coloniser, of labour by capital and so forth, of new forms of governance, certainly produce a new subject as the object of practices of population management as Foucault suggests. However, this does not simply replace one form of being with another, but produces a splitting. Csordas (1994) argues that 'the body has no existence of its own in the indigenous worldview and no name to distinguish it'. The consequences of objectification through colonial discourses and practices are what produce the figure of the colonial subject as an object. This is made possible by a mode of governance which depends upon the singling out of the singular subject. It is this practice which instantiates dualisms as objects of governance and science, be it mind/body, subject/object, psychic/social. I would argue that this splitting is part and parcel of the splittings made possible by the incorporation of the Cartesian project into practices of domination – scientific, colonial, capitalist, for example. This splitting assumes that there are two parts, not simply a replacement of something by something else. Something has been split off and that split off part is hidden, occluded. In Csordas' example of colonisation, what is split off is the ways of being which existed before colonisation. How do those remain? As pain, memory, ritual, hidden, subverted, suppressed? Capitalism hides the labour used to produce goods. Neoliberalism hides the sociality of the practices which produce subjectivities, as though we and we alone produced ourselves through rational choice as a form of hyperindividualism. So, in arguing for a relational approach to video games, I am wanting to bring to light the occluded practices through which the production of video games play is accomplished.

If meanings are made by producing specific affective relations within practices (Walkerdine, 1988), it is through the practices of those relations that cultural and subjective endlessly flow through each other. By this I mean that when, for example, we remember where we were when we heard the news that Princess Diana had been killed, there are a number of embodied sensations to which particular meanings become associated, which exist in a set of particular relations, but those are intersected by the cultural affectivities and meanings circulating in relation to the death. We make an embodied link between those two sites and kinds of meaning, which are not fixed but endlessly circulating. Ricoeur (2004) in particular thinks of memory in this way. Our life histories produce different experiences of the same event. In particular then this constant play of signification is also the site of fantasy, the way in which wishes endlessly circulate. In video games, as I have argued throughout the book, fantasies of action masculinity are endlessly circulated. I argue that it is through our embodied engagement with the practices in which meaning is produced that those fantasies work in relation both to their mass circulation and in the specific temporality of life histories. Thus, also we see players playing, but we miss the relations through which games playing are assembled. The relations flow into each other and are constantly in flux.

What if abstractionism of thought/language makes us miss them, but it backgrounds them when they should be foregrounded? It's not that they are absent but that they are disavowed. A standard part of developmental psychological theory is separation – the becoming singular of the subject. Critical and discursive psychologists have attempted to critique this by stressing the production of meaning through discourse, but we are still trapped within the rational, rather Cartesian subject which flows from this approach. Could we not shift our gaze? What if instead of looking for the discursive production of singularity we looked for the ways in which, as Lacan tells us, the autonomous rational subject is a fiction, but not because of simply the symbolic ties that bind him, but because of the dynamic relations that flow through the life world, which historically, western approaches have attempted to elide because the Robinson Crusoe singular rational subject was needed both for capitalism and for liberalism as well as the superiority of colonial power.

In addition to this, as many feminists have argued, it is the maternal which is usually presented as the guarantor of the separate subject of liberalism. That is, we have an account which offers a necessary primary connection of the infant to the mother and then a necessary separation. I argue that understanding relationality this way makes the maternal relations do the work of all relations and thus occludes a primary relationality as fundamental to thinking about the ways that the world works. As I have argued throughout the book, the player is a figure and a fantasy. This fantasy is sustained by the occluded work of others – from mothers to sweatshop workers. It is the figure of the mother who, as Austin says, has to be space and in being space, woman cannot have space for herself. If it is mothering that has to hold both connection and separation, of course women are put in an impossible position themselves, always caught between trying to be separate and needing to hold connection, as has been obvious in the analysis of girls' game playing. However, I am not proposing a relational account which begins with the mother–infant relation for precisely this reason. Starting there and seeing this as the connection of connections, serves to obscure the problematic place in which this relation is located historically and culturally. It is in understanding how the separate subject is itself assembled that we might be able to look at the maternal connection in a different light. I suggest that this is a way forward for thinking through the issues that arise around masculinity and femininity with respect to video games. It is not simply that women need to become separate subjects as, for example, Braidotti (1991) argues, but that it is the creation of the fiction of separateness and the continual circulation of its sustenance within the social world, which is a problem.

Braidotti argues that by making woman synonymous with unrepresentability that is the precondition for logocentric thinking instantiates woman as the transcendental desexualised bodiless origin of logocentrism, the non truth of truth. This is done by a long tradition of male academics (Braidotti discusses Derrida in particular, but we might also add Freud and Lacan as well as many others) who put themselves as masters of that truth, while fixing the truth of woman and denying her the right to speak of her relation to this truth. This re-establishes their mastery and her silence in continuity with a long standing masculine tradition (Braidotti, 1991). Derrida (1985) in fact appears to glorify the mother, making her responsible for the living mother tongue as against the dead paternal language – the latter being the whole philosophical tradition of argument. It isn't that Derrida leaves woman out but that he in Sue Austin's (2005) terms only allows her to be space, to be that which makes subjectivity possible and that in addition which guards against the dead paternal language but only for him, for masculinity. Secomb (1995) adds that at many moments in the dominant philosophical traditions woman is not so much exploited or excluded but is central to, end entombed or imprisoned within, the philosophical story. That is, I think that woman is made to hold so much that there is no space for her and nobody actually takes seriously the lessons to be learnt from addressing relationality. Irigaray (1985) says that the woman's status as an envelope for the masculine subject is inseparable from the work or act of man, notably in so far as he defines her and creates his own identity through her, through this determination of her being. But he denies her an existence because he subverts and destroys her.

I think we do have to look to how the maternal is used as a guarantor of the logos within western thinking. I have argued elsewhere that maternal work is turned into play in order to hold the responsibility for the production of a rational liberal and autonomous subject. Is woman then the connection which makes separation possible? This is certainly how she is viewed within almost all developmental psychology. In order to be a separate autonomous subject, the child must first be fully connected and bonded and must gradually separate to become autonomous. I think the idea of the mother entombed is precisely that this is where woman is stuck. Because she is connection she is necessary, but because she holds connection she can never be truly separate – never secure the Logos, but worse, if the story of connection and relation becomes a developmental story, which places its origin with the mother, she has to somehow hold all the connections inherent in the life world as well as the repudiation of them! Judith Butler (2004) reminds us of the 'ontological primacy of relationality' (p. 150), arguing that:

> 'we' who are relational do not stand apart from those relations and cannot think of ourselves outside of the decentering effects that rela-tionality entails. Moreover, when we consider that the relations by which we are defined are not dyadic, but always refer to a historical legacy and futural horizon that is not contained by the Other, but which constitutes something like the Other of the Other, then it seems to follow that who we 'are' fundamentally is a subject in a tem-poral chain of desire that only occasionally and provisionally assumes the form of the dyad. I want to reiterate that displacing the binary model for thinking about relationality will also help us appreciate the triangulating echoes in heterosexual, homosexual and bisexual desire, and complicate our understanding of the relation between sexuality and gender. (p. 151).

So Butler is emphasising relationaity as primary but recognises that in any simple sense the dyadic maternal or indeed couple relation can never be understood as holding relationality – that there are always others, even though this quote seems to privilege an originary moment, which I am arguing against. This is an important corrective to any work which assumes that we are simply talking about a re-evaluation of the mother and connectivity. What I am talking about is the disavowal of relationality. A relationality which is associated with the maternal relation and whose denigration is at the heart of the central component of Robinson Crusoe separateness which is at the heart of what Couze Venn (2002) calls Occidentalism. I want to emphasise that the maternal relation is only one aspect, not *the* aspect, of the disavowal of relationality. The maternal relation simply gives us a way of thinking about ontology as the gradual production of separation as a developmental accomplishment. This developmental story begins with the mother, but if relations are every-where, this story is also part of much larger stories and greater disavowals in which the world is seen to work through the actions of thought upon it, through the thought of singular actors who construct the world in the form of that thought. It is this act which places the mother as central and then denigrates her, and it is this act which disavows the relationalities which make the world work and which Occidentalism refuses to see. I argue that relationality has been radically backgrounded so that we are led to deny its existence, but this denial is a defence against the recognition that it in fact is everywhere, but demands that we look differently. I think this has profound implications for a kind of work which could go on, and which is beginning to emerge. My own attempt to work towards a relational account has, I am sure, many problems and inconsistencies. I have been aware throughout the writing that attempting to work in a different way, is continually challenged by a tendency to keep returning to given ideas. However, I hope that, inconsistent as it no doubt is, it may help pave the way for further developments in relational ways of working.

Foucault (1986b) argued that the masculine subject is the one who is dependent on nothing. This subject only gains status by obliterating relationality and remaking the world in his vision of separation, while at once making the maternal hold all connections. But capitalism depends upon workers, colonialism depends on the colonised, children depend upon mothers, men depend upon women and so forth. A long history of disavowals creates our world of singularities. I argue that when we understand how this works, the chimera that constructs the disavowed and separated objects of the life world falls away.

Notes

1 Introduction

1 It is worth noting that activity is also a category which is taken to describe masculinity. Men and boys have to act, as we shall see in Chapter 2. The danger of passivity, we might suggest, is also a danger of femininity, of not being man enough to resist.

2 Video Game Research

1 We might also point out that within psychoanalysis, there is a difference between an object world and so-called internal objects. These are objects which gain a particular place within the unconscious and are not the same as those objects in our conscious everyday world. For example, an object or person that assumes particular significance in the unconscious may be something from a different time at which something got fixed within a painful affect. Moreover, those objects can act within the unconscious. Within a Kleinian approach, projected and introjected objects can act upon the subject. It is this which gave rise to a stress on relationality within psychoanalysis and the development of approaches based on object relations. I do not explore the link between internal and external objects in this book, but suggest that it would be an important and fruitful line of analysis to take this work further, because it would add a further important layer to the mode of analysis, which would specify that relationalities must be understood as being much more complex than might be thought simply from studying social relations.

3 Video Games and Childhood Masculinity

1 We could speculate that this move from heroics as a spectatorial activity as in film and television to the necessity for the hero to be an embodied physical activity relates specifically to the decline in male manual work within the global North.

4 'Remember Not to Die': Girls Playing Video Games

1 I am aware that one of the constraints of this research is that girls do not play by themselves and are also being surveilled by the researchers while playing. This means that we do not have any sense of whether they play in the same way on their own in private. It is has been suggested to me on several occasions that perhaps some girls are more openly aggressive and more desirous of winning when they can practise alone, which would allow another fantasy to emerge. While we cannot know about this, it is certainly a possibility which

we can access in a complex way in other parts of the data. For example, in interviews with girls, they claim lack of interest in practising, but in interviews with most parents there is a noticeable management of girls' playing by refusing to let them practise anything but 'educational games'. This means that in fact these girls do not get the opportunity to practise to win in anything but that which is sanctioned as suitable for education. I read this as an anxiety about over-masculinisation on the part of parents as well, of course, as a desire for their daughters to succeed at school.

2   There is an interesting difference between those girls who would rather choose her for her 'to be looked-at-ness' and those who like being active. We could specify this in terms of the anxiety about femininity, which would preclude too much movement onto the side of masculinity. However, it is beyond the scope of this chapter to discuss this in any detail.

3   I am also reminded here that in, the film *Tomb Raider*, Lara Croft does the heroics but the men are rendered mainly as incompetent buffoons. It is this counterpoint which allows her heroics to dominate, so that we are offered a different version of masculinity to the standard heroic model. I wonder therefore whether female bravery cannot be shown to exist alongside masculine heroics? However, as Helen Kennedy (2002) argues Lara Croft is shown as the equivalent of an avatar controlled by a man, as she is seen as acting out the will of her father and not the agent or originator of her own actions at all.

4   Though of course, as we know, both Kristeva and Clover are talking about masculinity and the mother. The consideration of how girls and women might like violence is a different matter, see Muriel Dimen (2004).

5   We can think of her reference to an inner topos as energetically and affectively linked to an outer topos through which affectivities are carried and circulate both within and through bodies and the social realm.

6   Freud first begins to talk about energy in his early work. In an appendix to Vol. 3 of the Standard Edition, the editor gives a section on the emergence of Freud's fundamental hypotheses (62–68). He argues that Freud first came up with the idea of a neuro-psychology of psychic functioning. The idea of defence was based on a more basic idea, stated in the Lecture in SE 2, 38 which is what became known as the theory of cathexis. This means occupation or filling – something that fills the gap or space.

> There is perhaps no other passage in Freud's published writings in which he so explicitly recognises the necessity for this most fundamental of all his hypotheses: 'that in mental functions something is to be distinguished – a quota of affect or sum of excitation – which possesses all the characteristics of a quantity . . . which is capable of increase, diminution and discharge. . . . '
> The notion of a 'displaceable quantity' had, of course, been implicit in all his earlier theoretical discussions. As he himself points out in this same passage, it underlay the theory of abreaction; it was the necessary basis of the principle of constancy . . . ; it was implied whenever Freud made use of such phrases as 'loaded with a sum of excitation' (p. 48 above), 'provided with a quota of affect' (1893c), 'supplied with energy' (1895b) – predecessors of what was soon to become the standard term 'cathected'.
> In early work he spoke of 'displacements of excitability in the nervous system'.

At first Freud thought of these cathectic excitations as material events – the nervous system had recently been discovered as chains of neurones, so he literally saw cathexes as chains of neurone links through the general laws of motion, coming to the basic idea of a cathected neurone filled with a certain quantity and at other times empty. He thought it would be possible to state psychology in neurological terms, as became common, but he later abandoned this idea and applied his concepts to purely mental phenomena. So cathexis came to have an entirely non-physical meaning in Freud's later writings. So he in fact comes up with an idea of psychical rather than neurological energy as in bound and free cathectic energies. He uses cathexis as an analogy 'between psychical operations and the working of a nervous apparatus conceived in terms of energy' (Laplanche and Pontalis, 1980, 63). This relates to things like the idea of introjection where it is assumed that a certain amount of psychical energy is used when moving from an actual object to an intrapsychical object. So what we have here is relation between external objects and objects created in the psyche so to speak. This can relate to external objects, e.g. in a phobia or a fetish, in which the object is in each case, though differently, injected with a huge force or psychic load. This can be related to how relations flow through objects, places, people, etc.

Unpleasure is a rise in the level of affective energy which is then later discharged. This gives us pleasure and is a sensation of discharge.

Freud also thought that energy had a quota of affect – the psychological representative of an energy or drive has two parts – the affect as the translation of the energetic drive and the idea or group of ideas cathecting it. In other words cathecting an idea takes a load of psychical energy or affect.

Laplanche and Pontalis say that aggressive energies can therefore be understood through a sense of a driven psychic energy (or death drive) which breaks up the unities of the life force or libido. In shattering the life force, aggressive energies are directed against the self in guilt, for example. In Austin's sense then, we can understand that the force of such a self-directed psychic charge serves to block a sense of aliveness. While women are spending all their time holding the space of the nurturant other, this turns their life energies in on themselves, through feelings associated with not being nurturant enough. This effectively affectively blocks the possibility of using this psychic energy for her own life, which has to be subsumed to other-directedness. In doing this, she creates the space for the other to express a life force, which she can only channel.

5 Rethinking Violence

1 See, for example, Freud's (1930) *Civilisation and its Discontents*, Standard Edition, XXI.
2 I deal with the issue of aggressive fantasies and energies raised in relation to the work of Sue Austin in the last chapter, and more generally with what Freud meant by energy and aggressivity in note 6 of Chapter 4. I would argue, following work on vitalism in sociology (*see* Fraser, Kember and Lury, *Inventive Life: approaches to the new vitalism*, 2005) that aggressive energies are not the same as positing a psychobiological predisposition to aggression, but this is a complex topic and deserves some unpicking of its own.

3 Although the avatar Kirby is not specified as male or female, it is a firm favourite with some girls, who do seem to treat it as feminine.

8 Becoming a Player

1 Burman (1994) criticised my desire to go beyond developmentalism (Walkerdine, 1993), arguing that developmentalism was absolutely prevalent in many areas of the world to describe and define children in a variety of surveillant and regulative practices. While that is absolutely correct, we can understand the effectivity of developmentalist discourses and practices as one aspect of the complex network of relationships that I have attempted to set out in the last chapter and therefore a forgetting of the imperialism which creates these children as an object of Western regimes of power/knowledge and modes of regulation.

9 Playing the Game

1 In all psychoanalytic theories, it is the position of the mother as powerful in the life of the child (but to be controlled, put down, denigrated, by an attempt to control that being who controls you, to be free, to dominate), which is at the heart of psychoanalytic accounts of masculinity. In other words, the defended against pain is constituted in bodily feelings, and later relations through which the affective is carried. 'Timothy' may need to express dominance because he may feel an embodied anxiety which he does not understand and cannot control, if he is dominated. His action to bid for dominance, in this account could be understood as defending against an anxiety or a pain he cannot bear. This anxiety and pain is then built into the social practices of masculinity, for example, which themselves are constituted defensively. For Lacan, for example, this defensiveness is embodied in the symbolic systems which he calls the Law and in language. But it is also felt in the body, possibly as feelings we cannot bear or do not want to feel. We can place this both in history in terms of the defences which have to be marshalled to come down on the side of masculinity in any one place and at any one moment, but we can also locate the production of the unconscious, the unbearable feelings which cannot be spoken, within the experience of children and the intimate practices and relations of the domestic, family life.

2 I want to stress that I am not talking about the interior per se. There has been much written on the historical emergence of the idea of interiority (e.g. Steedman, 1995). However, this assumes that historically there was previously only an exterior. I do not believe that this is correct. The issue is not that there was no interior but that the interior/exterior was configured quite differently. For example, people who believed in a spirit world placed many of the aspects we would now call interior in the shadowy forces that were in a liminal place. Freud placed them elsewhere. Christianity placed them in sin. Australian Aboriginals traditionally understood themselves as indistinct from the landscape through which they walked, which they narrated into being, through the stories they told and sang and painted about it. They produced it and in doing so it produced their being within it. There is no absence of interiority – it

is simply differently understood and configured. The issue comes with the separation of the two realms, an explanatory interiority which, in Csordas' (2002) terms describes an individual body as an object. In this sense, it is deeply caught up in power and dominance and becomes the province of a psychology with a distinct sense of the personal as explanatory and an equally separate social realm explained by sociology. It is this splitting, which we could term the historical production of a binary, which creates the opposition which I am at pains to dismantle. It is *not* solved by placing everything within the exterior, social, sociology. The aim is to dismantle the binary and to demonstrate the necessity of rethinking exteriority/interiority as part of a complex explanation of how sociality and subjectivity works.

10   Conclusion

1   An approach to relationality as applied to subjectivity is begun in Walkerdine (2006).

References

Adorno, T. W. and D. J. Levinson (1950) *The Authoritarian Personality*, New York, Harper & Brothers.

Althusser, L. (1977) *'Lenin and Philosophy' and Other Essays*, London, New Left Books.

Ansell Pearson, K. and Mullarkey, J. (2002) *Bergson: key writings*, London, Continuuum.

Anzieu, Didier (1989) *The Skin Ego*, trans. Chris Turner. New Haven, Yale University Press.

Arendt, Hannah (1998) *The Human Condition*, Chicago, University of Chicago Press.

Austin, A. (2005) *Women's Aggressive Fantasies: a post-Jungian exploration of self-hatred, love and agency*, London, Routledge.

Bakhtin, M. (1981) *The Dialogic Imagination*, Austin, University of Texas Press.

Baudrillard, J. (1998) *Selected Writings*, ed. Mark Poster. Palo Alto, Stanford University Press.

Bergson, H. (1911) *Matter and Memory*, London, Allen and Unwin.

Bernays, Edward L. (1961) *Crystallizing Public Opinion*, New York, Liveright.

Billig, M. (1999) *Freudian Repression: conversation creating the unconscious*, Cambridge, Cambridge University Press.

Billig, M. (1999b) 'Whose terms? Whose ordinariness? Rhetoric and ordinariness in conversation analysis', *Discourse & Society*, 10: 543–58.

Blackman, L. (n.d.) 'How do the many act as one? Suggestibility and the problem of contagion'.

Blackman, L. and Walkerdine, V. (2001) *Mass Hysteria: critical psychology and media studies*, Basingstoke, Palgrave – now Palgrave Macmillan.

Blanton, W., Greene, M. and Cole, M. (1999) 'Computer mediation for learning and play', *Journal of Adolescent & Adult Literacy*, 43(3): 272–8.

Bolter, J. D. and Grusin, R. (1999) *Remediation: understanding new media*, Cambridge, MA, MIT Press.

Bortoft, H. (1996) *The Wholeness of Nature: Goethe's way of science*, Edinburgh, Floris.

Bourdieu, P. (1991) *Language and Symbolic Power*, Cambridge, Polity.

Braidotti, R. (1991) *Patterns of Dissonance*, Cambridge, Polity.

Braverman, H. (1974) *Labor and Monopoly Capital: the degradation of work in the twentieth century*, New York, Monthly Review Press.

Brennan, T. (2004) *The Transmission of Affect*, Ithaca NY, Cornell University Press.

Buckingham, D. (2000) *After the Death of Childhood: growing up in the age of electronic media*, Cambridge, Polity.

Burman, E. (1994) *Deconstructing Developmental Psychology*, London, Routledge.

Butler, J. (1990) *Gender Trouble: feminism and the subversion of identity*, New York, Routledge.

Butler, J. (1997) *The Psychic Life of Power: theories in subjection*, Stanford, Stanford University Press.

Butler, J. (2004) *Undoing Gender*, New York, Routledge.

Cassell, J. and Jenkins, H. (1998) *From Barbie to Mortal Kombat*, Cambridge, MA, MIT Press.

Clark, N. (2005) 'Ex-orbitant globality', *Theory Culture Society*, 22(October): 165–85.
Clifford, J. and Marcus, G. (eds) (1986) *Writing Culture: the poetics and politics of ethnography*, Berkeley, University of California Press.
Clover, C. (1992) *Men, Women and Chainsaws*, London, British Film Institute.
Cole, M. (1996) *Cultural Psychology: a once and future discipline*, Cambridge, MA, Harvard University Press.
Cole, M. (1999) 'Culture-free versus culture-based measures of cognition', in R. J. Sternberg (ed.), *The nature of cognition*, Cambridge, MA, MIT Press. pp. (645–64).
Cole, M. and Scribner, S. (1973) *Culture and Thought: a psychological introduction*, New York, Wiley.
Cole, M. and Traupmann, K. (1981) 'Comparative cognitive research: learning from a learning disabled child', in W. A. Collins (ed.) *Aspects of the Development of Competence: the Minnesota symposium on child psychology*, Vol. 14, Hillsdale, NJ, Erlbaum, pp. 125–53.
Cooper, J. M. (ed.) (1997) *Plato: complete works*, Indianapolis, IN, Hackett Publishing Co.
Cowie, E. (1997) *Representing the Woman: psychoanalysis and cinema*, London, Macmillan.
Csordas, T. J. (1994) *Embodiment and Experience: the existential ground of culture and self*, Cambridge, Cambridge University Press.
Csordas, T. J. (2002) *Body/Meaning/Healing*, New York, Palgrave – now Palgrave Macmillan.
Curtis, A. (2002) *The Century of the Self*, BBC Television.
Damasio A. R. (1999) *The Feeling of What Happens: body and emotion in the making of consciousness*, New York, Harcourt Brace.
Deleuze, G. (1992) *Difference and Repetition*, New York, Columbia University Press.
Deleuze, G. and Guattari, F. (1977) *Anti-Oedipus: capitalism and schizophrenia*, New York, Viking Press.
Deleuze, G. and Guattari, F. (1987) *A Thousand Plateaus*, Minneapolis, University of Minnesota Press.
Derrida, Jacques (1981) *Positions* (trans. Alan Bass), London, Athlone Press.
Derrida, Jacques (1985) *The Ear of the Other: otobiography, transference, translation: texts and discussions with Jacques Derrida*, Christie V. McDonald (ed.), Peggy Kamuf (tr.) New York: Schocken Books.
Descartes, R. (1984), 'Meditations on first philosophy', in *The Philosophical Writings of Descartes*, Vol. II, ed. John Cottingham, Robor Stoothoff, and Dugald Murdoch, Cambridge, Cambridge University Press.
Dimen, M. (2004) *Sex, Feminism, Psychoanalytic Feminism: from political correctness to irony, pleasure and danger revisited*, Conference 'Pleasure and Danger Revisited', Cardiff University.
Donaldson, M. (1978) *Children's Minds*, London, Fontana.
Elliot, A. and Spezzano, C. (1999) *Psychoanalysis at its Limits: navigating the post-modern turn*, London, Free Association Press.
Facer, K., Furlong, J., Furlong, R. and Sutherland, R. (2001) 'Constructing the child computer user: from public policy to private practices', *British Journal of Sociology of Education*, Routledge, 22(1).
Foucault, M. (1973) *Madness and Civilization: a history of insanity in the age of reason*, New York, Random House.
Foucault, M. (1977) *Discipline and Punish*, Harmondsworth, Penguin.

Foucault, M. (1981) *The History of Sexuality Vol. 1, An Introduction*, trans R. Hurley, Harmondsworth, Penguin.

Foucault, M. (1985) *The History of Sexuality, Vol. 2, The Use of Pleasure*, trans R. Hurley, Harmondsworth, Penguin.

Foucault, M. (1986) *History of Sexuality, Volume 3, The Care of the Self*, New York, Pantheon.

Foucault, M. (1986b) in P. Rabinow (ed.) *The Foucault Reader*, London: Penguin.

Foucault, M. (1989) *Archaeology of Knowledge*, trans. A. M. Sheridan Smith, London, Routledge.

Fraser, M., Kember, S. and Lury, C. (2005) 'Inventive life: approaches to the new vitalism', *Theory Culture and Society*, 22(1): 15–27.

Frayn, D. H. (1998) 'Unconscious communication and its relational manifestations in the analytic process', *Canadian Journal of Psychoanalysis*.

Freud, S. (1922) *Group Psychology and the Analysis of the Ego*, International Psychoanalytical Library Institute of Psychoanalysis, trans J. Strachey.

Freud, S. (1928), *The Future of an Illusion*, Standard Edition', 21: 1–56. London, Hogarth Press.

Fromme, J. (2003) 'Computer games as part of children's culture', *Game Studies*, 3(1).

Gauntlett, D. (1998), 'Ten things wrong with the "effects model" ', in R. Dickinson, R. Harindranath and O. Linne, (eds), *Approaches to Audiences*, London, Arnold.

Gee, J. P. (2003), *What Video Games Have to Teach Us About Learning and Literacy*, New York, Palgrave MacMillan.

Gee, J. P., Hull, G. and Lankshear, C. (1996) *The New Work Order: behind the language of the new capitalism*, Boulder, CO, Westview.

Geertz, C. (1993) *Local Knowledge: further essays in interpretive anthropology*, London, Fontana Press.

Geraghty, C. (1991) *Women and Soap Opera: a study of prime time soaps*, Cambridge, UK: Polity.

Gill, R. (2006) 'Rewriting the romance: Chick Lit and postfeminism', ESRC New Femininities Seminar, Open University, Milton Keynes, April 2006, 10–16.

Gorz, A. (1982) *Farewell to the Working Class*, Boston, South End Press.

Hall, S. and Jefferson T. (eds.) (1976) *Resistance Through Rituals: youth subcultures in post-war Britain*, London, Hutchinson.

Hansen, M. (2004) *New Philosophy for New Media*, Cambridge, MA/London, MIT Press.

Haraway, D. (1991) *Simians, Cyborgs, and Women*, London, Free Association Books.

Haraway, D. (1992) *The Promises of Monsters: a regenerative politics for inappropriate/d others*, in Lawrence Grossberg, Cary Nelson and Paula Treichler (eds), *Cultural Studies*, New York: Routledge, pp. 295–329.

Haraway, D. (1997) *Modest Witness@secondmillennium, Female Man meets Oncomouse: feminism and technoscience*, New York, Routledge.

Hardt, M. and Negri, A. (2000) *Empire*, Cambridge, MA, Harvard University Press.

Hayles, N. K. (1999) *How We Became Posthuman: virtual bodies in cybernetics, literature, and informatics*, Chicago, University of Chicago Press.

Henriques, J., Hollway, W., Urwin, C. and Walkerdine, V. (1984) *Changing the Subject: psychology, social regulation and subjectivity*, London, Methuen.

Himmelweit, H. T., Oppenheim, A. N. and Vince, P. (1958) *Television and the Child*, Oxford, Oxford University Press.

Hollway, W. (1984) 'Gender difference and the production of subjectivity', in J. Henriques, W. Hollway, C. Urwin, C. Venn, and V. Walkerdine, *Changing the Subject: psychology, social regulation and subjectivity*, London, Methuen.

Hollway, W. and Jefferson, T. (2002) *Doing Qualitative Research Differently*, London, Sage.

Horkheimer, M. and Adorno, T. W. (1972) *Dialectic of Enlightenment*, New York, Herder and Herder.

Irigaray, L. (1985) *This Sex Which Is Not One*, trans. Catherine Porter. Ithaca, Cornell University Press.

Irigaray, L. (1991) 'Bodily encounters with the mother', in M. Whitford (ed.) *The Irigaray Reader*, Oxford, Blackwell.

James, A. and Prout, A. (eds) (1990) '*Constructing and Reconstructing Childhood: contemporary issues in the sociological study of childhood*, Basingstoke, Falmer Press.

Jeffors, S. (1993) *Hard Bodies: Hollywood masculinities in the Reagan era*, New Brunswick, NJ, Rutgers.

Jenkins, H. (1998) ' "Complete freedom of movement" ': video games as gendered play spaces', in J. Cassell, and H. Jenkins, (eds) *From Barbie to Mortal Kombat: gender and computer games*, Cambridge, MA, MIT Press.

Jenkins, H. (2004) 'The War Between Effects and Meaning: rethinking video game violence', *Independent Schools*, Spring.

Jones, G. (2002) *Killing Monsters: why children need fantasy, super heroes, and make-believe violence*, New York, Basic Books.

Kennedy, H. (2002) 'Lara Croft, feminist icon or cyberbimbo? On the limits of textual analysis', *Game Studies*, 2(2).

King, G. and Kryzywinska, T. (eds) (2002) *Screen Play: cinema/videogames/interfaces*, London, Wallflower.

Kristeva, J. (1982) *The Powers of Horror*, New York, Columbia University Press.

Lacan, J. (1977) *Écrits: a selection*, London, Routledge.

Lahti, M. (2003) 'As We Become Machines: corporealized pleasures in video games', in M. Wolf and Bernard Perron (eds) *The Video Game Theory Reader*, New York, Routledge.

Laplanche, J. and Pontalis, J-B. (1980) *The Language of Psycho-Analysis*, London, Hogarth Press and the Institute of Psycho-analysis.

Latour, B. (2005) *Reassembling the Social: an introduction to actor-network-theory*, Oxford, Oxford University Press.

Lave, J. (1988) *Cognition in Practice: mind, mathematics and culture in everyday life*, Cambridge: Cambridge University Press.

Lave, J. and Wenger, E. (1991) *Situated Learning. Legitimate peripheral participation*, Cambridge, University of Cambridge Press.

Le Bon, G. (1897) *The Crowd: a study of the popular mind*, London, T. Fisher Unwin.

Manovich, L. (2001) *The Language of New Media*, Cambridge, MA, MIT Press.

McDougall, W. (1926) *An Introduction to Social Psychology*, Boston, John W. Luce and Co.

Mitrani, J. (1993) ' "Unmentalized" experience in the etiology and treatment of psychosomatic asthma', *Contemporary Psychoanalysis*, 29 (2) 314–42.

Morley, D. (1986) *Family Television: cultural power and domestic leisure*, London, Comedia.

Mulvey, L. (1974) *Visual Pleasure and Narrative Cinema Film Theory and Criticism: an introduction*, Gerald Mast, comp. New York, Oxford University Press.

Neale, S. (1983) 'Masculinity as Spectacle: reflections on men and mainstream cinema', *Screen 24* (6): 2–16.

Newman, J. (2002) 'What it feels to be in the Tomb Raider or Vib Ribbon gameworld is, however, of paramount importance', *International Journal of Computer Game Research*, 2(1).

Oliver, M. and Pelletier, C. (2005) "Activity theory and learning from digital games: implications for game design", in *Proceedings of Digital Generations: children, young people and new media*, London, www.gamesconference.org/digra2005/papers

Piaget, J. (1947) *The Psychology of Intelligence*, London, Routledge.

Piaget, J. (1972) *The Psychology of the Child*, New York, Basic Books.

Plato (1977) *Complete Works*, ed. J.M. Copper, Indianapolis, Hackett.

Potter, J. (1996) 'Discourse analysis and constructionist approaches: theoretical background', in J.T.E. Richardson (ed.) *Handbook of Qualitative Research Methods for Psychology and the Social Sciences*, New York, Wiley.

Potter, J. and Wetherell, M. (1987) *Discourse and Social Psychology: beyond attitudes and behaviour*, London, Sage.

Radway, J. (1984) *Reading the Romance: women, patriarchy and popular literature*, University of North Carolina Press.

Rehak, B. (2003) 'Playing at Being: psychoanalysis and the avatar', in M. Wolf and B. Perron (eds), *The Video Game Theory Reader*, New York and London, Routledge, pp. 25–46.

Ricoeur, P. (2004) *Memory, history*, trans. Kathleen Blamey and David Pellauer, Chicago, University of Chicago Press.

Ringrose, J. (2006) 'A new universal mean girl: examining the discursive construction and social regulation of a new feminine pathology', *Feminism and Psychology*, 16(4): 405–24.

Riviere, J. (1929/1986) 'Womanliness as masquerade', 35–44 in *Formations of Fantasy*, ed. V. Burgin, J. Donald, and C. Kaplan, London, Methuen.

Roberts, D. F. and Henry, J. (1999) 'Kids and Media @ the new Millennium', Kaiser Family Foundation Report, Diane Publishing, Stanford University.

Rose, J. (1983) 'Femininity and its discontents', *Feminist Review*, 14, 78–91.

Rose, N. (1999) *Governing the Soul: the shaping of the private self*, (2nd edn), London, Free Association Books.

Rotman, B. (n.d.) 'Mathematics: an essay in semiotics', University of Bristol mimeo.

Rotman, B. (1988), 'Towards a semiotics of mathematics', *Semiotica*, 72(1/2): 1–35.

Ryan, M. L. (2001) *Narrative as Virtual Reality: immersion and interactivity in literature and electronic media*, Baltimore and London, Johns Hopkins University Press.

Scribner, S. and Cole, M. (1973) *The Psychology of Literacy*, Cambridge, MA: Harvard University Press.

Secomb, L. (1995) 'The entombments of feminine being', *Australian Feminist Studies*, 21.

Shotter, J. (1993) *Conversational Realities: constructing life through language*, London, Sage.

Stainton Rogers, W. (2003), *Social Psychology: experimental and critical approaches*, London, Open University Press.

Steedman, C. (1995) *Strange Dislocations: childhood and the idea of human interiority, 1780–1930*, Cambridge, MA, Harvard University Press.

Stephenson, N. and Papadopoulos, D. (2006). *Analysing Everyday Experience. Social research and political change*, Basing stoke, Palgrave Macmillan.

Stopford, A. (2005) 'Psycho-social research', *International Journal of Critical Psychology*, 10.

Studdert, D. (2005) *Conceptualising Community: beyond the state and individual*, Basingstoke, Palgrave Macmillan.

Thompson, E. P. (1968) *The Making of the English Working Class*, London, Penguin.

Thompson, T. (2005) 'In Caracal, Romania', *Observer* Sunday 13 March.

Thrift, N. (2004), 'Intensities of feeling: towards a spatial politics of affect', *Geografiska Annaler* Series B, 86: 57–78.

Tulloch, J. and Jenkins, H. (1995) *Science Fiction Audiences: watching Doctor Who and Star Trek*, London and New York, Routledge.

Tulving, E. and Donaldson, W. (1972). *The Seductions of Materialism and the Pleasures of Dualism . . . Organization of Memory*, New York, Academic Press.

Urry, J. (2003) *Global Complexity*, Cambridge, Polity.

Urwin, C. (1989) 'Wonderpeople: children's use of superheroes in child psychotherapy', paper presented at Birmingham University, October 1989.

Urwin, C. (1995) 'Turtle power: illusion and imagination in children's play', in C. Bazalgette and D. Buckingham, (eds) *In Front of the Children: screen entertainment and young audiences*, London, BFI.

Urwin, C. (2001) 'A psychoanalytic approach to language delay: when "autistic" isn't necessarily autism', *Journal of Child Psychotherapy*, 28(1): 73–93.

Van Looy, J. (2003). 'Uneasy lies the head that wears a crown: interactivity and signification in Head Over Heels', *Game Studies*, 3(2): http://www.gamestudies.org/0302/vanlooy/

Venn, C. (2002) *Occidentalism*, London, Sage.

Volosinov, V. N. (1994) 'Marxism and the Philosophy of Language', in *The Bakhtin Reader: selected writings of Bakhtin, Medvedev, Voloshinov*, ed. Pam Morris. London, Edward Arnold.

Vygotsky, L. S. (1978) *Mind in Society: the development of higher psychological processes*, Cambridge, MA, Harvard University Press.

Wajcman, J. (1991) *Feminism confronts technology*, Cambridge, Polity.

Walkerdine, V. (1981) 'Sex, power and pedagogy', *Screen Education*, 38: 14–23.

Walkerdine, V. (1984) 'Some day my prince will come: young girls and the preparation for adolescent sexuality', in M. Nava and A. McRobbie, (eds) *Gender and Generation*, London, Macmillan.

Walkerdine, V. (1984b) 'Developmental psychology and the child-centered pedagogy: the insertion of Piaget into early education', in J. Henriques, W. Hollway, C. Urwin, C. Venn and V. Walkerdine, *Changing the Subject: psychology, social regulation and subjectivity*, London, Methuen, pp. 153–202.

Walkerdine, V. (1988) *The Mastery of Reason*, London, Routledge.

Walkerdine, V. (1993) 'Redefining the subject in situated cognition theory', in Kirshner, D. (ed) *Situated Cognition: social, semiotic and psychological perspectives*, Mahwah, NJ, Lawrence Erlbaum.

Walkerdine, V. (1991) film: *Didn't she do well*, Working Pictures.

Walkerdine, V. (1997) *Daddy's Girl: young girls and popular culture*, Basingstoke, Palgrave – now Palgrave Macmillan.

Walkerdine, V. (1989) *Counting Girls Out*, London, Virago.

Walkerdine, V. (2006) Thinking subjectivity beyond the psychoanalytic/discursive divide, ESRC Identities Programme Public Lecture, University of the West of England.

Walkerdine, V. (2006b) 'Workers in the new economy: transformation as border crossing', *Ethos*, 34(1): 10–41.

Walkerdine, V. and Lucey, H. (1989) *Democracy in the Kitchen? Regulating Mothers and Socialising Daughters*, London, Virago.

Walkerdine, V., Lucey, H. and Melody, J. (2001) *Growing Up Girl: psychosocial explorations of gender and class*, Basingstoke, Palgrave – now Palgrave Macmillan.

Walkerdine V., Lucey, H. and Melody, J. (2002) 'Subjectivity and qualitative methods', in T. May (ed.) *Qualitative Research in Action*, London, Sage.

Whitford, M. (1991) *Luce Irigaray: philosophy in the feminine*, Cambridge, Basil Blackwell.

Wilson, E. A. (2004) *Psychosomatic: feminism and the neurological body*, Durham, NC, Duke University Press.

Wolf, M. and Perron, B. (eds) (2003) *The Video Game Theory Reader*, New York, Routledge.

Woolgar, S. (1991) 'Configuring the user: the case of usability trials', in J. Law (ed.), *A Sociology of Monsters. Essays on power, technology and domination*, London, Routledge, pp. 57–102.

Wundt, W. (1904) *Volkerpsychologie: eine Untersuchung der Entwiicklungs gesetze von sprache, mythus and sitte*, Leipzig, W. Engelmann.

Zizek, S. (1997) *The Plague of Fantasies*, London, Verso.

Index

action, 152
action masculinity, 35, 39, 45, 73, 89,
    144–5, 180, 215
  management of, 87
active subject, 8–12, 17
Actor network theory, 13, 28–9, 146,
    166
addiction, 90, 101, 104–5, 127, 144
affect, 17, 19, 20, 22–8, 30–1, 146–9,
    157, 165, 166, 173, 187–8, 214
  affective work, 69
after school videogame club, 3–4, 14–15
  aggressive fantasy, see under fantasy
Althusser, L, 5–6, 11, 16–17, 150–1
America, as site of gun crime, 83
anxiety, 25, 35–6, 67, 188–90, 205
  see also pain
apprenticeship, 154
Austin, S, 31, 69, 165, 179
assemblage, 33, 48, 135, 146, 168,
    173, 206, 212
  see also Deleuze
associative sociology, 146–8
avatars, 26, 35, 97–8
  competing for choice of, 181–5
  cute and cuddly, 51–3
  favourites, 52
  female, 49, 140
  femme fatale, 53
  mothering, 53

becoming, 14, 26, 153
  becoming masculine, 144
  see also Deleuze
behaviour, problem, 132
Benjamin, J, 167
Bergson, J, 20, 23
board games, 131
body, 22-3, 26, 48, 194, 197
  feminine body, 27
  see also embodiment
Braidotti, R, 216
brothers taking over, 115
Butler, J, 71, 217

capital accumulation, 150
Cartesianism, 2–3, 13, 138–9, 152,
    154, 169
  Cartesian subject, 9, 215
  see also rational subject
Centre for Contemporary Cultural
    Studies, 5
Changing the Subject, 16, 17, 152
cheats, 143
children, 8, 47, 155–6
  childhood involves action, 103–4
cognitive psychology, 23, 25, 155, 166
competence, see under player
competition, 43–5, 54, 98, 117, 128
complex circuits of exchange, 146
complexity theory, 146
consumer, 138, 142, 150–1
consumption, 5–8
context, 22
controllers, 30–1, 59, 165, 179–80, 213
Cowie, E, 31
crashing, 174
crowd psychology, 6–7

Daddy's Girl, 12
Dan, 77, 95–7
defence, 26, 27, 189
  see also pain
Deleuze, G, 14, 135
Deleuze, G and Guattari, F, 28, 33,
    146–9
Derrida, J, 70
Descarte, R, 34, 166–7
developmental psychology, 1, 13, 169,
    222
discourse, 14, 21, 33, 48, 146, 174,
    180–1, 185, 187, 215
disembodiment, 13–14, 20, 26–8
  see also rationality
dominance, 164, 174–5, 179–80, 185,
    187–8, 214
dream analysis, 31
dying, 47
  see also killing

231